WOMEN

AMERICAN WOMEN IN THEIR OWN WORDS

MARK BAKER

POCKET **STAR** BOOKS

New York   London   Toronto   Sydney   Tokyo   Singapore

A Pocket Star Book published by
POCKET BOOKS, a division of Simon & Schuster
1230 Avenue of the Americas, New York, NY 10020

ISBN: 0-671-73361-3

First Pocket Books printing May 1991

10 9 8 7 6 5 4 3 2 1

POCKET STAR BOOKS and colophon are trademarks of
Simon & Schuster.

Printed in the U.S.A.

WOMEN
American Women in Their Own Words

ON THE "NEW WOMAN"

"It's scary. All of a sudden, it's happening. I woke up one day and I became my mother, except with an advanced university degree. . . . I'm picking up after my boyfriend and apologizing to the maid for the house being dirty. Oh, my God, no. I'm turning out just like her."

ON FRIENDSHIPS WITH WOMEN

"Going out with the girls was always something to be snickered at. Now it isn't at all. Hurray! That's the woman's part that I finally value. Once you value other women, you value the femaleness in yourself."

ON BABIES

"People's reactions show that they do consider male babies much more desirable, which says something about how women are perceived."

ON THE FAST TRACK

"I'm a single-faceted success. I'm very successful in what I do. I'm not as successful in what I am. Somewhere along the line I got confused. I began to believe that what I do *is* who I am."

ON RELATIONSHIPS

"Men don't want to be trapped. Guess what? Neither do we."

Books by Mark Baker

Cops
Nam
Women

This book is dedicated to the memory of
Nora Elizabeth Taylor
1908–1987

Acknowledgments

The women whose words fill these pages were generous with their time, their intelligence, and a bit of their souls. Their enthusiasm for this project inspired me. I would like to thank them again here at the beginning of their book.

Very few writers have the luxury of working with an editor whose judgment they can trust and whose ability they can rely on. Bob Bender is that kind of editor. Esther Newberg, my agent, stands up for me against the world and always tells me the truth. She's determined to keep my two sons from going hungry.

I'd like to thank Frank Fortunato for being the devil's advocate, Bruce Margolius for his hospitality in a place very close to his heart, and John Davis for all his technical guidance in this age of computers.

Helena Angel, Susan Beecher, Ferne Cassel, Peggy Grossman, Robin Johnston, George Moon, Loretta Nash, Helen Pantzis, and Gary Smolek entrusted their friends to me to be interviewed. Gloria and Bob Baker and Joan O'Sullivan are always there when I need them. The following people fed and housed me as I traveled all across the country, and provided support and encouragement: John and Cindy Davis, Nancy and Tim Conaway (aka Cracker and Raoul Robino),

ACKNOWLEDGMENTS

Cathy and Peter O'Sullivan, Bebe and Richard Elliot, Magic Michael Cranmer, Marty Perlman, Penelope Weiss, Bob Luzzi, and Kathy Pohl (even though she didn't think this one would work). Ray Ottenberg deserves special mention for welcoming me back to his home on several occasions, even though he knew my arrival meant at least a foot of snow would fall on Washington, D.C., no matter what the season.

I'd like to thank my son Sean for letting Dad work and then taking me to the park to blow off a little steam. Thanks to my son Noah for arriving two weeks early when time was of the essence.

The most important person in my life and to my work is Veronica. She is my strength and my consolation. We have been married ten years now, and I love her more every day. I wish I were a poet so I could put my love for her into words.

Contents

PREFACE   xi

INTRODUCTION: WOMEN TROUBLE   1

1. WHO THEY ARE AND WHAT THEY WANT   7
2. SUGAR, SPICE, THINGS NOT SO NICE   55
3. BREATH 'N' BRITCHES   110
4. NEVER DONE   177
5. RAPE   238
6. FOUR LIVES   293

Preface

When this book first appeared in 1990, it was met with a resounding silence. That's an author's worst nightmare: Not bad reviews. Almost *no* reviews. Not critical letters and threatening phone calls. Little response at all. Having had the temerity to write about women and be a man—something no male writer has had the foolhardiness to do in almost twenty years—I expected indignant harumphing and perhaps even some angry screams or derisive laughter from the public at large, particularly women. My hope for this book was that it might start women and men talking to one another about the remarkable changes that have engulfed all of us over the last twenty-odd years, during the most sustained feminist revolution in the history of the Western world.

I knew why men weren't saying anything. They were scared. They'd been excluded long ago from any dialogue about feminism and women's new roles in modern society. Most of the men of my acquaintance knew better than to broach this subject in "mixed company" after their first few male chauvinist faux pas in the early 1970s. If they did not fawn over the radical feminists' line or if they stumbled against a few thousand years of their own cultural baggage and ended up with a foot in the mouth, the iron door was slammed in their faces. Since then, unless addled by drink or infatuation, they fall into sullen taciturnity and try to look like wallpaper whenever conversation turns to the subject of gender and equality. Besides, we are members of the dominant sex, so we know we can just sit it out and then turn the conversation back to baseball or work at the first opportunity.

Personally, I was tired of behaving that way and feeling separated from the trials and aspirations of half the human race. I wanted to talk about it, honest-to-God conversation with fellow human beings about what the hell has been happening to us and what we're going to do about it. I've always found the best way to nurture a conversation is to listen. So I did. The result of my conversations with women is the work you hold in your hands now.

Then silence. A big blank wall of it.

My first reaction was, "Well, you must have screwed up, Baker. You didn't get it right after all. It didn't speak to women, so they didn't talk back." I began to call some of the women I'd interviewed. They were the ones who could tell me if I'd gotten their stories wrong, if I'd picked the important pieces or settled for dross. Here are a few of their answers:

"Reading what I told you, I realized what a *bastard* my first husband really was to me. That hurt."

"I got almost all the way through it, but it started making me so sad, I haven't been able to face finishing it."

"When we talked, I picked out the big moments in my life and gravitated towards the hard stuff. When I saw it in print, it all came back and those things were just as painful again. And I cried again."

"I'd read great big chunks, then I'd have to leave it alone for a week or so, because it made me so angry. Women are still getting the shitty end of the stick."

Whatever its flaws may be, whatever misinterpretations I may have made simply on account of my being male, I believe I did get the story right. I read and reread these women's stories. I re-examined my motives and my own relationships with women. The one big failure of this book may be that in my effort to be evenhanded I wasn't blunt enough. I'm more convinced than ever that this book tells a big piece of truth about women in America today, and that truth is scary —so scary that women don't want to talk about it. This truth is especially frightening because it's not complicated or abstract. It's simple. It's obvious.

The truth is that life is difficult. Real flesh-and-blood people live messy, unpredictable lives full of compromise and contradiction. For the majority of women, feminist ideals are a luxury, and life choices are more often than not based on the pragmatic business of getting through each day in a man's world.

The truth is that at some point in life all of us are ruled by—if not tormented by—our upbringing and are weighed down with hundreds and hundreds of years of Western cultural and religious tradition. Women have not been able to throw off those burdens in a mere generation, and it will be many more generations before all the outdated sex roles, archaic laws and gender discrimination disappear from our society. It will probably be even longer before men get used to the idea of women as equals, if they ever do.

The truth is that for all the great strides toward equality with men they have made in the last twenty years, women have only begun to approach that goal, and already there are signs that they may be slipping backward.

The truth is that this book is really about the joy and

pain of being a human being, especially a female human being. As it turns out, I discovered there's a lot more pain for women than joy. There's so much pain, disappointment and humiliation that most women would rather try to ignore it than talk about it.

So consider this fair warning, gentle reader. This is not one of those books that reassure you everything's going to be all right and that you already know all there is to know about life. All the puffed-up political rhetoric, all the sexy media dreams, all the gleam of idealism has been leached out of these stories with tears and sweat. It's not a pretty picture. If I were a young woman reading this book, it would scare the hell out of me.

This book will challenge you to face some hard truths about women, about men and about America. When you've finished reading, whatever your reaction to these stories turns out to be, maybe some of you, men and women, will have the guts and the love to start talking to one another about your lives. I'm convinced that is the next step we all have to take if we're ever going to make life better, more balanced between feminine and masculine, as fair as life can be. There's been enough silence.

M.B.

Introduction:
Women Trouble

You know, you could get into a lot of trouble talking about this," Susan warned me. She had spent several thoughtful, emotional hours telling me the story of her life. Her warning came as the interview was drawing to a close, and I asked if she would talk in a more generalized, philosophical way about what she believed to be the differences between women and men.

"You could get into a lot of trouble talking about this. I believe there are tremendous differences between men and women, but I have a really hard time with that in my own mind. Where do they come from? Why do the differences exist? Are they self-imposed? Are they genetic, cultural, environmental? It brings up all the questions that we've been trying to grapple with as modern women."

I was looking for trouble. Susan was one of the first of one hundred American women I interviewed for this book. I asked them to talk about what has happened to them in their lives and what is happening to them now. Through their individual stories, I wanted to assemble a composite portrayal of the experience of being female in contemporary America, in the women's own words.

Many people think they know as much as there is to know on this subject. There are men who feel they have been bombarded with more sermonettes on the status of women than they care to hear. Many women will assume that from their own experiences they already know all about the subject.

But if what men think they know is dissected, it often turns out to be a Frankenstein's bride stitched together hastily from their casual conversations with women, TV sitcom images, some *Cosmopolitan* magazine coverlines, a few snippets of feminist rhetoric read years ago in college, a handful of newspaper stories or magazine articles, and a snapshot of Mom. Meanwhile every woman is inadvertently locked into her own social, economic, and regional sphere, virtually cut off by circumstance and convention from any tangible personal contact with women outside her community, class, and occupation.

There has been phenomenal progress in the advancement of women's rights toward equality with men in our society. Some American women alive today embody the most far-reaching changes in the stature and power of women in our history, and perhaps in all of history. Yet, a stroll down any shopping mall in the country suggests strongly that the majority of women are living the same lives their mothers lived twenty years ago.

Because some women have managed against the odds to liberate themselves, most of us tend to believe that all women are more or less liberated. If a woman has taken over control of her life, we assume that she has ascended to some state of grace, beyond the reach of trouble, pain, and doubt. The lives of real human beings are never so uncomplicated. I wanted to get beyond the easy answers of commercial formulas, political dogma, and sexist rhetoric to those real people and their stories.

The one hundred women who talked to me hail from

fifteen states scattered all across the continent, Alaska to Florida, Vermont to California, and many points in between. The oldest woman was eighty-seven, the youngest was eighteen, but most of the women in this book were between the ages of thirty and forty-five. Those are the women of my generation, the women who have been the most personally involved in and affected by the women's movement, whether or not they would describe themselves as feminists.

The interviews generally took place in each woman's own domain, ranging from a mansion in Beverly Hills to a tiny apartment in an urban ghetto, from a spacious office with spectacular views to a cramped basement cubicle where the only view was of the shoes and ankles of passersby on the street above. I was in neat rural farmhouses and untidy double-wide trailer homes. But most of the interviews were conducted in the tract houses and apartment complexes that crowd the suburbs. The majority of the women I interviewed were white and middle class, although my interviews included a few black women, one woman of Mexican-American descent, one Asian-American.

Three-quarters of them had been married at some point in their lives. Half of them were married when I spoke with them or had some other more or less stable relationship with a man. Five women told me they were lesbians.

Although I was asking them to tell me about their *entire* lives, that is impossible to do in two or four or even six hours. What usually happened was that a woman gave me a particular version of her "life story," perhaps in terms of her career because the interview took place in her office. Another talked mostly about her relationship with her children, because she had just left them with a baby-sitter so we could conduct our interview without distraction. I talked with one woman in her mother's house in the room that had been her bedroom as a child. Now it

3

was the place where her mother kept a personal library and went to write. That interview was almost exclusively about the woman's relationship with her parents, especially her father. A few women were not interested in a chronological life story. One woman said, "I don't want to talk about my childhood. I just want to tell you what I'm doing right now."

Each of them decided where to start and finished where she pleased. I rarely interrupted with a question unless I lost the line of the narrative or the conversation ran out of steam. I promised them all anonymity, so they would feel freer to be frank with me, and then I simply listened.

The women in this book were obviously aware of my gender. I am sure that awareness shaped their conversations with me significantly. They may not have told me the same things in the same way that they might have told them to another woman. There are events that they may not have told me at all. I do think that the circumstances of our meetings—anonymous, unalloyed, purposeful—helped to ameliorate this situation. Many times women's statements were prefaced by some variation of, "And women will kill me for saying this, but . . ."

There was also a deeper personal meaning for me in Susan's warning of "trouble." As an old friend of mine, she is aware that for about two years I was an editor for Larry Flynt's *Hustler* magazine. For the next year and a half after that I was the executive editor of *Forum,* a digest-size compendium of readers' letters published by Bob Guccione's *Penthouse* organization. I told all the women I interviewed about this part of my past and I was never turned away because of it.

No book could be sufficiently exhaustive to contain The Truth about the lives of the millions of women living in the United States. This book does not pretend to be a scientific study with control groups, statistical accuracy, and cold objectivity, nor am I an expert in sociology, anthropology, or psychology. But I think many American women will see themselves, or at least important elements of their lives, reflecting back at them with a keen intensity from these pages.

Women and men *are* different, whatever the reasons for those differences may be. Each sex wonders what the other is all about, how their minds work, what it is like to be inside the other's skin. We are not opposites; we are more alike than unlike. But those differences are what keep us apart. If this book causes some readers to think more deeply with empathy about the differences between men and women, I won't mind a little trouble.

1. Who They Are and What They Want

I was present for the birth of both my sons. For all my encouragement and wild, rhythmic breathing, I was still little more than an observer. I stood by, in awe of my wife's pain and courage, holding her hand, tears running down my cheeks, both times that our children appeared out of her body. I thought, "How wonderful that must be, to bring life into the world." And then, "I'm glad I'm not a woman."

My year gathering interviews for this book was like that experience in some ways. Looking into women's eyes and hearing them tell me their stories had the immediacy—and sometimes the terror—of seeing a loved one in pain. The plain details of how they grapple with daily existence were infinitely more powerful for me than all the rhetoric and philosophizing about women. I finished these interviews with a renewed respect for women—and a more profound understanding of how they live their lives. But I could only sit and listen, then echo their words here, with a male admonition: I wouldn't want to be a woman.

Women don't want to be men either. One woman articulated the consensus when she said, "Given the choice, women would rather be women. Very few want to be men. There are a lot of men who are envious of women. This sounds crude to say, but you don't find many women who have a gender problem— who literally want to become men. It seems to be widely true in the opposite direction—a lot of men wish they were women. They perceive women's lives to be nicer, which maybe they are. The reason they might be nicer is that there is less pressure from the rest of society to live up to something."

For most women, that's still true. They are not being coerced into change; rather they are choosing new professions and trying on new character traits. The freedom to explore has been exhilarating, they say, but the times are changing fast. Women find themselves in competition with each other. They undergo more inner conflicts than ever before. As women pry open the doors to their dreams, they find themselves increasingly driven by peer pressure to excel—as men are—but in an ever-widening range of roles. "Women are turning the feminist movement around and becoming their own worst enemies, putting their own sex down," another woman told me. "They take on all of it—wife, mother, housekeeper, career woman—and then get angry at someone else because they haven't taken it all on, too.

"I watch my little sister who won't even finish high school now, because she's afraid that she'll have to go out and prove herself in this really great career. She's terrified. My other sister is spinning her wheels. She has all kinds of talent, but she doesn't want to tangle with it, because you either do absolutely 100 percent, and you're on top of the world, or you're a failure."

The majority of contemporary women were reared with most of the old gender stereotypes, so that even those women on the cutting edge of innovation often find their rational selves at odds with their subconscious impulses. Here is how one woman describes that confusion: "It's scary. All of a sudden, it's happening. I woke up one day and I became my mother, except with an advanced university degree. I thought I was going to turn out more like my dad, but, no, she's there. I'm picking up after my boyfriend and apologizing to the maid for the house being dirty. Oh, my God, no. I'm turning out just like her. Except my fiancé and I can't be Mom and Dad. Sam's not going to be the breadwinner and I'm not going to be a housewife. That's all there is to it."

Expectations are running very high among women that institutions will change, men will change, that they themselves will change. Disappointments have been correspondingly intense. "Women were thinking they could have a full-on, high-powered career and a family and a husband/wife relationship which was sustaining and supportive of one another—two human beings making it through the world. I don't see that as being very realistic anymore. I've tried it. What was happening was that things were kind of crumbling at home, because Mom wasn't around for the kids, and my husband and I were rushing in and out of each other's lives. It didn't work for us. It didn't work for me."

It is a time of turmoil and contradiction in the lives of American women. Here are the voices of three women, all in their forties, all very independent and productive, yet still aching for fulfillment:

"I fear getting older. I had my forty-fourth birthday this year and I definitely feel what it means to be a woman approaching or at the end of her childbearing years and not having had one."

"I would like to find someone to share my life with now. It doesn't have to be marriage necessarily. If I thought I was never going to find that in life, I think I would end it. That's how important it is."

"It's weird. You wake up and think, 'What happened to the nuclear family that you were supposed to have?' I have this little coterie of friends who are in the same position I am. Most of my female friends are very successful; they earn a lot of money—much more than I do. But we're going through this period of wondering, 'What is it going to be for us?' "

In this chapter—and throughout the book—you will not be reading feminist abstractions about who women are or male chauvinist platitudes about what women want. These are conversations about survival, the human condition, and the pursuit of happiness. These are women talking straight from the heart about being alive in America today.

The most profound and biggest revelation for me—which sounds stupid and basic—was to understand that men were not like me. I always wanted to believe that they were, that we were all human beings who thought the same way and felt the same way and that we were all in this thing together. That's partly true. We are in it together, and we're all human beings. But we're not the same.

Women have balls, you just can't see them. They're not hanging out exposed.

Men are more Oriental. They are into saving face. I don't know if it's because women's role for centuries was to have kids vomit on them or shit on their laps, but face is not as big a deal for us. You would think that would work to our advantage in the world, but for some reason it really doesn't. I could never figure it

out. Every man I've ever known after he does something that would be generally perceived as embarrassing spends the next two or three hours going, "Did I
disgrace myself? Was it embarrassing?"

So what? Men seem to have so much more at stake
in things. I wouldn't want to be a man. They have a
much harder row to hoe.

Toys. He's much more concerned about his toys than
I am. I have books and dogs and birds. He has toys. I
bought him a remote-control car. He loves it. He loves
his little model airplane. He washes his truck all the
time. He loves his truck.

If my car got wrecked tomorrow, it would bother
me, because the insurance probably wouldn't pay off
the loan, but it wouldn't kill me. Right after he bought
his truck, somebody took a key and ran it down the
side. The whole side of his truck was ruined. He called
me up, and it was the closest he's ever been to tears.

"It's all scratched," he said. "It'll never be the
same again." I tried real hard to be nice about it and
not say something smart like, "Oh, they don't paint
trucks anymore?"

Men have a strong sense of magic. They think everything just happens. They don't see the mechanism behind it. He doesn't clean at all. I do all of that. I tell
him, "How do you think it gets like this? All these

books got in order by themselves? One day they jumped up there on the shelf and got in alphabetical order. Isn't that neat? The records? Same thing. They're easier to find in alphabetical order, David.''

"Oh, is that what they're in?"

He doesn't see order. He has one drawer with shirts in it and that's all that's in there, just T-shirts that he wears to work. There's a drawer with jeans and another drawer with underwear and socks. If *he* puts the clothes away, the jeans end up in the shirts, the socks end up with the jeans. It doesn't hit him when he looks at it. He doesn't go, "Oh, these are all T-shirts." He goes, "If this drawer has all my stuff in it, and here's some more of my stuff, it all goes together."

I have to say, "The garbage needs to be taken out." I noticed that it needed to be taken out. Why doesn't he? I walk into the house, and it smells like a garbage can.

"I don't smell anything," he says.

I pick up the baby. "This baby smells like poop."

"I didn't smell anything."

"Well, put your nose up to his butt."

"I still don't smell anything."

Men are allowed to be creative because they don't have to think about all this shit. They don't have to think about the fact that the rug is dirty or that the milk needs to be bought or that diapers need to be changed. They don't think about the details, so that's why they get to write the books and make the films and run the companies. They don't have to worry about that crap, and you can only do so much in a day.

If there's two of you, *somebody*'s got to worry about the crap, unless you don't care if your house is a big wreck.

Unfortunately, I'm like the main character in Herman Hesse's novel, *Steppenwolf,* in the scene where he sits on a landing and he smells the wax as he watches the housekeeper polish the floor. His room is a wreck, but she cleans the house and keeps the plants dusted. He sits there and just soaks in the wonderful odor of her cleanliness. He loves it, but he hates himself for loving it.

I'm the same way. I hate myself for loving this order, but I do like it. I like my house clean, but I spend my whole life making it that way. So I don't get to write the books and do the photography. It's just so silly.

Women are like that. Women like to have things clean, but by the time we're done cleaning, there's nothing left to do. We're old. We look back at how we spent our lives and we cleaned the house. "I had a clean house." Put that on my tombstone.

My mother's pattern as a role model was as a workingwoman, who also was the person who put dinner on the table. My father did nothing in the house. My mother made slipcovers, curtains, fixed things, hammered nails into walls, put in light bulbs. When my father came home, understandably he was very tired, but he never felt that he was responsible for doing anything in the house. My mother did it all and she was also working sixty hours a week in her own business.

The legacy that she left me was the expectation that I, too, would be a working mother, and that I, too, would take care of all household matters. Through the several career changes in my life, through two marriages and a child by each marriage, I kicked myself around a lot for having the same role. Yet, I'm well aware that role was fashioned by this wonderful role model of mine who just managed to do it all. Except she seemed to do it all without as much resentment as I have.

What the consciousness-raising of the last twenty years has done for me is to let me know that it's okay for me to be angry about doing it all. Angry at myself, for allowing myself to do everything, and periodically angry at my husband for not taking on more responsibility by himself.

The cry of greatest anger is, "He'll do it if I ask him to. I don't want to be the top sergeant in the household, always asking. It's easier to do it myself than to beg for help." I know I'm not alone in that. I also know that my mother had nobody to bless her if she felt that way at all. I never heard her say, "I wish your dad would do more." She just didn't expect it.

So if the changing attitudes have done anything for me, they've just made me a bit more annoyed at myself and often *very* annoyed at my spouse. I know that the proper thing when I'm feeling this anger is just to establish rules in the house and not do it to myself any longer. But I'm my own worst enemy.

We did an interesting role-playing thing early in our marriage. I made out a whole list of the things that had to be done just to live. Then I made three columns and checked off the things that fell in different categories. Things that I not only don't mind doing, but that I prefer to do either because I had more talent or because I enjoyed them, things my husband enjoyed doing or preferred to do or had a natural bent for, and then this category of all the others that had to be done that both of us found onerous. We split up the onerous ones.

That went along kind of nice for a while. Then I began to feel a certain amount of resentment, because shopping in the supermarket for the week's food was on his list, and he often didn't do it. Although cooking was on my list, I wouldn't have the ingredients, so I wound up shopping for everything. I began shopping so often that before I knew it my side of the list was unbalanced.

After about six years of bitching about it, I created a revolution. I just yelled and screamed and had a fit. I'm not a screamer, but I had chewed on this for a long time.

"We're reversing roles!" I said. "I'll do the banking, you do the cooking."

"You're kidding," he said. My husband does not cook very well. He doesn't have any experience with it and he doesn't like it.

"That's only fair, isn't it?"

He happens to be a very rational man. I presented the fact that for six years I had done these things, and now I wanted a shot at doing his things. I didn't say it had to be an equal six years, but I certainly wanted a shot at trying it. There wasn't any logical reason to say no, so we switched roles.

I really became sensitized to the fact that banking and paying the bills is really very onerous and takes a much longer time than I had supposed it did. There were a lot of things on his list that were not pleasant tasks.

I don't know whether it was that sensitivity or the fact that I ate an awful lot of bad meals, but we switched back again. We didn't even talk about it, we just switched. I adjusted after a while to the fact that I take more responsibility for the household.

Every once in a while I say, "This is not a hotel! You are a rotten roommate! I don't ask you to pick up my underwear and stockings!" It's not something to get a divorce about. I honestly recognize that it takes two people to make that situation. I'm a product of role modeling and I cannot seem to exercise the self-discipline to let all the laundry pile up at the foot of the bed and not care. I just can't do that. So it's my problem, not his. It took a lot of maturation, and every once in a while, I have to remind myself it's not that bad.

My dad is one of these people who probably doesn't know where the Coke is kept in the house, because I've never seen him get one. "Can I have a Diet Coke?" He doesn't know where they come from. They drop out of space.

I've seen him cook maybe twice. One time when my mother had to get a late plane, my father made grilled cheese. It was so black, my sister and I wouldn't eat it. So we had Twinkies for supper. Other times when my mother left, we had Oreos for supper. Oreos and Coke. I knew where the Coke was.

My mom was one of these people that you couldn't sit in her house for one minute before she's running to make you eat or drink something. My mother used to iron pillowcases and all my dad's handkerchiefs. It was frightening.

I wait on my boyfriend and I hate it. My boyfriend will drop stuff on the floor and instead of telling him to pick it up, I pick it up. I don't say anything.

I'm a lawyer. I cook dinner. I read cookbooks. I never thought I would do that and I'm doing it.

You got a lot of miserable people, because they're doing things they don't really want to be doing. More men are in that situation than women. Men get up in the morning and have their breakfast. They go to work. They work. They come home. They read the paper. They have dinner. They nod to their children. They watch television and they go to bed. There is no absorption in anything else. They work harder and harder, until you lay them to rest, and that's their permanent retirement.

For so many years, we women were under the thumb of society. Women could become nurses or teachers or social workers . . . or social workers or teachers or nurses. Or they stayed home. If it became imperative that they make a living, and—God forbid —they didn't have an education to do it, they went into the factory or to secretary school. There were damn few who went into anything else. God knows men tried like all get-out to keep us out. When we finally shook off the shackles and said, "Hey, listen, you guys, my brain's got the same compartments as yours and I can use it just as well," it was something we wanted to do as opposed to something we had to do. That puts a whole different light on it.

Women don't feel all that locked into anything. "I got a great job, and look, I do this so good—surprise, surprise. So forget it, I'll try something else." I never particularly felt that I was pressured to prove myself at anything except for myself. My only worry was to be as human a human being as I could possibly be. That's it. There was never anybody standing over me saying, "What do you do for a living? How much do you make a year? What was your bonus?"

There is more peer pressure on men. Women can

do whatever we choose to do. We don't have to do nothing. Therein lies a great difference emotionally between men and women. We are not the donkey following the carrot. You are.

Women tend to be more self-examined, tend to reflect on our lives more than men—not that we necessarily learn anything from it.

Women reason better than men. As a general rule, we give more thought to both sides of a question, because we are so used to taking care of other people and wondering how they feel. Very few men will sit and think, "If I do this, he or she is going to react this way." Every woman I know does that. The man who does is very rare.

This is not to say that I don't do things wrong. I still do. It's not to say I don't do things that will piss people off. Even knowing it's going to piss them off, I'll still do it sometimes. The difference between me and my male friends is that I think on it, and I know what's going to happen. They don't even stop to think on it. They can't put themselves in somebody else's place.

That's what it all comes down to. Women can put ourselves in other people's places and see their perspective. Whether it affects our behavior or not is another story, but we can do it, and I don't think men can.

Men have a hard time understanding women. I'm not sure why. It's hard to know when you are a woman, because you understand other women perfectly well. Men are the big enigma. They say things they don't mean. They misinterpret things you say. They don't even understand other men.

Communication is the biggest stumbling block. Men communicate differently than women. Women speak with actions and expressions and attitudes. Men say things in words. Men and women can almost never express things so that they understand each other.

I used to spend a lot of time hating women. I never wanted to be friends with women. I didn't like them. I thought they'd screw you over the first chance they got. They were sneaky and you couldn't trust them at all. Most of my women friends—girlfriends, when I was younger—did exactly that. If it was a choice between you and a guy, it was the guy. If you both liked the guy, then forget it. It was all-out war. You could be the closest friends in the world, it didn't matter. I guess with a few exceptions, that's still the way I feel.

It took me fifty years to know who I am, to find out and look at it. Women. I like women. That's recent, though. All that time, I was the product of a female society that told me that if you were a bright woman you would not like women's company, because they would want to talk about laundry detergent and recipes. They did not talk about interesting things. Men talked about interesting things.

I went to the theater with men, to the opera and museums with men. I had men for friends and avoided being with women, who really seemed to lead dull and mundane lives.

In the past few years, I have begun to have a new respect for women and their accomplishments, maybe because I am surrounded by more accomplished women than I ever was in the 1950s or 1960s. When a woman admires me, I think that's fantastic. That's a whole new mentality for somebody of my generation. Young women of today may value each other's opinions of themselves, but I wouldn't have valued a woman's opinion twenty years ago. If a woman said, "Hey, wow, you're great, you've done so many things," I just would have tossed that out as I tossed out my mother's opinion. Who cares? What does she know? Stupid people don't know anything.

There's a whole half of the world I spent more than half of my life dismissing, that now I see are very competent, terrific, capable creatures. They're fun and interesting companions. When I was twenty-five or eighteen, I would not have enjoyed going to a movie or the theater as much with a woman as with a man, but I probably enjoy it more with a woman these days. I don't think this is a function simply of the fact that I am married now and I'm not seeking male companionship. It's just that I really have come to a new conclusion.

I now recognize that women are fun to be with, that they very often have retained a sense of playfulness where some men have lost it. The men had it when they were younger, but as men get older, they seem to misplace that. Maybe they seek their playfulness or sense of humor with younger women, I don't know.

Whatever it is, it's not at all apparent to older women that they're fun anymore. With younger women they are, but with women of their own generation they tend to be serious.

Going out with the girls was always something to be snickered at. Now it isn't at all. Hurray! That's the woman's part that I finally value. Once you value other women, you value the femaleness in yourself.

My cousins, who I grew up with like sisters, are all married and have children now that are in college. They don't treat me the same and it's real hard for me to be the same. I'm not the same. It's a price that I didn't know that I would have to pay for moving out and moving up. It really hurts me, because these are people that I loved dearly.

But then I'm there with them for two hours and I'm like driven insane. How long can you talk about hairdos? How long can you talk about whether the hemlines are going up again? How long can you talk about Joan Collins? Give me a break.

When I get like that, I don't blame it on them at all. It's like, "Look what you've done to yourself. This is crazy. This is not okay to become impatient and infuriated and distant from these people who you love so dearly."

My cousin and I are six months apart. We were hanging around the same high school getting drunk and having parties. She's doing something entirely different than I am, and I can't sit there with her anymore for more than a couple of hours. That's sad to me. I don't like that at all.

My women friends are the most important relationships in my life. Trusting, open, honest, not really judgmental. We tell each other the truth. My women friends have sustained me through it all. We are there for each other. When I was married I felt safe, and I didn't have to be with my friends much. But I know now how much I cherish them. I'm more intimate with my friends than I am with my husband. They know me better. I think we'll be around for each other always, no matter what happens with the men in our lives.

I got to tell you, I used to have a really great sense of humor. I just sort of lost it when I got married. Now that I'm separated, I'm beginning to get back my sense of humor. It's a prime value to be able to laugh, not take it all so fucking seriously. Laugh at it and laugh at yourself.

I can do that with my women friends. That's one criteria I've chosen my friends by. I want them to be there and I want them to laugh at themselves and at the messes that we're making out of our lives and still love each other. We all make messes in some way, I'm convinced. Everybody I know does. I make the worst mess, but I'm also the funniest.

I've been through my childhood and my adolescence. I've been married and I'm a widow. I've had other relationships with men that have been significant. I'm in a relationship now with a man. One of my children is twenty, so he's a man. I have a less naive and a deeper appreciation of the role men play in life and what men are. My expectations of them are more grounded in reality. I've gotten a rounded, as well as a deeper, picture of men and a better one. Kind of the long view.

I used to be angrier with men than I am now. Angry, because I expected them to be stronger and the ones who would take far more responsibility for their lives and our life together. I expected something of them that is probably not where their strengths are.

On the other hand, I always thought men weren't the ones you could talk to. You hear a lot about men not being good talkers, that women are the ones. But if you catch them when they're not watching a basketball game on television, if it's the right moment and you're not intruding on their need to really relax with a beer and the TV, turning from channel to channel to channel, they're very good talkers. They are perhaps not great gossips. For that you have to rely on women. But they're very good talkers and they can be just as loyal as women, maybe more loyal.

When I was younger, I demanded more expressions of intimacy. I thought men should be capable of more clarity in their intimacy, and that translated into being better gossips than they are. Now I believe intimacy is expressed in other ways. There are shared experiences that often are silent.

Therefore, I've changed my mind about how capable men are of intimacy. They're just as capable as women are. What they aren't so capable of is remembering the nitty-gritty details about what she said and he said and then she said in a conversation, or taking responsibility for being the one who has to make sure there is milk in the refrigerator and all the shirts get washed and the shoelaces get bought. Women have always done that and I think we always will, no matter how powerful women's rights movements become.

Men can be good friends and comrades. You can't expect the same things from men and women friends. I don't think you should. I like being with other women and talking with them. Most women I'm friends with like to talk about all the details of daily life, which is why you have to keep up very close contact with women. You can't miss a couple of weeks or months, because then you miss the details and you don't know where to begin again, except for those few real close friends who are friends even after years. I enjoy and need female friends very much and insist on getting out at least once a week—more often if I can—to be away from my kids, away from work, and away from male company, to be with women friends just really to *gab*.

Women experience relationships with one another in terms of talk. Men and women don't. Probably men and men don't. I don't know about that. You're doing things with a man and watching a man and having him watch you. There are so many ways that you climb over that wall between people—which is always inevitably there—to touch one another. It's not, by a long shot, primarily talk with a male. That's the least of it. When a woman forgets herself and starts to blabber with a man, it becomes self-conscious and uncomfortable. Men aren't cut out to do that.

Men enjoy amusing one another. Women can do that with men, but that's not what women need. That need is fulfilled best by another woman. To try to squeeze that out of a man all the time has got to end in disaster. By disaster, I mean a fight. That's a difference between men and women. Not necessarily a shortcoming of men or women. Differences should be respected and understood. It's a difference in degree.

It's nice when men can still be romantic. One of the bad things about this new forced talking is that then men aren't as likely to sing to you the old sweet songs or just walk holding your hand. I would greatly miss those things. I wouldn't give them up for talk. I'd rather talk to women.

24

All women I talk to, who are involved with men, complain about them in great detail, as do I. That's not to say that they don't love them and respect them and honor them. But they have to complain about them, because men can be a handful. It's the same way you love your kids, but you have to complain about what's happening with them. You have to put it on the table in front of you with somebody and get some perspective on it.

All this anger that's been generated in some degree by the women's movement has been a fairly destructive force. I recognize that it's helped women get better pay, better jobs, and more freedom to play in the sports arena and to drive taxis and to become physicians. All that is wonderful, but it's been at enormous cost to human relationships. It's taken a huge personal toll, particularly between men and women, but also between mothers and their children, women and their husbands, children and their fathers, because it demanded something both of men and of women that wasn't a possibility: the kind of equality in the home that is impossible for most people to come by. To define the roles and the responsibilities of men and women the same way is foolish. It has led to a lot of anger and false expectations, or has been a vehicle for other kinds of anger.

Frankly, too much has been said about the women's movement and about what men should be and how a man should have to act. It's all too self-conscious. I've gone through periods when I thought, "Men are dogs." But basically, I don't feel that way. This whole thing of trying to make a list of things men *have* to be or of the ways in which men have failed to be these things really doesn't allow any individual man to just be himself in a relationship and to let the woman be herself. You're always standing there with the check-list. That's such a bad way of interfering in the lives of real people. You can conceptualize this stuff. You can talk about it and gossip with your girlfriends on Tuesday night, but in reality, except for the influence it's had on getting men to become more vulnerable and to open their hearts in a way they wouldn't before, the rest has been real destructive. Maybe it's worth it for some woman who wanted to play on the baseball team or wanted to get into a career that's only been for men, but it doesn't seem worth it to me.

The important thing that has come out of it is men's openness about their feelings for children, how it's okay for them to schmooze around with kids and be affectionate and bathe them and change their diapers and do those things that do represent intimacy—the *only* way you can be intimate with a baby, because a baby is a physical creature. Men used to feel babies were vegetables until you could play ball with them. "Hand it to me clean and pressed." That's changed.

Men who really involve themselves with the care of babies—touching them, wiping the baby's vomit off them—that makes them vulnerable to a relationship at a level that men never had an opportunity to have before. Grown women are threats. No matter how close you are and how much you trust your beloved, that's still a grown person who could hurt you. A baby never could, so you become vulnerable to this little creature who can hurt you more than you ever imagined anyone could have. Men experience some of the things that mothers have been experiencing since time began. That single fact has so significantly and positively changed men and changed men's relationships with women and with children that maybe the high price was worth it, but I don't know.

The best men are men who let themselves be vulnerable. The only way that happens—*really happens* —is when they let themselves love a baby.

I don't know why I'm going on and on about that . . . except that it's all I really have to say. That's the distillation of all I've learned in forty-five years.

I'm getting so much shit from my peers, because I don't want to have children. It's weird. I don't understand it.

The older you get, the less you are the center of existence and you realize how it might be nice to have another person in your life that you love and can help grow. That's wonderful. I might want children in my life someday, but I don't want my own baby. I don't want to go through that. I don't think it's important for me, but I get a lot of flak for it.

Women get angry. "What do you mean you don't want a baby? That's the most joyful experience a woman can ever have. How could you cheat yourself?" One friend said, "It's a shame. All the people I know who would be the best parents aren't having children." That's just a kind of backward pressure.

I was at the point of having my tubes tied, not having any children at all. We would adopt children. "We aren't prepared to bring kids into this world. Let's take some kids who are already here and don't have anybody." We both felt real good about that concept.

I'd read and been counseled; we'd both been counseled. I'd booked an appointment three months in advance to go in and have the tubal ligation procedure done when we got back from vacation.

At six o'clock in the morning the day we were to leave for that trip, a phone call jolted me out of my sleep. This very sterile voice at the other end said, "Mrs. Crenshaw, this is the clinic. We have had a cancellation this morning for the operation that you are scheduled for three months from now and we thought you might like to come in and fill this gap. There is one condition; we're going to have sixty doctors there viewing the process. We just wanted to know how you'd feel about that. You're welcome to take the spot if you want to.''

I'm just coming out of my sleep and this person is firing all this information at me impatiently. ''Do you want to take this spot? Because we have ten other women we can call.''

Suddenly this Orwellian, *1984*ish image just zipped in front of me. An image of myself as this object, this specimen, on a table in an amphitheater with all these doctors peering through glass, looking down at me. ''Here's a woman who's made the decision not to have any children, and here's the whole process that we have in place that will end any birth control concerns she has.''

''No,'' I said, ''I don't want this morning's appointment. And you can cancel my appointment for three months from now.'' That did it.

My parents were married for twelve years before they had me. My father was almost fifty years old when I was born. My mother was almost forty, so I was more like a grandchild instead of a child. I don't really know how much they wanted to have a kid. I really interrupted their life-style dramatically. My mother let me know that every day of my life. As a matter of fact, she always said to me, ''Don't have kids. Don't have kids. They ruin your life.'' I'm sure she was just projecting her own feelings back on to me.

I was five months pregnant when my mother died. She told all her friends how happy she was that I was having a baby, but she never said to me directly—not once—that she was glad for me. She just said, "You'll never go to Europe. You've got a kid now." She was the voice of doom and gloom.

When I first realized I was going to have this baby, I really, really wanted it to be a girl, because I didn't know any little boys. I thought, "It has to be a girl or I can't relate."

My girlfriend had amniocentesis. She called me up and she was so happy that she knew that her child was a girl. My first reaction was jealousy—jealous that she knew, because part of me really did want to know. Now that she knew it was a girl, she only had to concentrate on one species of name.

Then about the seventh month, because of the way I was carrying, men would say to me, "Oh, that's a boy. I know that's a boy." I was really resentful. I wanted to say, "Shut up. How do you know?"

I also resented that my mother-in-law kept saying, "Oh, that's a boy." When I would say, "You know, it could be a girl," she would be adamant that it was going to be a boy. She acted as if girls were second-class citizens, an undesirable sex to have. The consolation prize for being pregnant would be to have a girl. Boys are the only offspring worth having.

The doctor said, "It's a boy," when he was born. I wasn't surprised. In fact, by the time he was born, I couldn't have cared less. As long as it wasn't a dog, who cared? "Just get out!" My husband kept saying things during my labor like, "Just think of the beautiful baby who will be coming out soon."

"Who the hell cares about the baby? Just get this stuff over with," I said.

Now I'm really glad that he's a boy. It's all in my mind, but he seems less fragile to me. The first time you're a mother, you're really worried about how inept you are. He seems to be indestructible, made out of rubber. I'm sure female babies are no different, but psychologically it seems that way.

People give you such praise. Our cleaning lady acted as if I had done this amazing thing to have a boy. She was impressed, because she saw me as this little puny nothing and it showed some great strength to have a boy. People's reactions show that they do consider male babies much more desirable, which says something about how women are perceived.

With all these racially motivated violent incidents, the leaders of the black community keep saying on TV that a black person's life isn't really worth anything in America. Well, obviously, female life isn't too valuable either, here or anywhere else.

The first time I got pregnant I was shocked. We weren't using birth control, so it shouldn't have come as a total surprise. But it did. How did this happen?

My first thought after I found out I was pregnant was, "This is incredible." My second thought was, "Okay, now I'm going to have to start over and do it right." I had a miscarriage. Somehow I knew it was going to happen all along. I still wasn't prepared for it.

The night before the miscarriage, I dreamt it. In the dream, there was a split in the earth and it opened up. Out came these crawly, wiggly, slimy things. It terrified me, but I knew that I had to get hold of them because my husband would want to see it. It was very scary, but I did do it. Then I went around to all of these other women and talked to them about it.

The next night I had the miscarriage. I had been spotting during the day. I knew that wasn't a good sign. Suddenly, in the middle of the night, there was this gush. I went to the bathroom and the fetus came out in the toilet. I knew that I had to get it out. I knew that John had to see it. I was almost four months along, so it was fully formed. It was exactly the experience from my dream.

Since then, I've heard that this is not so startling, that women's bodies do know it before it actually happens. It's being communicated, but the brain doesn't understand, isn't ready. I wish I could have just gone to sleep.

The second time was very different. I knew I was pregnant immediately. I was frightened through the whole nine months that it would happen again. John remembers me sleeping all through the pregnancy. I was just conscious of the baby all the time.

Now I have a four-year-old. She's just incredible. She changed our lives unbelievably. Every moment it surprises me.

I stayed home for her the first three months and felt like I was going crazy. I've always been independent. I was thirty-six when I had her. That's a long time to be independent. I had no experience with babies whatsoever. I hadn't even baby-sat.

My entire day was spent nursing and diapering and it was crazy-making. For the first time in my life I started watching daytime television. I didn't watch the soaps, but I watched the talk shows. They saved me. I am grateful to them. There was intelligent life while I was nursing this baby. She wasn't a good baby or a bad baby, but she was a baby and she gave nothing back.

Then I thought, "I'm the assistant director at work. I'm in charge. I'll just bring my baby to work." I got permission, brought her in, and set her up and it was disastrous. Nobody said, "What the hell are you doing with a baby here?" But I didn't have any help whatsoever from any of them. Nobody even said, "Oh, what a cute baby. Can I hold her?"

I'm in this new phase, which is the staying-at-home-mom phase. For one thing, it is a wildly enviable situation to not have to go to work every day. It's a throwback to pre-women's lib. I have a girlfriend who is the vice president of the finance division of a big company out West. Every week she calls me and every week she says, "Aren't you bored? What is it that has meaning in your life?"

"Since when," I ask her, "did putting together asinine magazines have any meaning? What is this meaning stuff? How much meaning is there for you working in a bank? I can do basically what I want to do in my day and don't have to answer to a lot of other people, and that's the most liberating thing in the world."

Someone will say, "I don't see how taking care of a baby or cooking meals or vacuuming is meaningful." It's not, but the day is frantic for the most part. I have to look at it as, "Is it more meaningful than making a list of creative article ideas (none of which will ever come to fruition) for a week, so I can go in and talk to this publisher and be scored for it by this guy, too?" I think it's great not to have to go into an office every day. I feel very comfortable with that.

I had a lot of trouble with the name business. I wanted to keep on using my maiden name, but after you have a kid it gets even harder. You call up to make a doctor's appointment and you don't have the same last name as the kid, so you totally confuse them.

They don't know what name to put the records under. So just because of the kid, I ended up using the new name.

It was a simpler adjustment than I thought. But all my girlfriends were horrified. I do not have a single girlfriend who does not give me shit about having changed my name. They act like I've become a traitor and slapped the women's movement in the face. But I don't see that this has anything to do with your identity. Listen, to the whole world I am my Social Security number anyway.

I'm really worried about what I'm going to do with myself later. I don't want to just get a job when the kid or kids get older. Say my husband becomes wildly successful and a name brand. I don't want to be, "Oh, that's the famous guy's wife." There is still a great desire for something of my own.

If you're in a high-powered kind of profession then it's even worse. You've abandoned your job and a lot of places don't hire you back. Or they'll hire you back as some menial kind of thing, which is why some women feel the necessity three weeks after their baby is born to go back to their regular job and hire somebody else to take care of their kid.

I don't believe in that. I would never have had a baby if I intended for somebody else to take care of him. Pee in my hand, throw up in my hair, that's what this is all about. It's easy for me, but it's not to the Cashmere Sweater Club. Those women are having the worst time, the women who keep their careers and then hire some Spanish person to take care of the kid. The kid doesn't learn English, but learns great Spanish, and cries whenever he's left with his parents. That's pretty scary.

I was talking to a woman last night who is a career woman who just had a baby. She said to me, "You know, you have a baby and all your feminism goes out the window. You are biologically tied to this child." She's finding herself less and less willing to go to work and to do what she should be doing there, leaving this child at home. When I think about that, not personally but in generic terms, I say, "Why can't we as a society allow for that? Why do we make women choose? Why don't we value child rearing? Look what happens when you don't rear your children right." You'd think it would be a big issue, that we would structure things so that women could have that time and not lose their career momentum, that they could be paid to do it.

The majority of workingwomen don't make very much money. It's just a struggle for them to pay the rent. There's no glamour about this at all. They're just surviving. It drives me crazy to see the disparity between what they pay men and women. Single parents should be paid a differential or something. It isn't right to have all these kids growing up in poverty with these women who are at work all the time.

We run a big child-care program, kindergarten and day school here. These women drop their kids off to us in the morning and at six o'clock they pick them up. We do the best we can, but I'm not sure that's the way things should be. I'm willing to run the program. Somebody's got to do it.

Needless to say, I was really surprised when I did get pregnant and sort of shocked. I hadn't used any birth control in years and just figured I couldn't get pregnant. But I was real happy. I thought, "This is great, just what I need. This is really going to make my life come together." But I hadn't said, "I think I'll get pregnant."

There was a problem. I was having affairs with two men at the time, and I really wasn't sure which of them was the father. One of them was a younger man of Spanish descent and the other one was a black writer I met through my work. I figured at least one of them is black and one of them is white, so when it really happens I'll know what the deal is. It'll be real clear right off the top.

The killer is that the younger man had decided that he didn't want to see me anymore. I was too old for him. Wouldn't you know it, the very last night that we were together, that was the night that I got pregnant by him. To tell you the truth, I've never seen him since. He's never seen our son.

My other boyfriend, the black man, is one of the most sensitive people I've met in my whole life. When I told him I was pregnant, I said, "I don't know if it's your baby. It might be the other guy's baby, I'm just not sure."

"If anything," he said, "I think what you really need is a friend right now, somebody to help you do this whole thing. Let's just act like it's my baby. Then we'll take it from the top if it's not. But let's not tell everybody about this because, see, I have another woman." He had a long-term relationship with another woman. *Falcon Crest* has nothing on me. And he didn't want to put her through all the grief that she would go through, plus this news would probably break up their relationship. I could understand that. I figured, "Having a man hanging out with me for part of the time while I'm pregnant is better than not having anybody to hang out with me at all." Plus I really loved him and wanted it to be his baby.

I was really embarrassed to call up my relatives and

tell them, "The truth is, I don't know which of these guys the father is." I figured it would be better to prepare them for me having a little mulatto child than the other way around. It would be easier for them to deal with like this. But since I wasn't seeing the younger guy anymore, I told all the people where I worked that it was *his* baby, because they knew the writer and the other girlfriend. I don't know how I even thought of all this at the time. They say that pregnant women don't get enough oxygen to their brains, because the babies are sucking it all up, so maybe that's the reason. I had to really work at keeping my stories straight.

I was prepared from the beginning to deal with this on my own anyway. This is my kid and this is my trip. It's really nice this one guy was so supportive through the whole thing. That made it a lot easier. But it wasn't his kid. I decided it would be better to move and be with my family after he was born. It was a real good opportunity for me to pack up and leave, start a new life, wipe the slate clean, and see what happens after that.

This might be a better place for me to find a man that was either divorced or had some other kids. Statistically it probably would be, but in reality a relationship is next to the furthest thing from my mind. I'm kept so busy in daily life and dealing with my son, Ian. I rarely go out. I don't have much of a social life. Ian is my main man now. I jokingly tell everyone that this is the best relationship I ever had with a male. But it's true.

I'm really glad I didn't know how much work kids were before I had Ian, or I might have reconsidered. I'm not saying that I'm sorry I made this choice by any means; I've never regretted it. But you can only realize how much work it is to have a child when you do it yourself.

My roommate got really mad at me the other night

because Ian wouldn't stop crying and I finally screamed, "Stop crying!" She was sick and I was trying to fix her some dinner, do dishes, and take care of him, all these things at once. She goes, "That's got to be the stupidest thing in the world, screaming at him to stop crying."

I bit my tongue, but I wanted to say, "I paid for him. He's mine. If I want to scream at him, I'm going to. If it relieves some stress in me then it serves the purpose, because he's already stressed out. There's nothing I can do for him."

It doesn't matter if I never get married. It'd be nice. I'm not saying that there's anything wrong with that type of situation, having a mom and a dad. Given the choice, I would definitely go for it with the right person. But if it doesn't happen, I can make it on my own. It's not anywhere near to the worst thing that's ever happened to me in my life. I'm going to be forty this year. I still have a couple of good years left in me. And at least I have Ian.

Starting at age thirty-seven—I'm now forty-five—I pursued the business of adoption, to the extent that on three occasions I actually got as far as being able to have a child. But I got cold feet in every one of those instances. The most recent was two years ago.

I really think that family is the greatest thing, not necessarily my own experience of family, but my idea of it. Single life is not so bad, but it means that the essential things in life have to do with your work and your friends and yourself. It's too selfish, this single living. It leaves out a lot of substance of life, because it is so selfish. Life slips by without your noticing it. That's what happens with not having kids.

But this is my year to decide. This is the year that I'm either going to do it or not do it. Frankly, at this point, even if I said I'd do it, it would take me another two or three years to get the kid. So I'd be a very old mother. But I haven't closed the door.

I'm thinking about women who are very young and very poor, not necessarily homeless, but stuck with any number of young children and living on the edge of disaster. Living an emergency, surrounded by danger and death. I think how heroic it is of them to continue to keep on living and somehow managing to survive. There is a whole world out there of women and children who are living that way, a whole world of women who don't have the luxury to think about what men should or shouldn't be doing, or what women's rights are, about any kind of job much less a career, because they really can't feed their kids. Another reality.

I don't know whether to call myself an advocate. I'm the director of a bunch of programs that provide services to children who are poor or handicapped or at risk of going into foster care. Day-care programs, shelter programs, services to try to house people and prevent families from breaking up. I'm an advocate, because I don't think it's enough to provide services. The policies—especially the policies that affect the children of this country—have to change.

I work very hard with the issues of poor women which certainly have a lot to do with men, since they all have children. But men aren't playing day-to-day roles in their lives. They are only the seed bearers. Men aren't officially in their lives, because they aren't on their welfare budgets. Men are only in their lives as a danger of hurting.

My own life is in contrast to the lives of the people with whom I work and whom I mingle. My life has been fulfilled. My own relationships with men have been exciting and deep, certainly not happy, but good and interesting and full of juice. They are two separate worlds and there is very little bridge. One is concealed and hidden. I live in both. Sometimes it is jarring coming back from one or the other. It's hard.

I wish I could go back to playing with kids and having the luxury of being focused on the spit-up on my shoulder. I'd like to be home with my little girl. I really wish this other world I live in didn't exist. I wish every child had a home and enough to eat. That's what moves me. It isn't fair.

It sounds terrible to say it, but in many ways, it's extremely liberating when your mother dies. You stop doing things and thinking, "What will my mother think about this?" You don't need anyone else's approval. At the same time, it makes you feel very alone. Even if you hated your mother and vowed that you would do everything exactly opposite, your mother is still a big influence on your life. Probably for women, men are not the biggest influence on their lives. Their mothers are.

When my mom separated from my dad, we began to get close for the first time. In a sense, she finally began to blossom. She had always thought of herself as un-educated, unimportant, and quiet, and it wasn't so. She was an avid reader and became freer after my dad left. She had been cloistered in a sense. And we were getting to really know each other.

One day, I'm working and my mom comes to the office. She says, "Can I have a cup of coffee with you?" She sat down and she had this funny look.

"What's the matter?" I asked her.

"I have cancer."

"I don't believe it. What makes you think so?"

"I just saw the X rays and I'm pretty sure that I have cancer."

"Let's not panic. I'll get the X rays and see about this." I called up and pretended to be my mother's doctor's secretary. I asked for the X rays and said somebody would be over to pick them up. Then I went over and got them. I took them to my doctor and he said, "Yep, it's lung cancer." So she had to go on and have the next test. That showed that it was the fastest kind of cancer. You only live three months after you find out you have it.

Those next few months we got very close. We would laugh about it, because it didn't seem real sometimes. She was packing up her recipes all the time, trying not to leave a mess when she was dead. She would give me a million instructions. We both agreed that we wouldn't do the radiation or chemo-therapy. They can prolong life a little bit, but not more than a month.

One night the kids and I were going to get her to go for hamburgers. We got to her apartment. My daugh-ter went to the door and said, "Come on, Grandma, we're ready." She was just a little ten-year-old at the time. She looked at me and said, "Something is wrong, Mom." I went in and my mother had had a stroke. She was sitting in a chair doing nothing, just staring. It was a horror that my daughter has had a long time getting over.

I call the doctor and the ambulance and they take her to the hospital. The stroke was caused by the cancer that affected an artery in her neck. But they're going to teach her to walk again anyway, because she still had a couple of months left out of her time. None of us had any money, so she had to go on Medicaid which was abhorrent to her.

I went to the hospital every day. Another one of my daughters was in college at the time and she would send letters. My mother would recognize the writing and start crying, but she couldn't talk. She could sing, but she couldn't talk. She only had the tune, not the words.

The only words my mother was left with were, "Yes, ma'am." That was all she could say to anything, "Yes, ma'am. Yes, ma'am."

One of the nurses told me something later which I wish I'd known sooner. She said, "Some women are left with 'Fuck you!' Be glad it's 'Yes, ma'am.' "

At least people respond well to "Yes, ma'am." Do you want to eat?

"Yes, ma'am."

Do you want to go to the bathroom?

"Yes, ma'am."

To die?

"Yes, ma'am."

When you reach the mid-forties, you get a sense of mortality. It's shocking. Once you have a sense of your own mortality then everything changes. There is your own physical deterioration and also that sense of a shortened period of time in the future. And you start assessing your life. Suddenly, the coin flips. You no longer think that you are invincible, that you can do anything, and that you have time.

Suddenly the reverse happens. You don't think you can do anything else than what you're doing. "Oh, my God, this is it. I'm trapped here for the rest of my life. How did I ever get to this point? I'll never be able to make any change. I'm too old. I'm too tired." That's what's dangerous. You have to work hard to battle against it.

On the other hand, with this age comes an extraordinary amount of self-knowledge, knowledge about the world and people. I sometimes think, "I must have been an idiot, so stupid in the past." You know so much now that you didn't know then.

Since I can't run away and go home anymore, I was thinking I may get structure through religion. Or I may just go to a psychiatrist instead. I've decided it's either therapy or become a Catholic.

This is really a confession: I always defined my life by a man. If you asked me anything, I'd begin my answer with, "He." That was all I was interested in, that's all I thought about. I was only involved in my emotional social life. I was never involved in what I was really achieving. I was always achieving something, but I never gave it any credibility. What was important was if I had a successful relationship with a man and if it was going okay. That was how I saw myself. If he was handsome or bright or successful, that was good for me, and that's what I would talk about.

But it was always a rocky world for me. I mean, why after twenty-one years, have I never been married and no relationship has been successful with men? I had a great time. I did erotic, fun things, exotic things, and was involved with all sorts of different kinds of people. Even if he were a junkie, I would fight not to let him go. I was scared to be on my own.

Somehow it changed. In the last five years, somebody who really had her feet in traditional values decided that she could do it on her own. I could work for a corporation and be an executive.

I was enormously glad when I got this job. That night, I got all the women friends I know together and had a celebration. It was like a coming-out party, coming out of this other mentality.

I changed. I really did. The first day that I walked into that office building, I was a different person. I felt differently about myself. I was achieving something on my own.

It was hard. I was still scared. I don't have a lot of that killer stuff that I think you need. But I had the capability. I always had the capability. What I think is, "Why didn't I have this mentality twenty years ago? I'd be so terrifically successful now."

Then a year ago, I thought, "Now, what happened to that other part of my life?" As soon as I took this path, I had no more relationships. I have not had a relationship with a man since I started this. It might have something to do with being forty years old, I don't know. There aren't a lot of men for forty-year-old women like me. I'm putting my energy to work.

But that other missing part of my life is very hard to reconcile. I think, "If I could have felt this terrific about myself all those times when I had a relationship with a man, I would have had it all."

To be honest, I'm with a lot of these women who are talking about "Be your own person," all this feminist movement stuff. They are years younger than I am, all probably educated faster than I was—a lot of Ph.D.'s. They do all this stuff about being feminists and wholeness. I think it's bullshit. I can do all that stuff, living alone, but it doesn't feel whole for me.

The minute they get a man, they change. They're not as angry, they're not as bitter. They're softer women. It's the truth. I don't like being around women who are bitter and angry and hate men. It really scares me for someone to get into that mentality.

After you've spent a long time alone—and I have—you just get fussier and fussier. You aren't as needy about just plain companionship, someone to listen to or to talk to, so you want someone who's interesting. Then you narrow things down even more. It becomes harder and harder.

My guess is that my life will probably be a lot like it has been, which is a sequence of people rather than finding one ultimate person, but if even the sequence wasn't available that would be dreadful.

Women who like men and want them and need them generally find them in one form or another, even if they aren't ideal. Mid-forties, a large urban area, it ain't easy to find them. Single women have a tough time of it, tougher than men. That's about the only thing I can deduce from living as much as I've lived. The options aren't as available to finding partners and sex and companionship. Things still aren't equal along those lines. Men still get to do the asking. They're definitely in the driver's seat. They're in power in general, in business, but they're also in power in terms of finding a relationship, in terms of marriage.

When a forty-five-year-old woman meets a forty-five-year-old man, chances are that man is not going to be interested in her at all. First of all, he can have virtually any woman. Partners from eighteen to sixty are possible for him. The likelihood is that he'll go for someone younger. So there is an unfortunate inequity in that regard.

In those earlier years, you can meet men—if you're interested in them and in flirtation and you enjoy it—from rides on public transportation, plane trips, walking down the street or through the park. The whole world is out there exciting for you. Then things start slowing down as you get older. You get to the point where when a construction worker whistles at you, it no longer is insulting. "Thank you very much." Then you get to the point that meeting strangers is not as exciting, it's not as possible, and you start worrying that it might be dangerous, too.

I do have a sense of romance left. It's hard to believe. It's double-edged, romance. It can keep you fantasizing your life away and never getting down to things and being realistic. On the other hand, it's the best stuff.

Most of my friends are married. For many years, they were envious of me, because of my single life—the running around, going to parties, meeting guys,

buying dresses, flying off here and there for some as-
signation. There's nothing more seductive than the
newness of a relationship and wanting to please someone. But I was envious of their more predictable lives
with family.

As things change, as I move into my forties, as these
marriages get older and the women get older, they
don't envy me anymore. Married women who got
married in their twenties and have stayed married,
they make peace with it by the time they've been married twenty years. Instead, their energy is concen-
trated on themselves in a new way now and on their
careers and, in some cases, on a more spiritual life.
So I ended up feeling sort of "retro." I'm still out
there doing what I was doing in my thirties—having
boyfriends, making appointments, breaking up, reject-
ing people.

I mean, it gets tiresome after a while. And you want
something. I see that you can get to a level of richness
with a very long-term relationship. It has lots of
compromises and unhappiness, but it's like achieving
levels of consciousness. I see that you can have
something different with that duration.

I think I'm going to go out of my mind with a man
around the house twenty-four hours a day since he
retired. I don't have any real privacy. He wanders in
the back door and out the front door, then in the front
door and out the back. It's rough. It's like if I went to
his office and started staying there twenty-four hours
a day with him.

It was forced retirement. But after all, he's seventy-
one years old. The problem is he doesn't have any

hobbies, doesn't go out with friends, he doesn't do *anything* except play around out in the garage. I've just been doing things and having a good time the last few years. I'm going places all the time. Even the work I do at the school district, I love it. But I also love being home—*alone*.

We've been married for forty-three years. We don't communicate much. In fact, when we first met, we didn't communicate much. It was a physical attraction, but we really did not have much to say to each other. He was all action.

We've never conversed. I can talk with dozens of other people, but I just can't have a conversation with him. He's too negative. I've known this all along, but I was too busy with the kids to care at that time. Then when the kids were all gone, I just went back to work, so it didn't matter.

If I get on the phone, he'll come and sit down in the next room like he's listening. It isn't that I'm saying anything that I wouldn't want him to know, it's just that I don't like people sitting there listening to what I'm saying. I feel like I'm being held back. It may only be me. It may all be in my head.

I'll sit in the living room watching TV with him for a little while and then go into the kitchen to get a cup of coffee. If I stay in the living room, he stays in the living room. But if I go into the kitchen and stay there for ten minutes, he's right in there: "What are you doing?"

Then I'll go upstairs to sew for a while. He won't talk to me when I'm downstairs. We don't hardly talk to each other. He'll come up and sit in the room with me and talk. That's odd. I guess he's lonesome and wants someone to talk to.

If he knows I'm going off somewhere in the car, he'll sit on the edge of the stove or in the dining room and wait and wait and wait while I'm getting ready to go. I forget half the stuff I'm supposed to take with me, because it makes me so nervous to have him sitting there staring at me all the time. Then he'll come to the door with me like I can't leave by myself. Then he'll stand on the porch in the doorway, looking at me as I drive away. Nine times out of ten, when I get back, he'll be sitting on the porch waiting for me, or he'll open the door just as I get to it, like he has nothing to do but sit and wait for me to come home again. I hate that. I hate having somebody just sitting and staring at me all the time.

I miss my privacy. It's not being able to be home alone, having somebody watching every move I make. I still do all the shopping, all the cleaning, all the cooking, all the dishes. He would do the dishes, but it's such an easy job that I just get in and do it as soon as dinner is over anyway. He doesn't do anything.

I want him to clean up the garage first. If I let him get busy in the house all the time, then he won't get that done to a point where he can spend some time out there doing things. He can make a lamp out of anything. He can build anything he sets his mind to. But he's got so much junk in there, that there's no room to build. So I want him to get that straightened out first.

I told him, "You've got to find something to do. You can't just sit around here all the time watching TV. It's not good for your health."

"I don't believe in this health business."

Don't believe in this health business? What does that mean? I'm not talking about fiber. I'm trying to maintain him. I don't want him to die. People who retire and sit around all day don't live long. Although, his mother lived to be ninety-three. His father's ninety-one. I don't want another twenty years of him sitting around here watching every move I make.

I feel guilty about the way I feel about him. I have

had practically everything I've wanted, practically the way I want it. If I say I want something, he'll say, "Go get it." If I want to go somewhere, he'll say, "Go ahead and go." He doesn't care as long as he doesn't have to go, too. So I feel guilty resenting him being at home all the time.

I have it lucky, I know. I have a husband who still acts like he loves me. I don't *know* if he loves me or not, but he acts like he does. There's no chance of a breakup. I just resent the fact that he's around all the time. Even one day a week, just to be home alone one day a week, would be like Christmas.

I don't always know that my husband admires me. I often have to ask for reassurance. Sometimes I don't have the nerve to ask. I just need it. I hope he guesses, because I don't feel very good about myself. The way I feel about myself is still very much a reflection of the way others see me. I'm still a child that Mother set to perform a dance on Saturday morning for the aunts. I still need admiration.

I periodically get kind of disgusted with myself and the way I look, getting older. My body doesn't respond the way it used to. I can't count on it. I have a pinched nerve that gives me problems and I swell up when I don't want to and I break out in the most terrible sweats at the most inconvenient times. My body is betraying me again like when I was a kid and I couldn't be a ballet dancer, because I suddenly got breasts and hips.

49

There's a woman down south of here who has a hundred and fifty-seven cats at the last count. She's always getting kicked out of her house and they're always taking her cats away. I'm afraid I'll be her. That someday I'll wake up and I'll have this house, all this stuff, and all these animals. I won't have anything else. The animals will be my whole existence. Then they'll come and take them away, because there're too damn many of them. That's my biggest fear.

It comes in waves. There are times I don't feel my age anymore at all. I go for days, weeks, months not thinking about getting older. Then there are days when it's a real painful prospect, getting older, being alone, getting sickly. The mothers of many of my contemporaries are sick. One fell and broke her hip and my friend's facing the caretaking. "Do I take care of her? Do I get her a housekeeper? What do I do?"

I hope when my mother dies, she dies, and it's no debilitating illness where I have to debate whether I should shoot her or whatever. I always kid her about that.

There are more women alive in older years than men. Marriage was never important to me. I didn't have a good example of it from my family life, but I certainly want and would like to live with someone. I still see that as something that I hope to get to in my life. Maybe I'm feeling that now because there are so many men I know who are either royal assholes, have an overwhelming wimp factor—which is the positive side of their personalities—or they're gay and dying of one thing or another. There aren't a lot of opportunities out there now for me in terms of a social life. I feel that is even stronger once you get older.

So when I get depressed, there's a lot to be depressed about. I try to defend against that, but it sometimes hits. It really scares me and it hurts. My friends and I talk about it once in a while, but we don't want to talk about it too much, because it really is depressing.

I feel like I haven't really given myself a chance to live yet, why should I worry about what's going to happen when I'm seventy? It's hard for me to even think of myself as middle-aged at this point, but I'm getting there and that's scary. It hits home.

I'd just like to be exactly who I am. My job doesn't seem as important to me anymore. I'd like to get married again. I'd like to have a companion. I think that would make me whole again. I don't want to grow old by myself. That's a real thought for me right now. My ex-husband's dad died in a hotel by himself. The only reason they found him was that the bartender missed him. Occasionally that thought comes to mind, dying alone.

What I want to do is to continue to grow and change, because change is good. In a lot of ways, I haven't changed much. I'm still out there picketing and protesting, trying to change the world a little bit. I love feeling like I'm making a contribution. I like to feel I have a positive influence on people. I'd like to think I could be a role model for people to look up to me. In order to do that, I have to look up to me. So I'm working on that, developing that other side of me that I neglected for a long time, the who I am rather than what I do.

I can do whatever I want, like my dad said. I have a lot to offer. Much more so now than I ever could before, because I feel stronger about myself.

But I waver. I get into these places where I say, "What's wrong with me? There's nobody out there and I'm going to be by myself. Fuck it! I don't care. I'll be by myself. I'll show them." That kind of stuff. But it doesn't happen very often.

In the next few years, women will let go of their anger toward men, quit being so dykish about things, and just soften a bit with sensibility. From there, women will be able to have relationships and a career and children and everything at once, but not have to be such soldiers about it. *Soldiers* is a good word. You can almost see them marching. Oh, God, it's devastating. "First I'll get a job and then I'll get a career and then a husband and then I'll get a kid. Hut! Hut! Hut! Hut!" They don't have to do it all. I just want to do what I'm best at and what comes naturally.

We have a long way to go. Our generation is right in the forefront of all this stuff, pioneers. We've had a lot of casualties. To a great extent, the inability of our generation to form lasting relationships has to do with the uncertainty of being the first to try things, not

WOMEN

knowing what your role should be. My grandmothers
didn't have a lot of choices, but in a way that can make
things easier. You didn't make a lot of mistakes because your life was one big mistake.

My mother is in the middle there. My mother didn't
have much ambition—just to get out of her family
home, live her life, and ultimately get married and
have children. That was the end for her. She's very
brilliant, a wonderful person. Look what she's con-
tributed. She's put four extraordinary people out into
the world who are doing things that are important, that
are contributing. That didn't happen by accident. So
her contribution measured against mine, which would
be greater? I don't know.

I look at some of my cousins' kids—seventeen-,
eighteen-, nineteen-year-old kids—they don't know
that they're growing up in a different world than we
grew up in. They don't really value the kinds of
choices they have now.

There's one particular girl whom I've been close to
—a second cousin of mine. She's nineteen and has
two children and is pregnant with the third one. My
first impulse was to tell her, "Don't do that! You're
crazy!" Then I thought, "Marilyn, how the hell do
you know? Why don't you shut up? Let the little girl
do what she wants to do. Are you sure you're right?"

I'm not sure. I'm not sure at all. Maybe we don't
really have a choice at all. We just do what we're
going to do, and choice is an illusion.

It's easy to see why people make such a big deal about
the differences between women and men. That makes
it so much simpler and easier to identify everybody.

53

Break all the things humans can do into segments, then assign them. "Here's what you should do. There's what you should do." Unfortunately, these divisions become prisons, tombs where people are sealed up in their category.

The women's movement has worked in the sense that much of what we fought for is taken for granted now. There have been a lot of strides made in the lives of women. But when things become difficult—economically, politically—the old ways rear their heads and almost immediately those little categories begin working again. Those old ways are always just underneath the surface. My mother was involved in the women's movement of the 1930s. She knows how people forget. It starts up and it dies down. It starts up again. The eternal struggle of people to be free. It's not seen that way. Women are a joke. They're not really oppressed. They're women, that's all they are.

Women are just flesh and blood. That's all we are. A bunch of organs and a brain. What's the big deal? We're part of everything else, too. Why must we make cruel and unjust demarcations between ourselves? That's true of all kinds of people. No people are inferior. No people are superior. They are just people.

There is such a wide range of things people can do, feel, be. We've just chosen some of those things as a way of holding ourselves together—that's what culture is. But it doesn't mean that stripped down we are any different. I don't believe any of us are.

2. Sugar, Spice, Things Not So Nice

Good little girls are nice little girls. Mothers and fathers admonish their daughters to be good, and beam with pride when the second-grade teacher gushes, "She's such a *nice* little girl." But when women talk about childhood, it is apparent that "nice" is not so nice. For a girl to be nice, she must lose something of herself.

Here are examples from the lives of three generations of women in one family—my family. The first is my grandmother, Nora Taylor, from an interview conducted not long before her death in 1987.

"I was born in 1908, about seven miles outside of Waycross, in Ware County, Georgia. In them olden days, boys was all there was in the world to them. They favored them over the girls. They said it was because boys would work. I don't know what they thought my mama was doing out there hoeing in the fields from daylight to dark.

"My younger brother, Luther, me and him never did get along, because he was mean, just as mean as the Devil. My daddy used to go to town and he'd buy us each a pack of chewing gum apiece and some candy and give it to us. I'd save some of mine, 'cause I knew we weren't agoing to get no more till he went to town again. No telling, maybe a week or more from that. Luther'd put all that gum in his mouth and chew every bit of that pack. He'd have it in his mouth so big that he couldn't hardly turn it over.

"Then, when he'd chewed it all, he wanted mine. And my mama'd say, 'Well, I'd give him a little piece, 'cause you're bigger than he is.' So on and so on and so on.

"I'd give him my chewing gum and he'd chew mine *and* his. That's just how selfish he was. Instead of them telling him, 'You've already chewed yours, now leave her alone.' They didn't do that, see. They called themselves teaching us to divide, but I always had to give up mine.''

My mother, Gloria Baker, was born to Nora Taylor in 1928. By that time, the family had moved from a sharecropper farm into the small town of Waycross. The boy, Layton, that my mother mentions, is her uncle. Because he was only two years older than she, the two children grew up virtually as brother and sister.

"There was a difference in the way they raised the girl children and the boy children. I always thought marbles were the prettiest things I'd ever seen. I didn't have any marbles, because that was something boys played with. Layton had a cigar box full of marbles. All I wanted to do was look at them. They were so pretty. They were cat's-eyes and you could look down into them and see the colors. Of course, I was not allowed to touch them.

"I wanted to play marbles with the boys. I can hear my grandmama and my mama saying, 'Gloria Amanda, get up from there. You're not supposed to be squatting down there, playing marbles. Girls don't squat around.' The boys would play marbles and the girls would stand around and watch.

" 'Layton's a boy. You're not a boy.' That was the answer you'd get if you asked 'Why?' There were just some things that boys did that girls didn't do. I never did understand it. Did I resent it? Of course, I did. I thought they were just being mean."

Cynthia Baker, my sister, was born in Dallas, Texas, in 1955. Our family was now middle class and suburban.

"I wasn't too good at being a nice little girl, but I never had doubts about being a girl. Mother will tell you, we'd go in the store and I was the one who picked out those dresses with the crinoline petticoats, because I wanted to be beautiful. I liked to run with the boys and do all the rough things, but I also wanted to be Cinderella, Sleeping Beauty, and all those lovely girls. I'd pick out the frilliest dresses myself, even though I knew how uncomfortable they were going to be. You know, beauty has its price. It does.

"For Easter Sunday, I always had a little white hat, a white dress, new white shoes, a new pocketbook, white socks with lace on them, and white gloves. Mother would wash my hair on Saturday night, then roll it in tight, teeny-weeny pin curls on my head. The next morning we'd brush it out, which was excruciating. Then she'd stick the little hat on my head. They were one-size-fits-all, so it had these pipe-cleaner-like things that could be bent in, so it clamped onto your head. I'd put on the little skirt that was always tight, because I was kind of chubby. The petticoat pricks into your legs and it hurts. It stuck out so that every time you moved, your butt showed in the back.

"My mother would walk by me and say, 'Cynthia, you're sitting bawdy. Put your legs together.' I don't know where the expression came from. Probably it came from Grandmom saying, 'Look at that little girl. Gloria Amanda, you got to teach her not to sit bawdy.' So, I'd sit there for a while with my legs pressed together. Of course, I had fat legs, so it was hard.

"Then my brother would come by and say, 'You're sitting bawdy. Mom, Cynthia is sitting bawdy again!'

Then Dad would come through and say, 'What are you doing? You're sitting bawdy.'

"There were ten years of my life where the only response I got from the other human beings in my house was, 'You're sitting bawdy.' Did you sit with your legs together when you were eight or nine? No. That wasn't anything I thought about either. I think I sat bawdy until I was thirteen or fourteen, until I finally got embarrassed about it. Then I crossed my legs, but my problem was with chubby legs—it was hard to cross them. I don't know how you all expected me to sit with my legs closed *all* the time."

In a girl's life, "nice" becomes an ominous word. Give way, don't be squatting around, don't sit bawdy. The boisterous, full-tilt run of childhood is arrested in midstride and replaced with more demure mincing steps. Nice becomes a bridle, or perhaps a gilded cage.

As girls grow older they discover that it's not nice to be too smart either. One woman told me, "I had a lot of girlfriends who, from ninth grade to twelfth grade, got progressively dumber, because that was what was expected of them. I could see them doing it. They may have gotten progressively more popular also, but they consciously checked out of academics. It was not something that did them any good."

Then after puberty comes another definition of a nice girl—she is a virgin. Consequently, the most radically rebellious act a girl can commit is to have sex. This woman's reaction was typical of those who chose to rebel: "I began screwing around when I was quite young. I was about fifteen. I had tremendous guilt about it, thought I was the only one, such a bad girl. Part of it was the pleasure, but part of it was to say, 'Screw you!' to everything and everybody, the church and my parents and all that."

Sexual rebellion among young women is less shocking today than it once was. But the shift in cultural attitudes concerning premarital sex has increased the social pressures surrounding a girl's sexuality. A woman who was a teenager in the early '70s explains: "Sex is always a peer pressure item, but with our generation it was how many men you could sleep with, how adept you became at having sex with men. It wasn't so much that you had a boyfriend that you did it with or that you lost your virginity. With us it was more like the body count. It was how cool you were if you were able to just be uninhibited and experiment with all kinds of drugs and different types of sexual things. For somebody sixteen or seventeen years old, that was tough."

For the nice girls who don't rebel—or who limit their defiance to outrageous hairstyles, loud music, and boyfriends with motorcycles—the only legitimate rite of passage from childhood to adulthood, the one acceptable escape route from the family, is marriage. "I ended up being married at quite a young age," one woman said, "because it was really the only way to leave home. Their pushing me into getting married was the only way my parents knew to handle the situation. It was the only way they knew for a young person to get out—the only way that would be *permissible*. So that's what I did."

For some of the women I interviewed, college was just a halfway house for the unmarried, a bivouac on the husband-hunting safari. One young woman told me, "Used to be that you went to college so you could meet a husband. The bottom line is that I think that's still true, just nobody wants to talk about it." For others, living away from home on a college campus was their first taste of real freedom. Education was their springboard to independence.

Whatever decisions a woman makes as an adult, whether rebellious, accommodating, or reactionary, she will always hear those words from childhood echoing in her head, "Be nice, be nice." All the women interviewed for this book grew up being coaxed, exhorted, and compelled in one way or another to "be nice." Today the tyranny of nice continues, unbroken. Here, again, is my sister, Cynthia, talking about a four-year-old girl she teaches in pre-school:

"I have this little girl who can out-boy any boy in my class. But Tuesday was Picture Day and she came to school dressed in this gorgeous pink dress, her white Sunday school shoes, pink socks with the lace on the tops, and a great big pink bow in her hair for her school pictures.

"By the time the day was over, the dress looked like it had been through a war. It had grass stains on it and dirt everywhere. She had done all the things that she does with the boys, climbing the swing set, running around, sitting in the dirt, and digging worms. But she had her girlie uniform on. It didn't stop her from doing anything she wanted to do, but I wasn't there when her mama picked her up, thank goodness. I don't believe her mother would have thought it was very nice."

For the first eight years of my life, I was the little princess. I was going to be the best. I was the most gorgeous. I was *it*.

My mother would smother me, then tell me I was obnoxious. Everything she wanted me to do, I wanted to do completely the opposite. Like, if we were coloring Easter eggs, her Easter eggs had to be perfect. Perfect! I wanted to slam all them decals on them, make the ones with the weird ears and the bloodshot eyes. She wanted to have the ones you take pictures of with gorgeous stripes and patterns. I'd put purple and pink and green all together and it would come out some really bizarre color.

I had very long hair, down to my knees. My mother, she loved that. She used to mess with that all the time, braiding it and twisting it and curling it. I'd have headaches from her playing with that stuff. She'd have it pulled back so tight, I'd look like I was Chinese. I just wanted her to let it go. *Let it go!*

I took all the barrettes and ribbons and things out of my hair, then I'd go swinging in the swing out over the dirt. I would lean way back and drag my hair on the ground. I liked that. That was great.

Then when I got to the eighth grade, she took me to the beauty parlor and cut it, because I wouldn't take care of it. It was in two long braids. They just cut them braids off right next to my head.

My father kept them. He still has them. It's weird looking at dead hair laying in somebody's drawer. They're still there. He's got my teeth, too.

I wanted it cut in a way, because that would keep her out of it. But then, after it was done, I was mad. I started rebelling.

Growing up, I always wanted to be a dancer. But my mother wouldn't let me take dance classes. She thought you had to be really tall and really thin. She said, "You're not shaped right."

I used to dance by myself in my room on tiptoes, because I didn't want anyone downstairs to hear it. Or

I would stand in one place and dance or get on the bed and dance. I didn't want anybody to know that I was dancing. I believed her about that for almost thirteen years.

I wanted to be a boy, because boys had freedom and girls didn't. It had nothing to do with sex as far as I remember; the sexual parts were not involved in this. I wanted to be a boy, because then you could join the Navy and see the world. Even though it might have been wrong of me to think that girls couldn't do such things, that was the feeling. Only boy characters in my books did things. What's the purpose of a girl? It didn't make any sense to me. Who would want to do that, just stay home and wear these funny clothes?

I had a best friend named Skip. He lived in the big house to the left of ours. He was adopted and the best-looking boy in the class. The girls were all jealous, because they thought we were boyfriend and girl-friend, but we were just friends. There was his buddy, Wesley, who was the brain and lived on the opposite street up the block. The three of us would hang out together all the time and play fantasy games—make the backyard and the porches into a ship. He would be the head swashbuckling sailor and I would be his girl and we would run into trouble and have adventures, running around the yard and climbing trees.

As the firstborn kid in the family, my parents let me do anything. They let me talk when I wanted and get up in the middle of the night and visit with their friends.

I got to kindergarten and they told me to be quiet. I didn't like that. The teacher would let me play the triangle if I didn't talk all morning, because I liked the triangle. I learned real quick to be "the good girl." Looking over my report cards, that was the only year Valerie talked too much. Then she started being a good girl.

Of course, they used to spank you in school. They had kids walk up to the teachers' desks and then they'd hit them with a yardstick in front of the whole class. It was so horrifying to me. I don't know that I actually got spanked. I remember this spanking so vividly, but I don't know if it was me or some other kid. I felt so much for the kid who did get spanked. I could just imagine what it was like for him to walk up there and bend over and get spanked with a yardstick in front of the whole first grade.

Even when I said my little prayer at night that my parents had taught me, the last line was, "And make Valerie a better girl." You always felt like you had to do better.

I used to take a little ring and stick it on the wrong finger so that I'd notice it; that was the promise to myself to do whatever I needed to be better, like tying a string around your finger. Then I'd look down on it and go, "Oh, yeah. I was going to be real good about this." That would be my little reminder that I had to be a better girl—got to be a better girl.

The problem is, you never can be that good. It just never happens. But you're supposed to be, so there's always this big effort. It doesn't go away. You're never done. You're never okay. You're never finished. You have to be better, which basically means you're never good enough. So there wasn't much satisfaction.

Things are always less satisfying than I want them to be; nothing is ever quite good enough. Nothing seems to quite work out the way you want it to be. Expectations—that's it—they're just too damn high. For me and everybody else. I don't know who had such high expectations for me that made me be this way, but it's in me. Everything falls short and I'm always pissed off at everybody, including myself. So I'm lousy to be with because of that. I'm too demanding. You end up being unhappy, because things don't work out the way you expect them to. It's a terrible way to be. I shouldn't be that way.

My mother wanted me to have the kind of life she had wanted for herself. She was a very dynamic woman in a small circle. She wanted me to be that in a larger circle. She wanted her kids to be geniuses, and she was vocally disappointed that we weren't. There was a constant struggle and we all grew up feeling that we had not met our potential.

I'd do something and get wonderful feedback and think, "This is great. I've done a wonderful job . . . but." There was always a little "but." That was her: "Oh, I'm so proud of you . . . but, next time . . ."

I grew up in a typical family, middle-of-the-road, Democratic, fundamentalist Church of Christ. My mother voted for who my father said. It was pretty simple, except for Kennedy. That was the one they had an altercation over. My mother wouldn't vote for Kennedy because he was Catholic.

As I grew up, my dad and I had really fun things we'd do. Come as You Are Breakfasts. Daddy and I would get in the car, go wake up my friends in the morning in their pajamas, and bring them to my house. Daddy would make pancakes. Everybody loved to come to my house. Now I have this perverse thought that Daddy just liked seeing the little girls in their nightgowns, but I'm not sure about that. I think Dad was pretty cool. You hear all this stuff and you think, "God, was Dad one of those? Not my dad. No."

I went to church Sunday morning, Sunday night, and Wednesday night. I didn't really buy it very much. I don't know why. I felt forced into it, but I was not so bad of a kid that I wouldn't go. I just wasn't very reverent. I'd talk and my dad would walk down the middle of the aisle and thump me on the back of the head.

I have very fond memories of some of that. My dad would play with my hands in church to keep me quiet. To this day, I love a man's hands. The same congregation is still there when I go home to see my mom and go to church with her.

My parents always chaperoned the school dances. Which was good news/bad news. The good news was that they did, and the bad news was that they did. We used to cruise Main Street as a family, Mom, Dad, and me. She'd say, "Oh, there's a cute one."

We'd all three eat dinner together. Then Daddy would go into the den. Mother and I would sit there, talk about our day and pick at the food. Oftentimes, after dates, I would get in bed with my mom and dad and tell them about my date. Daddy would go, "Shut up and get out of here, I need to sleep." On the other hand, I think he liked it, too.

They were wonderful parents. They were never out of line with us and they were very consistent.

My father was affectionate and we always got along very well. He was kind of distant talking about stuff. We talked about politics and school, but nothing personal.

But my mother was always completely accessible for all the personal stuff. You could go and talk to her and tell her anything. It was pretty amazing. In adolescence when you have problems anyway, there were always times when I could go to her and say, "Okay, let me tell you what I'm up to." I'd tell her everything. She wouldn't freak out and wouldn't punish me. We're talking drugs, sex, rock 'n' roll, some heavy-duty stuff.

"Maybe you ought to do this instead," she'd say. She'd give me some sounding-board stuff which was cool.

My mom is a very harsh woman, a very bitter woman. The things Mom said while she was drinking, she would never admit to when she was sober. Up until I was a freshman in high school, my memories of my mother were mostly of her going to work and not being around.

My dad was around. I never thought my dad liked me. Part of that was from what happened years back. I was eleven and a half years old and a neighbor kid come in and wanted to know if I was playing with my dad. I said, "What are you talking about?"

"You know, playing with his thing."

I got furious and I told the girl, "Get out and don't ever come into my house again." I kept that bottled up inside me for probably six months. I didn't say nothing, because this girl said it was her and my sister that was doing this. I didn't know how to handle anything like this.

Finally, it bothered me enough that I said something to Mom. Well, the next step is Mom and Dad split up a couple of years down the road. Then when Mom would get drunk it was, "If it wasn't for your big fucking mouth, I'd still be married to your father." But Mom would never say that to me when she was sober, ever.

I was thirty-seven years old last year and it was the first time my mother ever said anything to me referring to the fact that I had told her what Dad was doing and this is what brought on the divorce. Right then Mom was sober, and I said, "Mom, what did you want me to do? You were my other parent. You were the one I was supposed to go to."

My dad was molesting my sisters. He never hurt them physically; pain-wise there was never a hurt there. But see, believe it or not, as a child, when you see your dad all the time paying attention to your two other sisters, you wonder what's wrong with you. I was the one that was big. I wasn't petite like my sisters. I was the one that had the freckles and the red hair, and all I got was, "You're fat. You're ugly." I always thought he didn't like me. I always thought he hated me.

I was five-foot-seven by the time I was twelve. But just because I was that size, I was still that little girl inside. They forgot that.

I was very bright. All my life I got straight A's and was highly touted for being smart. At the same time, many teachers and many people were saying, "Why is this person an underachiever? With this intellect, she should be doing so much more." It really disturbed me. I felt my privacy was being tampered with. I did everything everyone expected of me. I was a model child and a model student. Really good and practically perfect. But people kept telling me I was capable of more. "Why don't you do more?"

I told my father, "When I grow up, I want to be an airline stewardess."

"God damn it," he'd say, "that's bullshit. You could be president."

"But I don't want to, Dad."

"All airline stewardesses are whores." All those things have impact. At the time, I just felt batted back and forth. No matter what I did, it wasn't pleasing the important people. Neither one of my parents finished high school, so it meant a lot to them that I be somebody. But they had very narrow ideas of what being somebody was.

At age fifteen, I finally confronted a teacher who was doing an IQ study. Same old story. "Now that I know what your IQ is," he said, "I wonder why you're not doing more."

"What is it I'm supposed to be doing? I really want to know. All my life people have been telling me this."

This particular teacher said to me, "You need to be a scientist."

"But I'm not interested in science."

"That's because you're a girl," he said—this was the first time I heard this, and it took years again before I understood, because this guy was really ahead of his time in one sense—"That's because you're a girl. You've been trained not to be interested." This was the early '50s and nobody had ever said anything like this to me before. I thought, "What the heck does this mean?" I got good grades in science, but I was not interested in it. I was just a regular kid.

Even though my parents had no formal education, my father felt very strongly about wanting to censor what I read. At the same time that he wanted me to extend and be somebody, I wasn't supposed to read anything at home. He didn't want me to read *Gone with the Wind*. He didn't read these things, he just had an image of what they were. He didn't really want to know; he didn't want to think about them. He would flip through a book and if he happened to see anything that appeared to him to be sex, it was out. I started sneaking all my books and reading on the sly.

In high school, I had to give a speech on venereal disease in an all-girl biology class. He called up the principal and forbade me to do it. My family was bigoted, but I was interested in all the racial issues. I was interested in war and had strong feelings against the atom bomb. "Shame on you. Don't say that."

I just went underground. Luckily, I had a few teachers who took me places—innocent, wonderful places, like the museum. My dad said, "Why do you want to go there for?" He meant it.

I'd say I was going out with my girlfriends and instead I would take two or three buses and go to the art museum or a library. At an early age I was going into jazz clubs with older people. My parents never knew that.

I went to a girls' school where we had to wear uniforms and curtsy. They were big on the trappings of ladylike behavior. It was a finishing school, which meant that there were pretensions. I could go on and on and on about the teachers and the values I learned in school, many of which I feel grateful haven't debilitated me forever.

I had a teacher who I hated. She once had an emerald cocktail ring made. She wore it to school and made us all try it on, because we had to understand the concept of "cocktail ring." Believe me, to this day, I don't know what that is. It was so abnormal, but I thought it was normal.

I was the tallest girl for a long time. I was very, very, very self-conscious about my height. Very self-conscious about everything, probably. I started wearing glasses when I was five. At the time, it was only the worst thing that could happen to me. I had no idea that I couldn't see. My parents noticed that I squinted a lot. Seeing better was good, but sticking out was bad. I realized at that point that this was going to be forever and ever. Also I was unpleasantly skinny. So I was tall, very skinny, and had these glasses. I felt like a freak, especially when puberty hit.

This girl-school mentality was frightening. When a delivery man would come in with the tomato soup delivery, we'd all take out our combs and primp, hoping we looked good for him. There was a lot of coquettishness that was taught, or learned somehow, at a very young age to the point of total craziness. The emphasis was on boys, the focus was boys.

I was a Girl Scout for a couple of years. We made vinyl minidresses as one of our projects. I still have mine. It looks like a bib, it's so tiny.

I wasn't athletically inclined. In fact, I probably got more gym excuses at school than anyone else. The really good part about sitting out of gym was that you could hold everybody else's jewelry and try it on.

In junior high school, I transferred to a coed school. I did really badly my first year, I was so boy crazy. I couldn't believe it. It was a disaster. I'd always been in control, and here there were boys everywhere. Sometimes they looked at me and sometimes they didn't. At this point my glasses were about an inch thick. Being tall was worse at a coed school, although there were people who were taller. There were senior basketball players.

Aside from the fact that I was distracted, this was such a better school than the one I had attended that I went from being the number one or two student to not being close to the top. That was a jolt. The one thing I had confidence in was my brain. It was a real struggle to subdue everything so I could study.

I was very shy all through school. I was really almost retarded I was so shy, especially with boys, but with anybody. It was pathetic.

I didn't get asked out much. That's a euphemism. Did I get asked out at all? Saturday nights were not big nights for me in terms of my social life. Saturday nights I would watch the "Mary Tyler Moore Show" with my brothers at home. My parents would be out. Sometimes I'd rummage through my mother's things and try stuff on. I'd read and watch TV. I had a lot of friends, but we didn't date. I don't think we knew that we could at the time. It turns out, the guys were dating girls from other schools where they were faster than we were. I had no idea that there was supposed to be anything more than having a crush on somebody who didn't notice you. I thought that was normal, that was satisfaction.

It was the night of the Moon Walk in 1969. At camp we had our one social of the summer. That's what they called dances at this boys' camp. I wore Becky's dress, because my dresses were so nerdy—although the word nerd didn't exist back then. Because I wasn't allowed to shave my legs yet, I wore Jodi's panty hose. One of the counselors made me up and somebody else took my glasses. The one thing I had that everybody did like was very long, straight hair. I didn't have to iron it or wrap it or anything.

So we get into a little bus and go to the boys' camp. We walk in. I have no glasses. I'm almost legally blind, so I really can't see anything. I was the first person to get asked to dance. It was very exciting. The guy told me he was the oldest guy in his bunk— he was fourteen. I was very impressed. I thought I was going to die.

Not knowing how to talk to a boy, and not being able to see him—I knew he was in the general vicinity —I would say things like, "Boy, the music's loud."

"Oh, well," he'd say, "why don't we go outside?" I thought he was going to rape me or something, so I'd say, "Well, it's loud, but *good* loud. Good. Good."

Then after they played "Sugar, Sugar" for the eighteenth time, we were told that if we all followed single file, we could go to the rec room and watch this historic event in space. But I couldn't find my counselor with the glasses, because I couldn't see. Finally, after what seemed to be hours, I actually just walked into her—Brownian motion. I put the glasses on, and—I swear this is true—the guy split. Thus confirming everything I knew. Even though I got asked right away to dance, I knew it wasn't me. It was Becky's dress, Jodi's panty hose, Linda's makeup, and all the stuff.

Sometimes people look at you like you're a china doll and nothing is wrong in your life. That gets frustrating when people have certain expectations of what you are and what you aren't, just because of the initial reaction of appearance.

Sometimes, you are expected to be dumb. People will not take what you say to be worth anything. You'll say something and everybody will just overlook it.

I remember my mom telling me when I was young, she said, "Be careful, because you are not going to be liked by the girls in your life." I was so young that I didn't understand that it was because I was pretty.

I was one of these girls where I was everybody's buddy. I was never the girlfriend type—not because I didn't want to be. I was made to be that way, because I was so big compared to all the other girls. I didn't have a little figure. You're put in this category where you're either going to be completely outcast, or you're going to be everybody's friend, because you're not going to be a girlfriend. That's how everybody made me feel up to this point. I'm not saying they did this intentionally. It's just the way it's always going to be. I was called "Fullback." How can you be the ideal cheerleader type, when you should be on the team?

It was my father's idea that I was going to be a boy. He was kind of disappointed when I turned out to be a girl. But as I grew up, he treated me like a boy in a way, encouraging me to do more things than he normally would have for a girl in the 1950s. He used to convey to me this idea that you could do anything you want, if you want to do it badly enough.

Mom, on the other hand, looked at me and my sister and decided that Melody was supposed to be the pretty one and I was supposed to be the smart one. Basically, she also told me that I *wasn't* the pretty one. She would say things like, "If you get married . . ." It wasn't a liberal kind of attitude, like that was just one of the many options that a female had in today's society. This was the '50s and she meant, "If you're lucky enough to get married, but I'm not so sure you will, because you're kind of not so pretty."

I used to think, "Gosh, Mom doesn't think I'm ever going to have anyone like me enough to get married to me." So I would work hard at school. I wanted to be smart anyway and I loved to read, but I thought, "I've got to do something. I'll have to support myself, because probably nobody's going to marry me." Melody had some of the same feelings. It was unconscious on my mother's part, but we both got the message: I was the older one and the smart one, therefore Melody was the younger, prettier one, and the dumb one.

Dad was more fun than Mom was. He would do more things. He'd go to the woods with you. There was a great tree where the older boys had built this wonderful tree house. It was real high and there were stumps all around, so you knew if you fell you'd be dead, because a stump would go through you and your heart would be on the top of the stump and the rest of your body would be on the ground. But Dad would tell you which limb to put your foot on, because you couldn't see. He'd get you all the way to the top of the tree, and then he'd tell you where to put your hands so that you could swing into the teenage boys' tree house and see what it was like.

Mother would have keeled over and died on the spot if she had even seen where we went, much less knew that Dad helped us get there. It was so thrilling. I got up there and my dad was the guy who believed that I could put my foot in the right place and not fall down and break my neck and kill myself.

One time when he was treating me like a son, he came home with a little mechanical car engine kit. It was an Easter present. "Here," he said. You were supposed to put it together. I didn't mess with it much, so he came up to my room and he said, "I see you didn't build the car. I wanted to see if you were mechanical, but I guess you're not."

That's all he had to say to me. He left and I took the damn thing apart and put it together and brought it to him.

"See," I said, "I can do it. I just didn't want to do it. I'm mechanical. It just doesn't interest me."

He wasn't going to tell me I couldn't do it. I don't know if he did that on purpose or not. Sometimes I think he may have set me up on that one.

He was the one who told us about sex. I was about eight or nine. My mother just giggled, turned inside out, and left the table when I asked, "How come when I went to get an X ray, the man stood behind a shield?"

"That's because when you have babies, the radiation can hurt the babies."

"But what's that got to do with a man? He doesn't have the babies. What difference does it make if he gets the radiation?"

My mother chokes on her peas and goes in the kitchen. My sister is only five, so she doesn't know what's going on. But I know that something is going on. So after dinner, Dad comes up to my room and explains about penises and intercourse. "You're kidding," I said. "I don't believe that."

"No, it's true," he said.

"You're kidding. How's it get in there?" I couldn't believe what he was saying. It just blew my mind.

I was young, but he said, "You're asking questions that make me think it's time for you to know some of this." He made me swear not to tell the other kids, because they probably wouldn't know. So I had this secret that I wasn't supposed to tell anybody. I was real law-abiding. I didn't tell anybody.

Then I kept wanting to see what one of these penises looked like. So I would walk around the door to his room when he was getting dressed, hoping to see something so I could figure out how this worked. He was real modest. There were no pictures. He had just told me that men had this part that worked in a certain way. Then when I finally saw a little boy, I couldn't see how that little thing was going to do all this stuff. Dad didn't explain that it grew. They didn't have magazines for girls to see what men looked like.

Then I'd go look at our boy dog and that didn't help. He was always coming at the females from the wrong direction from what my father told me about.

He was the one who also told my sister. She was about nine, too, when we sat down at the dinner table and she said, "Dad, what's *fuck* mean?" Then, of course, Mother and I both choked on our peas, because I knew what it meant by then.

Pretty soon, Dad went upstairs and told Melody. Later, she came into my room saying, "I don't believe it."

"Kind of hard to believe, I know," I told her, "but it's true."

I remember thinking, I'm probably the only person whose dad told them these things. Later I thought that it was all right that he did it. I was glad it was him and not Mom, because she would have made it seem funny. She was giggling and acting funny and I'm glad I didn't get that as my first encounter with what sex is. He was pretty clinical, but he also explained that it was something you do with someone you love and something that you do that is wonderful and you'll like it.

I couldn't believe *that*. "I'm not going to like that at all. Some guy sticking his thing in me." I couldn't even figure out quite where it went. It didn't seem like it was going to be very nice.

Unlike a lot of other kids with working parents, we'd get home from school and my mother and father would always be home from three o'clock until they went to work in the evening. They were in the restaurant and bar business. Their word was law. You didn't mess with them. It was authority. You had to respect them, because they didn't misuse that authority at all. If they were wrong, they apologized. My mother was always careful to make sure we understood that we couldn't expect justice out in the real world, but there was justice where we lived.

Except when they went to work. Then it became like *Lord of the Flies*. It was a riot, because all our teenage years my brother and I were free in the evenings to do what we wanted to do, as long as we looked like we were sleeping in bed by two o'clock in the morning when my parents got back. The prime directive was, "Don't let anything happen to the two younger children."

Every night my dad would say to my brother, "You're in charge here. You're responsible." He leaves. The moment he said that, my brother's responsibility would go out the window. You can look at the different personalities of my siblings and see that he's probably the one who shouldn't have been first. Or maybe by virtue of being first, that's what happens to you. He just couldn't handle any of that stuff.

We had been real close when we were babies. He is very serious and he worries all the time. I'm not. I never have been afraid of anything. So when we were little, if he had to go to the bathroom in the middle of the night, I'd take him and stand watch, to make sure nobody got him. He was scared to go by himself.

He always called me Baby. When he was about twelve and I was eleven, I went from Baby to Bitch from one day to the next in terms of his relationship with me. I was just being me, you know. I didn't think it was any big deal. When I first started messing around with makeup, he got real upset and went to my mother. He said, "You can't let her do this."

"She's going to do this," my mother told him. "It's all right." He couldn't handle that. So we had it tough with each other the next ten years.

My parents would leave at night and we'd get into vicious physical fights. I bought knives to protect myself. This was when we were fully grown. This is not funny stuff. I talked to a psych about it for six years one time.

It wasn't laying down the law, it was telling my younger brother that he would have to get on his bicycle and go two miles to the grocery store and buy him some Snickers. I said, "No, he shouldn't go."

"He's got to go."

We'd get into it. Or what channel we were going to watch on television. Or a million other things. Not that it's important, but you get into it, so then it's serious stuff.

Then the next morning, he would tell on me. I would never tell on him, because I would always max it out.

He was bigger than I was, so he could hit me at a distance and I couldn't do anything about it. So I'd have to reach a certain emotional pitch to have an impact. This is not pleasant, not something I would want to repeat in my life. I would get out a knife or something to protect myself and he would tell them the next morning that I was playing with knives.

"No, I didn't," I would say. Just a bald-faced lie. As long as I didn't admit it, what were they going to do, flog me? You want me to tell the truth, then you tell them how it started. Come on.

Like all kids, we had a conspiracy of silence. We didn't always tell. My parents did know, and he would get lectures about hitting me. There wasn't a whole lot they could do about it. We were getting older and older, and we started having parties together. People would come over. We'd be drinking and smoking and doing other stuff and then clean up before they got home.

Through all of this, when we weren't at each other's throats, my brother and I still had an extraordinary level of closeness and communication. I knew him real well. I don't know how well he knew me. I don't know how interested he was. But I knew his buttons. I don't mean to praise myself or appear blameless, but I could do a number on him real easy. To this day, I can do it.

One night, I stayed out all night. Mom came looking for me. She actually found me, but she didn't know it. I was upstairs at my friend's house. I could hear her downstairs: "I have a right to go and look! Okay? I do, too! All right, then I'm calling the police! That's it! I'm calling the *police!*" She sent the police after me.

"Aaaaaaah, I'm going to jail." She left and I got the hell out of there. I went to my sister Janine's apartment. "Janine? Janine? Let me in! Let me in!" I go in. She's standing there at the door, but there's still somebody in the bed. I'd gotten her out of bed with some guy. "Oh, sorry. Are you busy?"

My mom was real into this, "Where are you going? Who are you going there with? What are you going to be doing? Tell me exactly everything that's going to happen and what other parents think of it. Will you have all your clothes on?" So I could really fight with her about that. I called home and told her where I was.

My dad called from work, which is like a major, major occurrence. Dad does not use the phone. He doesn't talk or do anything like that. This is much worse than the police. Janine is on the phone with him and she says, "Yeah? Yeah. Okay." Then she turns to me. "Dad wants to talk to you."

I got on the phone and he didn't even let me say anything. "I don't care where you were. I don't care who you were with. I don't care what you did. But you lied to me about where you were and that is *not* okay. Now, you go home and you stay there until I get there."

"Okay, Dad," I sniffled into the phone. I just started crying.

When I got home it was the same thing, my mom chasing me around going, "Where were you? What were you doing? Who were you with?"

My dad got home and said, "I don't want to know anything. Don't tell me anything." It was like, "I know you were out fucking some guy and I don't want to hear about it, just don't do it again." I didn't really respect him until then. I respected him when I was little, but then we didn't talk again until I realized what was really important—my welfare and that I be honest with him.

When my brother went to Vietnam, my mother was like having a nervous breakdown. Really going off the deep end, wandering around, talking to herself and crying, knocking dishes around. If we didn't get a letter for a certain amount of days, it would happen and she would just go. I totally understand it, but it *was* weird. So I was just walking around, not saying anything. My dad never said anything anyway. Nobody wanted to talk to Mom, so we all sort of went into the living room and let her wander around the kitchen mumbling to herself.

One day I was going to school. For some reason, my dad was still home and he said, "I'll give you a ride to school." The school is three blocks away.

"That's okay, Dad."

"I'm giving you a ride."

"I guess I'm getting a ride to school." I get into his truck. We drive all the way to school and he never said a word. "Why is this happening?" I thought. When he stopped the truck and I opened the door to get out, he started talking.

"Your mother's having a real hard time," he said, "and I know it's hard for all of us. I know it's bad and I'm not sure what to do."

This is my dad. This is the most he's ever spoken to me in my life on a personal level and he came out with that. But that was it. In all my thirty-three years, that is the extent of my dad's personal conversation with me. But it was really neat and it gave me an incredible feeling. I'd always liked him a lot, but I never felt like I could really get through the eighteen inches of steel around whatever he really is. But at least I know it's there.

I started working when I was twelve. My dad sold restaurant supplies. When I wasn't in school, Daddy would take me to sell the supplies and we'd go into all these restaurants. I was Dolph's little girl and Dad was really outgoing. People either loved him or hated him. He was generally well liked. One of these restaurants, a Swedish smorgasbord, was walking distance from our house. One day I walked in there and said, "Can I have a job?" And they gave me one.

My mother said, "No." My father said, "Oh, she won't last a week. Let her do it."

I stayed six months and saved my tips. I went to my mom and I said, "Mom, I want to invest in stocks."

"Why do you want to buy cattle for, dear?" she asked me.

"No, Mom, Pepsi Cola stock is what I really want to buy." But I invested in Anodized Aluminum and made about five thousand dollars when I sold it five years later.

My dad thought I could do anything. "Of course, you can do anything." It was never a question of being a girl. Although there were definitely role expectations. I was going to grow up and get married and have kids. But in terms of what I could do, there was no question about it. I wonder whether there was never a question about the fact that I *could* do it or that I *would* do it. Maybe there wasn't an expectation that I needed to do anything. But I did continue working.

I was fourteen when the Beatles came out. They had a profound impact on my life, I know. I can tell you exactly where I was when I first saw them on TV. This was a whole new world. This was exciting. This was something worth paying attention to. The first album I ever bought was *Meet the Beatles*. I became a complete Beatlemaniac.

They were coming on tour. My girlfriend and I spent all our money getting tickets for a concert they were giving in Las Vegas. Her mother, who was ditsy, said she would chaperone us to go see the Beatles in Las Vegas. She was as excited as we were. She was not very bright. I was a teenager, so it was okay for me to be going nuts, but here's a mother who should have been doing something else.

After the concert, the Beatles were leaving Las Vegas to go to L.A. The new Las Vegas airport was just opened. I said to my girlfriend, "You know, if we go to the new airport, we're never going to get to see them. All the girls are going to go there. If we see them at all, they'll be little, tiny things way over there. Why don't we take a chance that they'll leave by the old airport to avoid the crowds?"

So we take a cab out to the old airport. There was me, this one other girl, and her mom with a Super 8 movie camera. Here come the Beatles in a limousine. They get out about three feet away from us. We're nuts, we're insane. There they are. They turned around and waved. It was great.

When we came back to L.A. and got ready to go to the Hollywood Bowl concert, I was a dyed-in-the-wool groupie. I turned all my intellectual energy into this. I said, "Let's go to the Hollywood Bowl first, so we can check it out, see how they're going to get in and out and what we can do about it."

We checked it out, so when we went to the concert, we already knew the whole setup. We decided that before the last song we would go and get into position where we thought they would have to be. As we were going down there, we could hear them playing. We've got to get there before they hit the last chord, because they take off real quick and split.

But everything's changed around. "What the hell is this fence doing here? There was no fence here before. What are we supposed to do now?"

Right then, this armored car pulls up and parks about twenty feet away from the fence. The last chord happens and out of the side of my mouth I say to my girlfriend, "You know, this looks really good to me."

A door opens in the fence. These guys come barreling out, setting up a cordon for the Beatles to run through. There was just one guy in front of me. I saw them coming and I thought, "What do I do now? Here they come. So? Now what happens? I should do something." So I reached over the guy in front of me and touched John on the shoulder which I thought was expected of me.

This was real fun. There were about fifty girls all over the city who were dyed-in-the-wool groupies. We had real good leads. We had each other's phone numbers. We'd get on the phone and find out who was coming in, where they were playing, where they were staying, what was happening. This was like an intelligence network. We met the Animals. We were hanging around with Herman and the Hermits, hanging around one evening in a hotel room with the Rolling Stones.

But we were like fifteen and sixteen, and the two other girls that I did this with and I were all "good girls." We weren't sure what we wanted to do when we got there. The best part, the most fun, was getting past all the security. Once you got face-to-face with these guys it was like, "What'll we do now?" Most of them were stupid. You would talk to them and they were boring and self-obsessed. They were twenty-two and here's this sixteen-year-old kid. "Put out, or I'm not interested.'' We weren't putting out, so they were real clear about when you should leave. We did it for the challenge.

One time the Beatles were staying up in the Hollywood Hills. There were about eight girls out there parked in front of the house all night long. The gates were closed and there's a security guard there. We all know the Beatles are in there. We're standing around, laughing and joking, just waiting to see if they come out.

About two in the morning, my girlfriend and I decided to go get hamburgers, so we took orders. When we came back up with the hamburgers, none of the girls were there. I said to the security guard, ''What happened?''

''They were let in.''

''We have their hamburgers. We have to go in, too.''

''No, no, you have to be invited.'' We didn't get in. My big chance destroyed by hamburger, which I thought had some poetic justice. In some ways, I'm glad I didn't meet them, because I might have been disappointed. Now since I never have, I can have all my fantasies, which is okay.

That was when I started my period and my mother didn't tell me nothing about it. I was watching some kind of cartoons on TV. Yeah. And I hurt real bad. I went into the bathroom and I was all full of blood. I freaked out. I told my mom, ''A-a-a-ayah! I'm dying! Something's going on!''

''Nah,'' she said, ''that just happens every month,''

and she threw them things at me, Kotexes. "Put these on and go to school." The whole day at school I was flipped out.

A couple of weeks later, they started showing us those movies in my health class. Then everything was okay. I figured it out. That was pretty rotten. Man, I didn't want to go to school.

She never told me about sex or anything. Never, uh-uh. In fact, after those films was when I started realizing something was weird around the house. My parents, they didn't sleep together. She always slept with me. Yeah. I kind of wondered what was going on, but I never said nothing. She told me it was because my father snored. She slept with me all the way up through high school. Great, huh?

My dad, he don't say nothing. I like him a whole lot. I remember I would always rub his back at night-time after dinner or rub his head. He'd let me do those kinds of things. He would always slip me things on the side. Give me money or take me somewhere I wanted to go. He was a bowler and I liked to go bowling with him. We went to the drive-in movie a lot together, the scary ones, the ones that she wouldn't go to.

But he would never say anything to my mother. He thought she knew what she was doing. She was right. She was a girl. I was a girl. He was a guy. She *must* know what she's doing, right?

I'd get that goody-goody treatment. I'd come home in tears from the bus stop, because some girl had said to me, "You weren't supposed to get straight A's, so-and-so is the best student in our class." Girls wouldn't play with me, didn't like me because I was cute or I had a nicer home or something. It was always something.

It probably drove me to this tremendous friendship I have with my mother, because I trusted her. There are very few women I trust, because invariably they're going to turn around and use whatever you tell them against you. I still believe that's true. I do know women who are really genuine and wonderful. But I'm still not trusting women.

I suppose if there is a person in my life that I will never, ever forgive for living, it's Rhonda. Jim and I had been going together for about three months. I just knew that we were going to be together for the rest of our lives, because he was the one for me.

One afternoon in study hall, Rhonda was sitting ahead of me and wrote a note that said she had overheard Jim talking to someone. He didn't want to be tied down. He wanted to see other people and he didn't know how to tell me. All that kind of stuff.

Of course, I wrote Jim a note saying that I thought we should be seeing other people and we shouldn't be tied down to each other and all that kind of stuff. I gave it to him and just wanted to die for two or three months. In fact, going through the rest of high school, for years, even after I was married, still even now, there is a little part of me that sighs when I think of that.

Two weeks later, guess who's going out with Jim? If I live to be a thousand, boy! I wouldn't give that girl water in the desert. That was high school.

In the summertime when school was out, everybody would go to this little putt-putt golf course and hang out. I'd go with my girlfriend, Dina. She was real Italian, big nose. She was a nobody, loner type, too. We met in Latin class. I don't know what we were. We weren't in and we weren't hoods. I never hung out with the hoods. The goody-goody girls were the ones that were laying all the boys. I guess we were dorks.

Then Dina started getting more attention that I did, because she started getting a body. She started growing tits, big tits. It made me mad. I knew what was going on. All the guys that I wanted to date were after her. She starts being nominated for homecoming queen and class representative for this and that. She was bad ugly, but she had tits. But when this stuff started happening to her, there were always all kinds of people over at her house, and she still hung out with me, so I'd be around these people, too.

For the junior prom, she fixed me up with her boyfriend's friend. They were both on the football team. He was gross, awful. Ugly and nasty, too. I tried to have a good time, but it was hard.

We were parked somewhere after the prom and he tried to get really weird with me. We were in the front seat, because he was driving. He had the car running and he was trying to feel me up. I jammed my foot on the gas pedal, *hard,* which made this real bizarre noise and scared the two in the backseat out of their skins. Scared my date to death. I said, "I want to go home *now!"*

Then he ran all around the school telling everybody how he laid me. He told the kid who lived next door to me, and his father worked for my father and it got around at work. Oh, yeah. Boy, I was pissed. My father came home and told my mother and she told me.

I couldn't believe it. I hadn't seen this guy after the prom. It would have been different if I was still dating the guy, but I never saw him again. I hated the guy after that. I used to call him The Pig. I didn't want his grimy hands on me. But my mom believed all this. So I had to go to school and straighten his ass out.

I yelled at him and told him he had to go tell my neighbor that it wasn't the truth. Dina's boyfriend was there and he was a friend of mine, too, so he started "saving my reputation." I didn't have any reputation at that point. I certainly didn't want that one.

My mother had a schedule: Stockings in eighth grade. Mascara at fifteen and regular makeup. Eye makeup later. So then you wear too much for two years—blue eye shadow up to my eyebrows. Plucking my eyebrows, that was a big deal. I had to fight for that one. I was sixteen. The stupidest part was I couldn't wait to do it and it hurts. There's no reason to do it at all. I plucked them so far that it was like I had one hair all the way across. I would spend hours doing this and I looked like a joke.

My grandmom encouraged me. She wouldn't say anything to me, but she'd let me do stuff. Like, I wanted to shave my legs when I was in seventh grade. My mother didn't want me to. I went to see my grandmother. She said, "Go ahead, here's a razor."

I shaved everything. Even my arms. I did. I don't know why. I didn't like the hair on them. I knew it was a big mistake after I did it, but I did it anyway. Everything, I shaved *everything*.

I had brains, but I just didn't use them, especially socially. This fellow used to squire me around. He was a very happy-go-lucky, overweight class clown. We got along really well together, so we went around to dances and parties and things like that.

My father came to me one afternoon and he said, "What's going on with you and Reggie? Is this getting pretty serious?"

"Oh, Daddy, we're just friends," I said.

My father never said a lot, but once in a while he waxed philosophical, probably after he'd had a couple of six-packs. In fact, my father used to run around quoting Nietzsche and I never knew that until about three years ago when I came across the quote, "Did God invent Man or did Man invent God?" My father used to say that all the time and I always thought he was so bright.

"Let me tell you something," Daddy said. "There is no such thing as *just* a friend. A friend is someone who would die for you and you would die for them. If you're not willing to die for them, don't call them your friend." That still stays with me. It's one of the few things my father ever said that I still feel.

Daddy also said, "Women aren't friends with men." I gave him the old, "Oh, Daddy," routine.

About three weeks later Reggie drove me home, opened the car door for me. When I got out, he didn't move. He put his arms around me and tried to kiss me.

And I laughed. You know, he never spoke to me after that night. I must have just killed him. I was always like that: If you don't know what to do, at least laugh. It breaks the tension. My sense of humor has always been my hardest armor.

I grew up in a very religious family. There was no drinking, no smoking. My father smoked, but my father snuck for thirty-two years to smoke. Mother knew he smoked, he just wasn't permitted to do it in the house.

If I didn't go to church on Sunday, I didn't step foot out of the house all day. Prayer meetings on Wednesday night. Sunday night I'd have to take my homework to church and do it there. I got absolutely nothing out of the church service, but, by God, I was at church on Sunday night.

Sex? Sex was taboo. You didn't even talk about it in my mother's house. Both of my older brothers *had* to get married. The only thing that I remember ever hearing talked about sex was, "They did it when they shouldn't have done it and it was dirty." They got these two girls in trouble and it was a detriment to the family name. It was really embarrassing to my mother.

As far as the female end of it, for my sister and me, there was never, ever mention made of starting your period. We never had the talk with Mother. There was no talk at all. These girls I ran around with would talk about starting their period when they were twelve years old. Me, nothing. I was wearing undershirts rolled up to make them look like bras, thinking that there was really something wrong with me. I was baking my birthday cake for my sixteenth birthday when I got my first period. I thought, "Oh, my God, it's happened."

My senior year in high school, I was up for prom queen, which is a big deal. This guy that I went with in high school was very scholarly, very stately. Mom and Dad just dearly loved this guy. We went "fishing" one day and things happened. I was a virgin until I was twenty-one, but I was human as far as playing around and fondling and things. One thing led to another and he got off on my leg.

The funniest thing was, in gym class the day before, we were all talking about the dreaded sperm, how it can crawl. I swear to God, I thought from that moment that I was pregnant. I was vomiting in the morning. My breasts were sore. I was three weeks late on my period, which I had never been. "Oh, my God, it did go up inside me!" I'm not real proud to admit this, but I did more exercise those three weeks than I've ever done in my life, hoping that if I was pregnant I would abort the baby.

When I was crowned prom queen, I still thought I was pregnant. They're crowning me, and I'm thinking, "What a slut! Here I am pregnant." I was only ninety-eight pounds when I graduated and I went down to eighty pounds during this period. I was a mess.

My boyfriend had a scholarship to go to school and be a lawyer, but we had all these contingency plans where he was going to drop out of college and go do factory work for my brother, and we were going to move in with my mom and dad.

It finally got to the point where I had to go to my mother and tell her I thought I was pregnant. I said, "I want you to know one thing: We did not make love."

"I guess we'll have to go to the doctor and see," she said.

After this, I went out and I looked it up, I read books about sex and I became an expert.

To show how sheltered I was, I couldn't figure out how a man and woman could make love. How does it work? I used to try for long periods of time to think it through, as though you could solve it by thinking it through.

Then I lost my virginity. I'd been living at home and going to college. I met this guy. His name was Edward. He was an okay person. He kept asking me to sleep with him and I kept saying no. Then one day, just at my door after a date, Edward asked me and I said, "Okay, yeah."

So we had to go back to his house. I knew what everything was, but I still hadn't figured out what would make it worth doing. He didn't know any more than I did. As a matter of fact, he had a book which he was trying to read while we were getting started. He kept checking with the text to see what we were supposed to do next. Neither of us knew what we were doing, but we did it.

There was a hell of a lot of blood. I was very proud of that, I must say. I didn't have an orgasm; I didn't even know what that was, but I wasn't a virgin anymore. Other than that it wasn't very special.

So then I went home; otherwise, my parents would have called the police. The bloody sheets were his problem. The next morning, I got up and danced around in front of the mirror, I was so happy I wasn't a virgin anymore. I was pleased as punch.

I knew that in my family you weren't supposed to do this. You were supposed to get married. My father saw it from the point of view that I should be taken care of. I thought, "Fuck this. What are they talking about? What can this mean? God, Dad must be crazy."

My mother found out I was running wild. She found my diary and read it. It was before I had intercourse, but I was heavy necking. Of course, I wrote steamy pages about this to Dear Diary.

She called the principal in my high school and had me sent home from school. She then called my father at his office, brought him home, and was herself absolutely hysterical. I came home and I didn't know what was going on. I thought somebody was dead or something. My mother was just out of her mind.

Finally, it came out. But she didn't admit that she read my diary, so I'm thinking, "Jesus, how do they know I'm parking in Thompson's Woods with no clothes on and all this stuff?" The diary just didn't occur to me.

I was grounded for three months. It was just awful. And where were their hidden eyes and ears? I couldn't imagine how they knew what I did on particular nights. Then there was a real enforced reign of terror where she'd say, "You're going to the movie at eight. It's over at ten. You have to be home at ten-fifteen."

Of course, what I would do is not go to the movie at all. Go directly to Thompson's Woods right away, drink beer, screw around, and be home by ten-fifteen.

Finally, a neighbor lady, who I used to do ironing for on Saturdays, said to me, "Betty, don't write in your diary anymore." So then I knew. She must have been my friend.

My first sex was in my boyfriend's house in his bunk beds, because he had a brother and they had bunk beds. We were in the top bunk and I was scared we were going to fall through. It was real good, it was. Frank was real kind. I should have stuck with him. It didn't hurt or anything. But I bled and that freaked me out. "Oh, well, I bled before. Mom ain't here to tell me what it is, so phooey." By this time I had decided that nobody would tell me what anything was anyway.

I forget how we got into it, but after that first time, we did it all the time. I don't know why I didn't get pregnant earlier.

My parents live on a hill and Frank and I would be out at dark time under a tree on that hill just going to town. My mother would be standing at the back door, calling, *"Melissaaaaah!"* And I'd just laugh. If she only knew, she'd have had heart failure. She hated him because he was half Mexican. She used to call him Tonto. Me and Tonto. If she had thought I'd have a little Tonto, she would have never talked to me again.

M y next older sister, who was termed "The Wild One," had gotten pregnant when she was sixteen. My parents forced her to get married. She had a miscarriage two months later. He beat the hell out of her for about a year. She ended up divorced when she was seventeen.

My father was convinced that they were going to be much more strict with me, which didn't get it with me. I was going to do whatever I wanted to do. I never said that to them. I'd just say, "Yeah, okay," and go do what I wanted.

So I got involved with somebody that they weren't particularly thrilled with, for whatever reason. I was a typical, lonely, fifteen-year-old kid. I ended up getting pregnant.

I didn't even want to tell my mother. But my mother who'd gone through this once before had been watching my periods and realized I hadn't had one. So she called my older sister and said, "Oh, no, she might be pregnant." My sister comes down and they take me out of school and drag me in to have a pregnancy test. "We need Sheila to come home. She has a family emergency." She *is* the family emergency. What else is new?

The big debate with my parents was abortion. "What are we going to do? We're not going to make her get married. We're not even going to let her think about that, not after what we did last time." So they decided we would try this new routine. I was due in August. Every day for the rest of the school year, I would tape myself up, *literally* tape myself up, so I wouldn't show, hoping that I could make it until June. And I did. By some ridiculous chance, I managed to never show my pregnancy all through the school year. But you couldn't talk about it. You break up with the boyfriend, of course, because that's what you have to do.

In June, they wanted to send me to a home for unwed mothers, but I really didn't want to do that. It had been tough enough. So they compromised and shipped me off to stay with my sister who had made the same dumb mistake, but who was now older and going to college in another part of the state. At the end of the summer, I would go to this home for a couple of weeks.

I wasn't allowed to make any decisions. They were telling me what I was going to do. At one point, I walked out of the house and had no intention of ever going back. But, at almost sixteen, that's hard to do. It was harder, because I'd always been close to my parents.

We were brought up to never do anything to make ourselves look bad in front of other people. That was my mother's whole theory of upbringing. This has made me give great first impressions. I interview for jobs wonderfully, because I know all the right things to say at all the right times. But it really preys on you after a while. You get into this thing where you're always pretending to be what everybody wants you to be, no matter what you really are. I was always very susceptible to that. My mother would say, "Don't do that. Nice girls don't do that." From the time I was knee-high.

It gets very confusing. You don't know what you want because you haven't been allowed to think about what you want. Even when I'd gotten into this halfway house, I always would appear to be happy. They made me sit down at some point and have a conference with this psychologist—who was always a nun in this particular place. She sat with me for about two hours and had me in tears for about an hour and forty-five minutes of that time, just asking me about things that I hadn't discussed with anyone. Because nobody had ever asked me. They don't talk about anything; they just do what they think is right. It gets to you. It drives you nuts, because there's no way to deal with it.

Then the big concern was, "Is she going to deliver in time to get back to school?" There was all this family stuff and I just sat there going, "For Christ sake, leave it. Let it go."

I delivered right on schedule and made it back to school by two days. Put the baby up for adoption, which has always bothered me. To know that somewhere I have a daughter who's sixteen right now, five years older than my daughter at home. I would never pursue finding that child. I don't think that's right somehow. Once you make that decision, then it's decided.

After the dust cleared and all was said and done, I was back to leading a fairly normal life. That was my second year in high school. That pretty much took care of the year.

When I told the boyfriend, he said, "So?" That's all I got from him: "So?" Then, "It's not mine." The normal, typical answers.

I'd always lived in a fairy tale world up till then. I always thought if somebody said "I love you" that they meant it. Even though I'd seen my friends going through all this same stuff, there was still this part of me didn't want to believe that this is the way it is. It can't be. It's just not the way it is. I thought he really meant that he loved me. I had the Walt Disney view of life from watching the old movies, the old love stories. From reading. That was my escape hatch for all those years, my way of saying, "There is a better place and a better reality than this one," instead of saying, "This is the way the world is."

When I was eighteen, I got pregnant illegitimately, using the terminology of the time. This was 1958. It was so different from today. Very taboo.

First of all, the father convinced me that it would "ruin his life" if I kept the child. I had no way of supporting it. I would have to quit college. So I agreed to an abortion. I borrowed the money from a family friend, making up a ridiculous excuse. We went to

Hollywood to have the abortion that he had arranged. We waited in this motel room. I'm crying and crying and crying, "How could this have happened to me?" I was in denial that I could even be pregnant. This was my first lover. How could it possibly be?

The abortionist came and examined me. That was gruesome. We set the time for the next day.

I went to a friend's parents' house to stay the night. She wasn't there, she was still at school. In the middle of the night, I sat up and thought, "I cannot do this. This is not right. Somebody else can do this, but I cannot do this."

This friend's parents didn't know why I was there, but at three o'clock in the morning, I knocked on their bedroom door and said, "Could I come in and talk to you for a minute?"

They were horrified, not by the pregnancy so much, but that I was deciding not to have the abortion. They said, "It'll kill your parents. You'll ruin their lives." When I didn't show up, the boyfriend called and said, "You're ruining my life." So far I was ruining quite a few lives. By the time I realized that I was pregnant, I had another boyfriend and he said it ruined his life, too, when I told him. "We haven't even had sex yet," he said.

"You didn't make me pregnant. This was months ago." He thought I was a terrible person for going out with him while I was already pregnant and not a virgin.

I borrowed money again and flew to my parents' home to tell them. That was a very excruciating experience. From the minute I walked in the door they knew something was wrong.

"What is it? What's the matter?" My dad ended up sobbing and crying. I'd never seen that. He was always an in-control, controlling person. He thought that he had somehow let me down.

"You're going to have to lie to all the great-aunts

and your grandmother and everybody," he said to me,
"because this will ruin their lives." He rushed out to
a pawnshop and he bought me a wedding ring. I had
to wear it around. I was to stay with them until the
baby was born.

I had a lot of feeling for him. He was doing the best
he could. It would have been easier if he'd said,
"Never darken my doorstep again." My mother
didn't know what to think, she was so upset.

I only stayed there for a few months. I almost had a
miscarriage and was physically sick, so I couldn't
work. My parents were taking care of one of my aunt's
children, so I felt like an extra burden on them.

One day, my dad got drunk, which he did on a pe-
riodic basis. He was picking on the little nephew about
tying his shoes and swearing at him. That was the kind
of thing I'd grown up with.

"I don't want to hear this again," I said.

"You don't have any rights anymore," he said. And
he threatened to hit me. This was what I expected and
now it came out.

"I always have rights," I told him. "I'm not going
to stay, because I don't want my child growing up with
this. I already went through it."

"Well, try to go," he said. "You have no money."

But I did have money. I'd borrowed money to come
home and I had a little of it left over. I flew back to
college. Friends picked me up and I stayed in the
apartment of a friend. I went on through the pregnancy on my own.

It was a wonderful experience of, "I'm okay, I
don't need them." I was lonely and I was poor and I
couldn't get enough to eat. I tried to get jobs and people just laughed at me—by this time I was pretty big
—but it didn't matter. I had friends. People were helpful. I did my part to help them back. But my friends
also thought I was crazy. Not one of them thought I
should keep this baby. They all said, "You're ruining

your life. You're making a choice that will stop your life. It's over. This is it. Good-bye." But I felt good about myself. I really could rely on myself.

Part of what happened was that I contacted the father and said, "I'm going to need help paying for the hospital."

"You must be crazy," he said. "I have fifteen fraternity brothers who will say that you slept with everybody." That was a bigger blow to me than anything else in the whole thing. I could not believe that somebody that I had intimacy with—even though not of a prolonged kind—would turn on me.

"You know that's not true."

"I know," he said, "but that's all I'll need in court."

That made me furious. It was a sign of the times, too. There was a double standard that went on. So I found a lawyer. I said, "I don't have any money, but after I've had the baby, I'll pay you."

He just liked my spirit. "I bet you would pay me," he said, "but you don't have to. I don't like hearing this kind of thing myself." He served this guy papers.

The guy got a lawyer. He called me and said, "I hope you know that by my having to get a lawyer, you're ruining my parents' lives." What the heck. I felt like a professional at ruining lives at this point.

He agreed to pay for the hospital, but his condition was that I talk to the Children's Home Society about the possibility of adoption. If he was going to be in on this, he wanted me to know that he didn't think I'd be a fit parent. A single parent? It wasn't done.

I got such a hard sell from those people. They came every week and said the same kind of thing to me: "What gives you the right to raise this child? You're going to work? Who's going to take care of your child? Women are supposed to stay home and raise their children. Why do you want to have a child? Just to

say that you've got one?'' It was women saying these
things to me.

They could have a wonderful home for the baby and
I could have other children. And this was one of
the wonderful lines: "And you won't even have to
tell your future husband someday that you've ever
had this child. No one will know that you've done
this. You can start fresh." They inferred, "Who is
ever going to marry you if you tell them this kind of
thing?"

I decided to have natural childbirth, which wasn't
done at that time either. I didn't know a thing about
birth. The doctor said, "That's very nice, but that's
not the way we do things."

So I had the baby by natural childbirth. There were
no classes, but I practiced the system from books. It
was a Catholic hospital and the sisters did not like it
one bit. Except for one. She kept slipping me Lifesav-
ers, winking at me, saying I was doing great. It was
the most wonderful experience I have had to date. For
a couple of moments, I thought I understood the whole
universe. I just couldn't hang on to it later. It wasn't
wonderful. I had a lot of pain, too. But basically it
worked. I came out of there feeling euphoric. I had
this huge, happy, healthy, beaming baby.

The next day in the hospital, a minister comes to
visit me, sent by the baby's father. He said, "How are
you?"

"I'm just fine," I said. "I never felt so good."

I'd never met this man before in my life and he said,
"Do you really think you have a right to that?"

"What?"

"All this happiness, when that poor little baby is
here without a father and with no prospects. You don't
even have a job."

I couldn't believe it. The same old "Shame on you"
routine. He'd been in contact with the Children's

Home Society. I ordered him out of the room. The euphoria went into hysteria and I shouted, "Get out! Get out!" This was the most horrifying, evil person, to rain on the one little piece of joy that I'd had in all this time.

I took them on. I got my lawyer and I said, "Let's have them over for a little talk." They all thought I was ready to capitulate. I told them, "If you take one more step, if you tell me that I'm not doing for this child what I should be doing, with no evidence, I will sue you." My lawyer was really behind me. He said, "I've never done anything like this and I don't think you have a leg to stand on, but it sounds good." They were not going to push me around. I scared them off.

I don't believe that anyone else knows what's good for me. I can listen to all kinds of suggestions, but I really am incensed when people think that they can tell me what will make me happy. People have the key inside themselves. They may go down a very winding path toward it, but they know what they need. Women especially have a good intuitive sense of what they need. Lots of women that I know have that sense about their own lives, but they hide it, bury it, for all these superficial reasons.

It is a risk. I know that I live my life intuitively a lot and there is the risk that I'm going to make a mistake and go down a wrong path. But who cares? Nothing is irrevocable. I learned that when all this happened. As long as you're alive, you can make another choice.

Years later, I found other women who did the same thing during that time period, but because it was not the thing to do, nobody talked about it.

All I know is that it was an event that happened and I emerged from it a woman. Hurray for me! It wasn't the end of trouble, but it was remarkable for the times. Eighteen-year-olds today—thank God—don't understand how remarkable that was.

I got a scholarship to go to a good state university, but my boyfriend decided that he was going to be the breadwinner and really I wouldn't have to work once we got married. I said, "Fine, I'll get a job and completely wash college out of my brain," which I could kick myself for every day. I thought, "This is the guy I'm going to marry." Being from a small town, I was convinced that's what you did. You got married when you got out of high school. In our case, he was going to go to college and then on to law school. I was going to make some money, save it, and we were going to live happily ever after.

I talked to girls I'd gone to school with, who had graduated, who had an apartment and a car. They were out running around, having a good time.

So I started my job on my eighteenth birthday. Within two weeks, I moved out of my parents' house and into an apartment with two girls I had been a cheerleader with. Within a month, I had broken my engagement and decided, "This life is all right."

I teach at a community college now. When I tell my students about what a big step this was and how revolutionary it was for women to be allowed to live independently off campus when I was going to college, I don't think they quite believe me. They look at me like, "You got to be kidding. This must be an exaggeration. Times were never like that." But they were.

In the same breath, I tell them stories about how we used to answer for one another during the two A.M. fire drills in the dorms that were designed to catch girls who were out all night. There was a real camaraderie among women to begin that movement toward independence, but we were still sneaking around—the guerrilla feminist movement.

My mother wanted me to go to college. I *had* to go to college. My parents started sending away for applications for me. I couldn't go nowhere out of the state. I wanted to go to Florida. Somewhere neat, different. The only place out of state they would let me go was Notre Dame. One of our relatives was a priest who taught there. Whoopee!

They drug me to a zillion different colleges all over the place to look at them. And I really didn't even want to go. I wasn't looking forward to it or nothing. I just wanted to hang around with my boyfriend and see what it would lead to.

My mother got all excited and started buying me clothes and footlockers and trunks. Sewing my name into everything. She sewed my name into every article of clothing I wore. Even my underwear. Wild.

My dad filled out the applications. They decided I was going to go to State University. Terrific. Oh, brother. So they carted me off down to college. My boyfriend came to see me a couple of times, but then it just didn't work out. I was too far away.

I had a wild time in college. When we got there I was the first one in the dormitory room, so I took everything. I took a bed, all the cupboards. I put all my stash in it and I sat there and waited. Mom and Dad went home. Then my roommates showed up. God, they were gross. One was four foot eleven and weighed three hundred pounds, but thought she was beautiful, a real man-killer. Her name was something like Bitsy. She had gigantic tits and she was always trying to get into my clothes. After she would wear them, they'd have those indentations in them and were all stretched out.

The other girl was real homely and tall and had a boyfriend she had been going with since first grade. They were getting married as soon as they were out of college. The boyfriend was there every weekend. Her name was Pamela Lovelace.

They were both from the South and had heavy-duty southern accents. They were both real smart and did real good in school. Not me. I did some wild things. I slept naked. What's-her-butt—Bitsy—didn't like that. She thought that was horrible. That was perverted. She couldn't handle it. I'd sneak out of the dormitories at night and stay out real late. We had to be in at ten. I'd stay out till midnight and some girl would sneak me in. Not my roommates, though.

We had a phone at the end of the hall and if it was for me, Bitsy would be making a big deal all the way down the hall about how, "It's for you again, Linda." Like I was real promiscuous. She was just jealous, because the other girl didn't care. She didn't make a big deal about it or nothing, really.

I didn't do no studying and I didn't go to no classes. All I did was get drunk there. I flunked out.

But something weird happened. We were changing roommates. Bitsy and Pamela were moving out and I was supposed to get two new people, but I didn't get anybody. They didn't seem to know that I had flunked out. So I stayed in my room for four months after I wasn't even supposed to be there anymore. I stayed on. I just wasn't in school. I partied for four months.

I had a boyfriend then—an older man. He was a senior. I spent time with him. Then I got nervous about what I was going to do. I couldn't keep doing this. My parents didn't know and I wasn't going to tell them either. So I called my grandmother, told her about it, and asked her to break it to my parents.

She did. They came to get me. My father was okay on the way home. He realized I wasn't going to be a chemical engineer after all. It was stone silence from *her*.

I always felt as soon as I got to college my life would start. When I did finally get there, I started dating immediately. I started getting un-shy. I became the life of the party very quickly.

My next-door neighbor in the dormitory had been Miss Teenage Somewhere-or-Other and she would walk up and down the halls naked, wearing her crown, holding her scepter, and examining her body for flaws. She had five guys who wanted to sleep with her every night. Five guys she had told she *would* sleep with them every night.

That first year everybody talked about sex. My first morning in the one communal bathroom, there were seven sinks and seven women washing out diaphragms. I didn't even know that's what they were. I thought maybe they were dirty soap dishes. I had no idea. There were people taking their birth control pills with great ceremony. For women in those years, that time of development, there was this real need to be openly sexual. It was so new to everybody. It was really taboo to be a virgin, very taboo.

I did not know at the time, but the floor I lived on was really the sluttiest floor in the whole school, the really eager freshmen women. Women, we weren't girls.

I could blame a lot of bad qualities on "I can't help it, I live here"—not promiscuity so much as a reluctance to take any guy seriously, juggling dates, and stuff like that—but that was only part of the story. I also was so shocked that there were men interested in me that I didn't know how to have a relationship. I just wanted to collect the admirers. I was sure that it wasn't going to stay that way. It was a novelty, and I couldn't believe it.

I decided my sophomore year that I wanted to transfer colleges for academic reasons. One of the schools I wanted to go to was about to admit its first female students. The other was a prestigious liberal university. For about six months I was trying to weigh the pros and cons between the two schools.

My pros for the liberal university were: I could major in creative writing. Everybody seemed to like it. It was a politically correct institution. For the formerly all men's college the pros were: If I date sophomores and juniors the ratio will be four to one. If I date sophomores, juniors, and seniors, the ratio will be six to one. If I also date teaching assistants, freshmen, professors, and the dean of housing, it's eighty-nine thousand to one. I couldn't get over it. If I date the janitorial staff and the maintenance crews, it'll be three hundred and fifteen thousand to one. All I could think about was all those guys.

But I finally decided on the university. I started getting a lot of "Dear sir" mail. "Now that you're a college man . . ." They were not ready for me.

It was wonderful to get away from that small town and all those people who knew everything that you did and didn't do and their mothers and fathers. The summer before I went to college, *Playboy* picked the school I was going to as the Number One Party School in the nation. All the girls from my hometown were supposed to go to the rival college, because that's where all the good girls went. But the university was a much better school intellectually. You knew you were going to be challenged.

I went there on my own money. I got loans and scholarships. I was completely free in every sense. It was the most invigorating, thrilling thing that ever happened to me. I felt like I was on a drug, I was so excited to be free. My mother didn't know what time I got home, nobody knew.

I wasn't going out with people; I was just doing whatever I wanted to whenever I wanted to do it. Talking, staying up late, going out for walks in the rain.

Those days are so crystal-clear in my mind, that sense of being free and also this feeling that anything was possible, anything. You could do anything you wanted to do. Here was your chance. You could be anything you wanted to be.

3. Breath 'n' Britches

There're only two things women have to know about men. One: They don't want to be trapped. Two: They're stupid." This woman was talking about meaningful relationships with men.

"It really is interesting to me," she continued, "how much men fight being trapped in relationships. That's code-red-dead from the beginning. Then it's just a question of *when* they get caught. It's not *if*, it's always *when* they stop fighting. They emit that little rabbit scream and it's over. It's so funny. Why don't they just acknowledge that this is going to happen and go about the business of making sure they get the right person, instead of making a big deal out of it?"

Love, sex, courtship, marriage. Men and women generally conduct their most intimate and complex relationships by succumbing to their most primitive instincts. Although many women will admit that they follow their hearts instead of their heads when it comes to love, they are convinced that men are truly Neanderthals of emotion, communication, and commitment.

"The part about them being stupid really refers to their perceptiveness—self-examination and intuitiveness about how other people are feeling. Women are reactive. You guys just *act*. Not a lot of times is there much thought about the emotional consequences of those acts.''

What makes this situation even more frustrating to women is the fact that men still get to do the asking and women still wait for men to approach them. ''A woman isn't supposed to come on to a man and most men can't handle it if you do. That's really a shame, but it's there. It's an issue that's talked about among women a lot. 'Why do we have to wait around for these assholes to come and ask us out?'

''But what happens if you don't wait and you make the play? It either works or it doesn't work, but there are so many implications to it. Did he know and did anyone else know? Was he embarrassed because somebody realized that I was coming on to him? Does he think he's going to go to bed with me right away or is it just a date? Does this give him carte blanche now? Does he think I'll do anything he wants? What it means is that a woman's sexuality is still not accepted by this culture.''

Unfortunately, that is true. However, women today do have more latitude to express their sexuality than ever before. Premarital sex is almost de rigueur for young women in American culture. One woman summed up the modern, casual attitude toward female sexual activity by saying, ''I was fairly promiscuous when I was younger, but it was standard for the times. The movie *Looking for Mr. Goodbar* had more effect on me about the dangers of picking up strangers than any of my own experiences did. Although I think the real moral of that movie was, if you pick up strange men, bring them home, and have sex with them, don't insult their technique, because *that*'s what will get you killed. Say, 'It's great, it's great,' and get them out of there.''

Perhaps the only other major change in the intimate interaction between women and men is that women are free to stay single today. Only two generations ago, any female who remained unmarried after the age of around twenty-five was considered to be an "old maid," an object of pity or suspicion. A woman's place in society is no longer necessarily determined by her marital status. Women can and do choose to live independently, making their own autonomous decisions. One woman told me, "After having been brought up in such a strict family environment, I loved the freedom of not answering to anyone for the first time in my life. I still have that. Although I really have blown it all out of proportion, this sense of independence. I'll spend the rest of my life coming in when I want to. That seems a bit excessive."

But most single women *are* looking for a man to share their lives. Even the most self-reliant and individualistic of them is often looking for marriage, "if the right guy comes along." Although today's Prince Charming may take the form of an armor-plated Dirty Harry or a quixotic Alan Alda, most women fantasize about a perfect lover/husband with whom they will live "happily ever after." Even among practical women with a more realistic outlook, expectations are very high. As one young, successful businesswoman told me, "I need commitment. That's probably the biggest pressure now. I get so neurotic. I don't want to handle the earning of the money, the balancing of the books, the paying of the taxes, the taking out of the garbage, and the feeding of the cat. I want somebody to do at least some of it. But I have to do it all. The illusion is that if you get married, somebody will do some of it for you, but you just end up doing more. 'Oh, shit, now I've got to do his laundry, too? This isn't what I meant.' "

Searching for the ideal man, many women spend their lives going from one disappointing lover to another. They are always leaving. A woman in her mid-forties described her own predicament this way: "I had a million boyfriends. I always assumed I'd be married again, that I'd have kids. Actually, when I got into my thirties and I hadn't gotten any of those things, even though I had the opportunity, it really started to make me nervous.

"I've spent quite a lot of time with the wrong men, men who are unavailable in some way, who wouldn't make a commitment. On the other hand, I've spent a lot of time with men who I cared for a lot, but I didn't want to marry. Both those things—never being able to make a commitment to those people who cared for me, who were good to me and good for me, and spending a lot of time with people who were terrible to me and were never going to stay with me—bring me to the conclusion that I don't want to get married after all. But I don't want that to be the case. I still feel that I can work it out. So I keep trying and looking. I still have hope."

Other women give up hope of ever finding a satisfactory mate and lower their sights. "That's when women are attracted to men they think they are going to change," another woman explained. "The fixer-upper type of thing. 'He looks okay, I can change him, I'll fix him up. It's a cheaper place, but I'll paint and rearrange the furniture. It'll look like a million dollars. It's not quite what I want, but let me get in there and spiff things up.'

"It doesn't work. When a woman is trying to change a man, the man picks up on it. Men are intuitive, too. Men have scent. They smell a woman trying to change them, picking and poking. That's when men just want to get out."

There are enduring, loving, inventive relationships between men and women, but those unions rarely have the storybook "happily ever after" quality women fantasize about. Women describe the experience as "teetering on the brink," "a constant give-and-take," "I sometimes wonder if we'll last another six months.'' Tension seems to play as big a part in balancing these alliances as does respect. The ability to fight fairly on a regular basis is as important as romance. The key word is compromise. But in fact women make the biggest concessions even in genuinely "equal" partnerships. "Men are allowed to have work and the woman and the family together in the middle of their consciousness. I know that everything I do, whether it's in my career or in my home, first takes into consideration the man in my life. Even getting to an important business appointment today in traffic, I was thinking, 'Later, I should pick up spinach, because he commented he wanted to have it.' It's that kind of focus women have that's very important in a relationship—those kinds of preoccupation and passion, obsession.''

Women who are unhappy in marriage can divorce without suffering much social sanction. They will not be called divorcées these days, with all the suggestions of risqué behavior or a shameful past that term used to connote. According to a 1989 report from the National Center for Health Statistics, there were 1,183,000 divorces in 1988 and the wife was nearly twice as likely as the husband to have initiated the legal process. Women shoulder as much responsibility for ending a bad relationship as they do for nurturing a good one.

The peripatetic coupling and uncoupling goes on. Young women enter the game with pop song lyrics for a marriage manual. Middle-aged women try to escape the panic of finding themselves alone by turning to the optimism of younger men. Loneliness is epidemic. Of all the women I talked to, only my grandmother at age seventy-nine seemed totally beyond the "battle of the sexes." When I asked her why she didn't find some nice old man to marry, she answered with a mild repugnance, "Oh, son, I don't want no more breath 'n' britches.''

My mother graduated from high school and went to beauty school. She had a fight with her mother, moved out of the house—which was something you just didn't do at that point in time—and went to live in a boardinghouse. She bought her own car, which she keeps telling me was a big thing back then, and wanted to buy her own beauty shop. Then, I don't know what happened, but my mother got married.

Maybe it was that certain age. Some women reach a certain age and think, "I've got to get married." She had been a career woman. She was getting up there. She was twenty-five.

"Why'd you marry my dad?" I asked her. "You have nothing in common."

"He was a good dancer," she said.

What jumps to my mind first is how much my life has been influenced by various men that I've lived with. That's alarming, because what really disturbed me about my mother is that she created her life around the various men she was married to. She once got really furious with me because of something I said. She was picking on me for having so many different boyfriends, and I said, "Why are we so different? Because you marry them and are faithful to them until they drop dead, and then you go on to the next one? It's just serial monogamy." That phrase had begun appearing frequently in *Psychology Today*.

My father died when I was six. He is a shadow person. I remember two specific incidents about him. One was when he bought a new car. The other was his trying to teach me how to ride a bicycle. He was too old. He just didn't have any patience. He traveled a lot and sent me postcards. I learned how to read from his postcards.

About a week after his death, this guy who my mother had been engaged to before she met my father —who had been my father's law partner—came into her life again. My mother and he resumed their relationship. This guy was married three or four times, but he seemed to like the wives' kids better than the wives. They'd run off and he'd be left with the kids. When he saw my mother was beating me up, he kept me and got rid of her.

By the time I was twelve I was back living with her. She hadn't stopped throwing things at me, but I was better at ducking. My mother married a furrier for a week and did not tell him that she had a kid. She showed up at the train station with this guy to pick me up when I got back from summer camp. "This is your new daddy," she said.

"Like hell he is," I said, like any smart-ass fourteen-year-old.

They got the marriage annulled about a week later. My mother told me for years afterward, "I could have been swathed in furs except for you. You had to open your mouth."

About two years after that, she married a retired attorney. He was an alcoholic. He was very quiet, invisible to me for the most part. I don't think she was happy or unhappy with him. My mother just couldn't be without some kind of husband in her life.

He got cancer. After a long, terrible illness, he jumped off the balcony of her apartment. He must have known that she was going to go off to the next guy, because she already had the next husband lined up as this one was dying. He was a friend of theirs. I found this note in her drawer twelve years after he committed suicide. It says, "The safety-deposit box is in the Western Savings Bank. Love to you and Martin." Then he jumped. He left the suicide note and a pack of cigarettes piled in the ashtray—two puffs off each one while he tried to steel up his nerves so he could jump off.

She continued to live in that apartment. I could never have lived in the place where my husband jumped off the balcony, but she did. He left her a couple of hundred thousand dollars and she got very clever at playing the stock market and at investments. She tripled the money on her own.

Then she lived with that one—Marty—for about nine years and he died of cancer. She died about six weeks after him of a massive heart attack.

She did not die because her heart was so faulty. She died because she could not foresee what was going to happen next in her life. She buried an inordinate amount of men in her lifetime. If I was a guy, I'd have been nervous about going out with her. It was like asking to die. She didn't really see herself in a grandmother role. She couldn't stand to be alone. Two days before she died she was talking about getting a facelift or going on a cruise. But I knew she really didn't have the heart to do it again. That was it. She felt like she had already dealt with as much as she could deal with and she just didn't want to get up the steam to do it anymore.

My requirements in terms of a mate were these: He had to have a sense of humor, be a little crazy. I had to be able to communicate with him and he had to be able to communicate with me. He had to be sensitive and caring and compassionate. I met this guy on the street.

I was working in the same office with a young

woman who was about to get married. She kept grumbling and grumbling that her husband-to-be's best friend was this wolf. If I would go out with him, at least she would know where her fiancé was and his friend wouldn't be leading him astray. It was going in one ear and out the other.

She and I were walking across the street one day at noon. It was December, and it was freezing out. All of a sudden she hollers, "Al!" This huge figure looms out of the blowing snow with a pipe and a coat up around his ears and I am introduced to this giant young man. He's a little over six feet. I'm five foot three, so anybody over five foot six is a giant to me. They're talking and then we left. I said, "Good-bye, it was nice to meet you."

"That's him, that's him!" she said to me.

"Who? Oh, the wolf."

"He's a musician." In my group, you didn't marry musicians. Doctors, lawyers, sure . . . but musicians? He was Juilliard educated, but that don't mean diddly-squat. A bum with a tenor horn.

I was twenty-four years old, considered an old maid, and I didn't care. I wouldn't say I was a maverick, how about a renegade? He called me up on a Friday night. "Where would you like to go?"

"The burlesque show in Union City," I said.

"Fine," he says, "I'll pick you up at six." And he took me. No other respectable young man at that time would have even considered it.

I had never been there and I was dying to go. I'll never forget it. We saw Rosita Royce and her Doves. They were pigeons and the damn birds got loose and flew all over the theater and it was marvelous. The comedians were hysterical and I had a wonderful time.

And he talked and talked and talked. My girlfriend was right, he was a terrible wolf. God! He really was. Let me tell you, that SOB spent hours that night telling me what a terrible time he had on New Year's Eve because he had to work. Sure, he had to work, but he had a girl with him. I knew it.

He tamed very quickly. He's one of the rare people in this world I look at and I just trust him completely. He's a dear, dear human being. Occasionally, I would still like to punch him in the nose, but I like him. I really do. We got married and that was that. Thirty-six years later and here we are.

I met my first husband the day I tried to get a job at the steel mill. I saw him in there. He was applying, too. My mother was bitching at me and that's how he noticed me. I was only seventeen and I couldn't work there. So I ended up moving in with my granny in town and working at the dry cleaner down the street.

I met him again at the dry cleaner's. He came in with a guy I knew from high school. We started talking and I went out with him a couple of times. Then I started going with him. I had a good time. He was crazy. Then he got me pregnant. Since I was with my granny, my mother didn't know nothing was going on.

You're not going to believe this. I don't know how she got suspicious that I was pregnant, but she started asking me about my periods.

"Oh, yeah, yeah, I'm okay," I said. "I'm having them." My mom started going through the garbage looking.

"Well, how come there's no things thrown away, then?"

"Oh, my God, now do I have to explain my garbage to you? I flushed them down the toilet. Really."

"What is going on?" my grandmother is yelling. "Will you leave her alone?"

I talked to Irv and I said, "What are we going to do? My mother's going to kill me. We got to do something."

He was at a weird period in his life, too. He'd gone to state college and was going to join the Air Force. Then I came up pregnant and I said, "You're not joining no Air Force. We have to get married. We have to. I mean, with my mother on my trail, I'm not going to live long when she finds out about this."

So we told my mother that we were going to a nearby town to visit some relatives of his, and instead we went to the next state to get married there.

All my girlfriends that I worked with knew about the whole thing and that I was getting married. They were all excited and gave me a little party at work. I went and bought my little outfit. I don't remember much about that day. We didn't talk much. I don't remember the justice of the peace or nothing. It all happened really fast.

Then we came back home and I went to my house and he went to his. We had wedding rings, but I kept mine hidden. He went to his mom and I went to mine.

This went on for about a month. I started getting bigger and bigger and bigger, right? I was wearing this corset thing, so you couldn't tell how pregnant I was. My stomach would hang out the bottom. He would come over every night like we were dating.

I started getting sick of that and my mother was irritating me. One day she said something to me and I blew up. "Listen," I said, "we're married. We've been married for a month now. Would you get off my back? And I'm pregnant, too. *Four months pregnant!*"

She went nuts. She took me to the family doctor who delivered me and asked him if he could give me an abortion. He panicked. He couldn't believe it. I was four months pregnant, and besides it was against the law. No way.

Then my husband's mom and my mom got together. They were talking about other ways to do it—to abort it. They made me sit in a mustard plaster in a bathtub. It was real hot, but it didn't work. Then his mother got this brainy idea. There's this stuff called ergot that you're supposed to drink and it will cause you to mis-carriage. So we went to a drugstore in the "bad part of town." We're standing there, the three of us, me with my belly poking out. She asked the druggist for this stuff and he freaked out. I went out the door and left her in there.

So after they tried all that stuff, they decided, "We've got to have a regular wedding with all the relatives, so no one will *think* anything."

"Fine, okay," I said, "where are we going to do this thing?" First, we were going to do it in the Cath-olic church. Everybody involved on my side is Cath-olic. We go and talk to the priest, but he wouldn't marry us unless Irv converted and we promised to have all our children raised Catholic.

Okay, fine. We'll try it the other way—Jewish. So we went to his temple and talked to his rabbi. The rabbi says, "Yeah, we'll marry you as soon as Tina takes these classes."

"How long do the classes take?"

"Four months."

"That's too long. It has to be right away. Sooner than that." So I took a quickie course in Judaism. I had to go to Hebrew class and religious class for three weeks. A crash course, but I passed.

It wasn't bad. I liked the rabbi. He was real nice. He looked like Victor Mature. Big smile and every-thing. We'd go over to his house and eat with his family. They knew I was pregnant and didn't care.

But the things they make you go through before the wedding, I couldn't believe. I had my wedding dress and I had myself squished into it so I didn't look too bad, too pregnant. I had a maid of honor and the whole bit. Everyone is waiting around and the rabbi says, "We have to go through the purification," or whatever he called it.

"What!?" I said. They were springing this on me. "How am I going to have time to do my hair? Get into that damn dress and everything before the wedding?"

"Well, it has to be done within a certain time before the wedding. And you have to do it."

So they took me down to Lake Superior in someone's backyard. I had this robe on without anything underneath it. I threw the robe off and jumped into the water. I had to go in Lake Superior naked and stay underwater for ten or fifteen seconds while he said all these prayer things over me. They were cleaning me up for my husband. I was dirty before. Yeah. I had to be purified to marry him. I loved that. I'm not sure they didn't just make this up.

My mother just bit her tongue. She was gritting her teeth during the whole marriage. We had a pretty big wedding and a big reception afterward. No one knew I was pregnant and when I did have the kid, no one said anything. There was no big deal.

With Mickey, one thing was leading to another. Finally, I was necked and petted long enough one night for him to penetrate me in the backseat of this 1949 green Ford two-door that he had. *Then* it was clear to me. I'd given him my virginity, he *must* be the guy that I should marry.

For a supposedly bright and intelligent girl who walked around doing a lot of bitching and moaning that people weren't very intellectual on a college campus and only wanted to go drink beer, I wasn't very smart. I decided to marry Mickey.

My mother was not happy. So I defied my parents. Dug in my heels, because everybody said this was not a good marriage, and I took a stand. I was this spoiled kid that my parents revolved around. It was, "I'm marrying this guy!" So there were tears, but I had my way.

I knew from about three months before the date of the wedding that this was wrong. We didn't get along. We used to fight with each other. We argued about everything.

"I can't marry this guy," I thought. But I had told my parents that I was going to marry him. I had *fought* to marry him, and I couldn't change my mind. We went shopping for wedding gowns. The invitations were out. The best hotel in town expected us. The band was hired, the photographer. They were making floral arrangements. I was stubborn. I couldn't admit that I was wrong, that's what it amounted to.

I married Mickey and we went to live in an apartment in somebody's attic in town. I proceeded to cut recipes from *Woman's Day* and *Good Housekeeping*. I had a little file box *full* of recipes. My parents were pretty much supporting us. His parents were kicking in, so we had a kind of monthly support check. Mickey was selling pots and pans door to door.

In the '50s, my entire mentality about the role of wife and mother was more influenced by outside sources than by the role model of my own mother, who managed her own business and worked when I was a child. There was such a strong ethic that if you were a caring, complete woman, you would make a perfect home, you would be a perfect wife, and you would be a perfect mommy. Somehow or other I broke that whole thing that was happening from my mom and went into what was happening in *Good Housekeeping* magazine and on television. Beaver

Cleaver's mother was the ideal. I would paper the baby's room and bake. "Hi, June, I'm home." That really was my image. Somehow my urbane working parents became sort of aberrations. They weren't what America and being an American college-educated wife was about at all.

It was worse after we got married. We didn't know anybody else who was married, so Mickey would go to the fraternity house, telling me the reason he was playing poker was that he wanted to win money to help support us. His fraternity brothers would tease him about how he had this gorgeous hunk of a wife at home and how he was the only one who could have legal sex on campus and why was he sitting there playing cards? The more they teased him like that, the more he stayed until three or four in the morning. I was home all by myself. A new bride, lonely. I didn't have anything in common with the rest of the girls who were still involved in dates and going steady and all that.

I thought I could win my husband away from the poker table at the fraternity house by making *Good Housekeeping* recipes—darling little things. When Valentine's Day came, I decorated the table with hearts and made a special meal. There was a theme for dinner at least once or twice a week. Fishnets with the tuna casserole, decorations. I stretched the budget, managed the money, I cleaned up the house.

One St. Patrick's Day, I got very angry at him. I had done this whole thing with the table. You know, we had green cupcakes and shamrocks and a special tablecloth and God knows what else I did, cut things out, decorated the whole damn place and made a special corned beef and cabbage. He came to the table in his underwear. So we had our first enormous fight.

By the end of the year, it was clear to me that I was really very unhappy with this guy, for a variety of reasons. He seemed irresponsible. He wasn't really being attentive and loving. The marriage was not romantic. No matter how hard I tried to be perfect, he didn't seem to appreciate it anyway. It wasn't fun and we argued a lot. We just had different points of view about a lot of things. What's more, I grew not to respect him intellectually. He was a philistine, he was a bore, he didn't have any sensitivity to poetry and literature.

So we had one very unhappy year of living together. I threatened divorce several times, but he always made it up being charming and funny and sweet.

I knew that I really wanted to leave him. But there wasn't anyplace to go except home, and then I'd lose the credit for the semester and how could I do that? I stayed with him because it was inconvenient to do anything else. I really didn't know how to arrange *not* staying. Nobody in my family was ever divorced, so I couldn't even carry the thought through to that.

In 1972 when the Democratic primary came along, I got involved in the McGovern political campaign. There were a lot of very dynamic women working there. They were in a consciousness-raising group at the time and they invited me to come along. I didn't know what consciousness-raising was really. I wasn't very well-informed. I was a very strong woman who didn't know where I fit in and I was carrying a lot of cultural baggage.

I felt like things just *zoomed*. I had found wonderful women whom I could relate to and talk to about things. I had a terrible sex life. Rick and I had no sex practically at all. I knew I was supposed to like sex, but I hated it. Our relationship had become very much best friends, which is wonderful for roommates, but not so wonderful for married people. I could finally talk about it. I could finally tell people and it was okay. I'd been carrying a lot of guilt around. It was like a womb, moving into a group of people I felt safe with. I found a home.

They were so different, very intellectual, and I liked that a lot. I felt dumb around Rick, I acted dumb, but I wasn't dumb. Rick had such a command of language; he was very bright and he could talk a great game. I was just in awe of him, but there were edges of it where I hated him. I hated feeling dumb. He could always do everything better than I could. He cleaned better than I could. He was a cook. I never cooked in my life. My dad cooked, so Rick cooked. I didn't know much about money. I had made five thousand dollars in the stock market when I was young, but I "didn't know anything about money." So there was a lot of conflict, a lot of confusion.

From the consciousness-raising group, I got involved with the National Organization for Women. Rick was very scared by all this. He felt nervous around women and uncomfortable. Absolutely threatened. He thought I went there and talked about our sex life. Which I did. He was right. He thought I went and told them terrible things about him, which I really didn't do. I always liked Rick, even when we had our worst times. But I liked him as a best friend.

"Slow down," he would say to me. "I'm with you, but you're moving too fast. Slow down." But once I went to my first consciousness-raising, bingo! I was gone. It was like releasing me. I had this imaginary vision of being chained down. I wasn't. Rick did not chain me down. I chained me down.

It was years later when I finally moved out. Then Ricky went to counseling after that, although he said to me at the time, "I know this is a waste of time. You already know in your mind what you're going to do."

"No, no," I said, "this is just a trial separation."
Liar, liar. I was lying and didn't know I was lying. He
knew it.

I thought I really wanted to get it together, because
I liked him so much. It was so confusing, because *I
liked him*. He's such a neat person. Everybody loved
him. You know, I didn't want to be the bad guy. How
could I leave this man who everybody liked so much?
That my mother likes better than me. That's right,
God damn it, she really loved him a lot. And he *was*
real good for me in a lot of ways.

When I left, Rick asked me if I was a lesbian. "Are
you leaving me for another woman?"

"No, I'm not, but how would you feel about that?"

"I don't want you to leave me, period. I don't care
if it's for a man or a woman. I just don't want you to
leave."

I've been doing so much divorce work now that I see
terrible things in relationships. I probably shouldn't,
because I'm just a dumb lawyer and it's none of my
business, but I ask people. I ask the men: "Was she
like this when you met her? Was she this much of a
bitch? Didn't you see flashes of this before you got
married?"

I ask the women the same things: "Did he always
act this way? Did he call you names like this? Did he
behave this way?"

Sometimes they answer me. Sometimes they don't
know. Sometimes they're real definite: "No, she was
real nice before." But the viciousness had to have
been there. I think you should be able to see it.

People hate each other so much. I don't know,

maybe it's worse to get married and end up like that than to just stay single, because I don't see how you go on. But they remarry and remarry. They do it over and over again after having something like that happen. There's got to be something wrong with you if you keep picking out the same kind of vicious Sue.

Most of my clients are men. In fact, I'm phasing them out. I'm not going to do any more male divorces. I know that sounds weird, but I'm tired of it becoming some kind of triangle all the time, which it does. The women are always thinking, "Oh, yeah, yeah, he's got this bitch representing him and she's after him."

Which I always think is just hysterical. "Yeah, right. I've seen his financial statement. Why the hell would I want to go out with him?"

Nobody thinks anything if she's got a male lawyer. Nobody thinks she's sleeping with him. But if I've got a male client, every wife on the other side has thought there is something going on. It was funny at first, then it got annoying, and now I just won't do it anymore, I'll cut it out. I'm going to start representing women from now on in divorces, no more men.

Being a divorce lawyer damages your personal life, at least with me. I was real strong for getting married until recently, but the more domestic work I've been doing, I just started asking myself, "Why would someone want to get married?"

I don't know if it makes any difference if you're married or you're living together, you're still going to be in the same kind of mess. But at least it won't be a public mess if you haven't made it legal. It won't be written down in some court reporter's file someplace where people can look back and say, "Yes, they were fighting over the bedspread." I've had people fight over pieces of china, *one piece*. She wants seven place settings and she'll give him one. He wants the other three to make it even. I don't know if it's marriage as an institution that does it, or if it's just people.

I didn't want to be divorced at thirty. That was the last thing I wanted to be. I had this image: Divorced women smoke a lot of cigarettes, wear a lot of makeup, have gravelly voices, and hang out in bars. This is very interesting to me, how my old preconceptions don't fit into the kind of person that I am.

Steven was the culmination of a series of bad relationships. He was all of my worst fears combined. We definitely locked into each other's needs and we made each other sicker and sicker. I became more and more controlling, and the more controlling I became, the more fucked up he became. I should think of a better way to say that. The tighter I tried to hold on, the more he backed out.

That meant in the beginning that there were problems with money and him never being able to keep a steady job. I would freak out about the bills, but somehow or another I would always manage to pay them. I was in control of all the finances. I had the credit cards. I had the checking account. I had everything. It wasn't like I was a silent martyr. I'd get pissed off at him, but I would always somehow scramble and make it work. The more he would become unreliable in that way, the more I would try to compensate.

He started doing cocaine. It was a gradual thing. He would cut back. Then it would get bad again. My life sunk to such a low level that the only reference point I had was things I'd seen on television or at the movies. I was dealing with a facet of life—drug dealers— that I never imagined would be a part of existence for a kid from the country. They were coming to the apartment. They would give him coke on credit, and when he didn't pay, after a while, they would call. This guy with a real heavy Colombian accent would leave a sinister message like, "Call Jorge . . . No message, *just call Jorge.*" That would be it. It was frightening.

There was this one drug dealer who would come up to our apartment to sell coke and Steven hung out with this guy. One of the things that freaked me out was the guy ended up being shot in the head a number of times and was found in a basket across the state line. I could never imagine that would be a part of my life. We had homicide squad detectives leaving business cards in our mailbox asking to talk to Steven, because they were questioning anyone who had any relationship with this guy. He was a professional. I think it is very difficult to stay alive in that business. You either die from the effects of the drug itself or you cross somebody or you end up in jail.

When this guy was murdered, Steven said he wasn't going to do drugs anymore. But then he did. He continued. He was addicted to coke, but I couldn't see it. I *refused* to see it at the time.

I had no way of knowing how much money he was spending, because he was getting a lot of it on credit. He would take the bank card and go take some money out of the bank. Usually, it would be after we had an argument. He would really act out. So I had the illusion that if I just behaved in a particular way, then he would stop doing this.

It got to the point where his behavior was violent. One night we were having a heated discussion and I walked out of the room. He came into the bathroom and threw me up against the wall. He's very, very strong. Then he pulled me into the bedroom and threw me on the bed. I was just like a rag doll. In the past, when we had argued and he had gotten violent, I could see it coming. Which was another illusion that I was in control. He took me completely by surprise.

Finally, I understood that there was absolutely nothing I could do, that it wasn't going to get better, that there was no way I could make it better, besides pulling back. That was a breakthrough for me.

Being alone terrified me. As unhappy as I was, the

prospect of having to just be with myself and focus on myself seemed worse at the time. I don't think I could have articulated it, it was just a huge feeling of emptiness that I had. Things got really, really bad. Really bad. I never would have thought that I would have held on for as long as I did.

Within a couple of months, I'd gotten in touch with a lawyer. The whole thing was supposed to be an amicable divorce. We'd just use one lawyer. The night we were supposed to meet the lawyer, Steven ended up spending the day in the hospital, because he thought he was dying, having a heart attack. He was hyperventilating. He had a major anxiety attack on top of being coked. At the time, he thought he was bottoming out, that it was the worst that it could be, because they treated him like a drug addict. He was just another drug addict who was having an anxiety attack. They strapped him down and basically ignored him.

At that point, I was numb to everything that had been happening to me. When I came home that evening, here's my husband, sitting on the couch, a physical and emotional wreck. I mean, the guy is dying from this drug, okay? He is trying to tell me what has happened to him at the hospital. By this time, I am starting to hate him—I *am* hating him. The television is on in the room and *Pee Wee Herman's Big Adventure* is running in the background. I start watching it and laughing while he's telling me his story. I was really starting to lose it. I was saturated. I looked at it as, "You did that to yourself. You're killing yourself. There's nothing I can do. I need to escape. I can't take any more. Now, I want a divorce and that's the day you choose to do too much coke, more than you usually do."

Obviously, our situation was becoming reality to him and it was more than he could handle, that we weren't going to be together. As strung out and freaked out as I was, I was much more capable of taking care of myself than he was.

Certainly, my choices and my behavior patterns were really fucked up as well. Basically, I chose someone who could not fulfill my needs and I chose him *because* he could not fulfill my needs, however much I wanted him to. From day one when I met Steven, I realized that here was someone who was very needy, someone who I could take care of. These things were very appealing to me on a very basic level. Now that's changed.

One thing that really helped me was to understand that I was responsible for myself. I was choosing every day to be in that situation and environment. I wasn't being victimized by it. I felt like a victim sometimes and I was frightened. But nobody was making me stay there. I did have a lot more choices than other people do in similar situations. I had family and friends and I had a job. I didn't have to go stay in a shelter, like some women have to do.

I had to go to family court and get an order of protection against Steven. I was having nightmares the whole night before. I'd made a whole profession out of protecting him, so how do I go to court and say, "I need protection *from* him"?

I was there with women and their children who had obviously been beaten by their husbands, bruised. I saw that this was my life and I'd better pay attention to what was happening to me. I can't pretend that I'm any different from any of these women anymore, just because I'm white and came from a sheltered, middle-class, suburban background.

I was talking to a woman not too long ago, telling her I was in the process of getting a divorce. She said, "You must feel like a failure."

"No," I said, "I feel like it's a second chance for me to change and grow in a different way." It's a time for me to look at what I've done with my life and to make choices about what I want to do now. The time hasn't been wasted, but I feel like I've chosen paths that have made it much more difficult to do what I want to do. That woman's words were like my old voice echoing, "You are a failure."

When people tell me that I'm strong, it's hard for me to take that in sometimes, but I've survived a situation that most people will never have to go through. When I look at my home now and where I'm at, I know I'm not just a survivor. I definitely had a victory. It was partly being very lucky and partly learning how to take care of myself. Maybe for the first time in my life, I understand what it takes for *me*.

There really isn't any safety net. This is my life and I'm making it up as I go along. It could all fall apart. I could lose my job, any number of things could happen that could change the entire structure of the way I live right now. That was kind of a weird feeling when I realized that. It's not secure. Nothing is. There's no backup anymore. Where do I go when I really need to feel safe? The answer is I have to make myself feel safe. I'm the only one who can do that. And that's a really tall order for me, because I've always looked to other people to create that feeling for me.

It's been a crash course.

I married this guy, my college sweetheart, the man who sexually liberated me. The marriage was really rough. We were very physically attracted to one another, very emotionally attracted to one another, but very competitive with one another.

He was an artist, welded metal sculptures, loved

being bizarre and eccentric. He was a night person and wanted to live at night.

I was a day person. I loved being up at five o'clock in the morning, taking my walk, watching the sun rise over the desert. Things had really turned for my career. I started working with these kids who were handicapped and I found my niche. This was where I belonged. I was teaching full time.

So we were battling all the time, and sort of thriving on it. There was a part of me that enjoyed the interplay. He worked in the restaurant business, because that gave him the freedom during the day to do his art. Then he would come home at two o'clock in the morning and he'd be up all night welding and doing stuff. He wanted me up at those hours. He wanted that companionship and I didn't want to be up. It was real stormy.

It really wasn't okay with Tom for me to have a career. He didn't like it. He wanted to run the show and he wanted me to be able to go to Mexico for two weeks whenever he wanted me to. It didn't matter that I had these other responsibilities or that I felt I had a commitment. He thought it was his place to support me and that I should be there like a possession. "You're here for my entertainment and my support and that's it. You can't do that when you're getting up at six o'clock in the morning and I'm just going to bed at four A.M." He wanted to have a leash on me.

It was real hard for me to come to terms with him. What I ended up doing was acquiescing to him and being real bitter and angry inside and not dealing with the anger and the bitterness. I let it build and build. It began to eat away at our relationship. I wanted to be my own person.

Finally, I wanted us to get some counseling and felt we should be apart. His attitude was, "If we can't work it out on our own, then we're not going to work it out at all. If this is how you are and this is how it is, then we'll just get a divorce.'' That was how his whole personality was, black and white. There was no middle ground. He lived black and white.

I got another place and we were separated for several months. During that separation, we saw one another occasionally. Always, I'd go into it with the illusion that we were going to work things out. He was very charming. I was very attracted to him physically. So there was a part of me that would just succumb to this, and then I would realize, "Wait a minute, I'm losing something of myself in this. I'm giving up something that is really important to me."

The renewed seduction was very much there and resisting was very hard. It was even hard to resist after we were divorced. I had moved away and when I came back to visit, I ended up sleeping with my exhusband. Which bothered me for a long time. Then it stopped bothering me while I had a great time. We knew what it was about, at least. We both went into it purely for the enjoyment of being together again.

Harold was in the family business. This is third generation, very real wealth. I'm from the wrong side of the tracks. I couldn't handle the money. I felt that somehow you were supposed to work toward something, you were supposed to suffer a little bit before you got all you got. You were supposed to earn it.

I loved his parents dearly. They became almost like parents to me. I think one reason I married him was because his parents were wonderful. His mother took me shopping. My mother never took me shopping in my life.

His parents bought us a house. On an acre. With a

135

tennis court. My mother-in-law said, "You shouldn't be cleaning that big house yourself. Use my cleaning lady." My parents never had a cleaning lady.

Still I couldn't handle the whole thing and Harold couldn't handle it. He was getting real moody.

"You know, Harold, we got to do more than spend money and travel. I need something. I need something to do." So I joined the homeowners' association and the local organizations. Harold got really uptight about that. He didn't like it. Friends said his ego was too big. He couldn't believe that he wasn't my whole life.

In November, we were supposed to go on a vacation to Cozumel. He came home one night and said, "I want to go by myself."

In January, on my twenty-ninth birthday, Harold gave me a sheet cake that said, "Bon Voyage," and filed for divorce. That's a good one.

I transferred to a new division in the company and met this guy, Ted, who I thought was really cute, but he was married. I'd been through that with a married man before, so I just kept watching him and smiling. He had called me twice when he was really drinking, saying he and his wife had problems. Thank God, I had the fortitude to say, "If you're unhappy, get out of what you're in. Then maybe you and I will talk."

I went to the neighborhood place on Christmas Eve when we got off of work early. Ted was not a bar person at all, but he went and we sat and talked. It was totally innocent. I took him back to work to pick up his car and we sat in front of my apartment in the car and kissed a little bit, but that was it.

His wife got wind of it and to make a long story short, they split up and got divorced. She at first blamed me for their marriage splitting up. But she and I are best of friends now, because she realized that I did not break up their marriage.

Ted and I ended up moving in together. We got along great, but I changed my whole life-style. I gave up my friends, and I didn't go out to the bars, and I didn't do anything that I'd done before. He would never ever go out with me. We did not do much at all. We visited my parents and his parents and went to the movies every once in a while. We camped and went fishing—things I thought were really boring, that I did because I thought it would make him happy. That's just not me.

We lived together almost a year and decided to get married. I thought, "This guy's a professional. He's got his head together. I love him." I thought I did at the time. I saw no indication of jealousy, of temper, of insecurity—nothing. But I guess there was no reason to see it. I really never bucked anything he ever said. The one thing that I remember the most that should have told me something was when a gay friend of mine called and said that he was coming through town and needed a place to stay overnight. Ted said, "I don't want no God damn faggot sleeping on my couch." I turned my back on one of the best friends I've ever had in my life. I said, "I'm sorry, you can't stay here."

Before I married him, before he and his ex-wife sold their house, she called me and said, "Rebecca, come out. I want to talk to you." I said okay. Ted was nervous about me doing it. I didn't understand why.

She took me through the house and showed me places where Ted lost his temper. There was a big hole in the garage wall, two that I can remember in the living room wall. All the doors were bashed. I thought,

"She made him do that. I'll never push him to that extent."

Linda was a perfect little wife; she mopped the floors three times a week and baked, and she really loved Ted, but it got to the point with her that his temper was too much to take. But I told myself, "She forced him to that. He loves me so much, I'm never going to see any of that."

Got married. Very, very, *very* small wedding. I didn't want a large wedding, but I wanted one bigger than what I had. But Ted is kind of backward, kind of quiet, and he didn't want it. So I said, "Fine."

The day of the wedding, my dad was so happy, he cried all the way down the aisle. My mom was just tickled to death that I was finally getting married at twenty-seven. I'd put her through a lot. My family really liked Ted.

The weirdest thing to me was, the year we lived together, five out of seven nights a week we made love. Our wedding night, we did not make love.

Two weeks after we got married, we rented this cute little farmhouse on the edge of town. He got the idea that he was going to lay carpet in this one room. I said, "Ted, if you've never done it, you're nuts. It's stupid to buy carpet and cut it yourself. If it's the wrong size, it won't fit." But he was going to do it, so he did it. He couldn't get the carpet stretched right. He picked up the hammer and threw it through the wall and started cussing fluently. I saw this look in his eye that I'd never seen before in my life.

He cooled off after the hammer incident, but the jealousy and the insecurity were still there. I'd made the mistake of telling Ted everything about my past before we were married. I mean everything. "That's fine, Becky," he said, "that's your past. That has nothing to do with us."

After we got married, it became his business. The jealousy was amazing. If I would see any of my friends on the street and I gave one of them a hug, he wanted to know how many times I'd been to bed with them. He couldn't imagine me having a platonic relationship with a man. I would walk across the street to avoid seeing a friend, because I didn't want the hassle. I would not speak to a friend because of that and that's not me.

I even blamed myself for that. Ted didn't have a past. He was married from the time he was nineteen. I know he slept with only two women in his life—me and his other ex-wife. "Maybe for me to tell him everything I'd done in my past was just too much for him. Maybe, if I can live with this, we can make it," I thought.

He never hit me, but the threat was always there, "I'm going to bash your head in." Sometimes I thought the threats were worse. "Why don't you just fucking hit me and get it over with?" I was scared of him and he knew it. I lived like that for six years, scared to death of the man.

In his defense, the only time there was ever, ever, ever any type of contact was when I was pregnant. Lamaze was a very important thing to me. He agreed to go with me, but he bitched the whole time. The two most important classes to attend, he just decided he wasn't going to go. He didn't have anything else to do. He just didn't agree with the class.

"Hey," I said, "I'm having this baby and I want to know what's going on here."

"I'm not going. Don't talk to me. I'm just not going." He got really upset with me and he shoved me down on the bed. Things like that really hurt and you don't forget them.

He had a very stressful job and I'd be the first person to admit it. He came home for lunch one day. I had put my little two-and-a-half-month-old baby down for her nap. I planned it that way, so I could have some free time with him. I'd fixed his lunch and I had it ready for him when he walked in. I'd been around him long enough by then that I knew from the look in his eye when he came through the door, "Look out!" He was livid about something that had happened to him that morning.

Jill started crying. I went in and got her and I was feeding her a bottle of water sitting at the table. Ted stood up and upset the kitchen table. He took the glass that he was drinking out of and threw it against the sink. It shattered. A piece of it cut my arm just above Jill's head. I was nuts. I took Jill in her room and locked the door, because I didn't know what he was going to do.

He left. I gave him some time to cool down. Then I called him and asked what the heck was going on. It was all that I wasn't giving him the attention that he thought he deserved. I said, "Ted, I think you better move out. I can't live like this." He moved out to the Holiday Inn.

My girlfriends came over and they said, "Rebecca, you can't do this on your own. You've got a two-month-old baby. He didn't mean it. What will you do by yourself?" He moved back in, which was probably the worst mistake I ever made.

We went to see a marriage counselor the third time we split up. I loved her dearly. But she was a female. He went one time and said, "If you think I'm going back to her, you're crazy. She's out for the woman, it was evident. This woman is siding with you."

I had a few holes in my walls, too. I always told people that we were trying to put the air conditioner in the bedroom, "and by God, the air conditioner went through that wall." I don't know whether they believed it or not, but anything was better than the truth. Not even my closest friends knew he did that. My family knew nothing. Ted was the saint of saints as far as they were concerned. I'd seen my mom go through two divorces with my older brothers and it tore her up, so I never wanted to bother her with my problems. Plus I never wanted to admit that I failed. I mean, I waited until I was twenty-seven to get married, and—by God—this was going to work.

We decided that we were going to the beach with his family on vacation. Everything was peachy keen. We had this understanding before we went on the vacation, "Ted, you get up at six o'clock in the morning and go fish if you want to and come back. And then I'm going to go lie on the beach. I'll watch our daughter half the day and you watch her half the day."

He went fishing and then came in and went to sleep. It was like our daughter doesn't exist when he's on vacation. I held it in as long as I could. He came down to the beach one day and said, "Don't you think she's had enough sun?"

"Yeah," I said, "why don't you take her back up to the cabin?"

"Don't tell me what to do!" and so on, right in front of everybody. So I took the kids back up to the cabin, being the obedient little wife that I was. I didn't want to be, but I was. He walked in and I thought he was going to kill me. He backed me into the bedroom and he said, "If you ever talk to me in that tone of voice around my family again, I'll kill you."

"Go ahead and hit me," I said. "Hit me right in front of your niece and your daughter and show them what a man you really are." He lost it then. He started beating—not me, but everything else around him. The two little kids were going nuts. I grabbed them up and we ran back out to the beach. I said to Ted's father, "If you can talk to him, do it. I'm done. He has scared me and he has threatened me for the last time. I'm not going through this again."

His father went to talk to Ted. Then he came back to me and said, "Ted says you did him wrong. You embarrassed him in front of his family. He wants an apology."

Believe me, I had a lot more nerve in that crowd than I did when it was just one on one. Toward the evening, we both agreed to take a walk on the beach. We walked for five minutes and didn't say a word. I thought, "Hey, if you think I'm going to do the talking, you're crazy. I'm not going to open my mouth and then be threatened to have my face beat in again. If you want to talk, go ahead."

Finally he did. "Do you really think it was right what you did this afternoon?"

"Ted, I'm going to tell you right now. I'm done living like this. I refuse to do it any longer. Don't talk to me. My mind's made up. I'm getting out of this." We cut the vacation short.

It was typical Ted when he got mad. When we got back, I unpacked the clothes, did the laundry, watched the baby. He laid. He did nothing. I guess he figured, "What the hell, if it's over, there's no sense in talking."

Ted stayed here in the house for two more weeks after I told him I wanted him out. It was awful. He stayed in one bedroom and I stayed in the one at the far end of the house and Jill was in between. He kept telling me he couldn't find an apartment. Maybe financially he couldn't. But it was funny. He'd come in at night and my bedroom door was closed. He'd have to knock on the door to get in. He'd come in and start yelling and ranting and raving and I'd say, "Get out. This is my bedroom." I was at the point with him then that I should have been six years earlier. I wasn't afraid of him anymore. I finally mouthed back at him and, boy, it felt good.

The evening before he moved out, though, we had a kind of a knock-down-drag-out here in the kitchen. No violence, just verbal. He said, "I don't give a shit. You're not worth worrying about." Then he said something that I will take to my grave with me. "My favorite recollection of you is seeing you cower in the corner afraid of me.''

"You son of a bitch," I thought. "Out of all the hurt that I've already been through, you have the balls to say that to me.''

Ted had this pellet gun in the basement. He threatened to commit suicide. "Fine," I said. "If you don't have any more balls than that, I'll tell your daughter that you committed suicide because 'you couldn't live with yourself." I said, "Go down there and kill yourself, I don't really care.''

He went downstairs and I heard this shot. "Oh, my God," I thought, "he did.''

When I didn't run down there right away, he came back up laughing. "Hah, you *really* didn't care.''

"I'm done caring, Ted. Whatever I felt for you is gone.''

He moved out the next day. There was a legal separation for a year, but two days after he was gone I knew I had done the right thing. It was like having five thousand pounds lifted off my shoulders. Not financially—it was taking a lot of money and saying goodbye to it. But to me the money didn't mean nothing.

After he moved out, it was like, I can sit in my recliner and read till two A.M. and he won't be out here saying, "Why don't you come to bed?" I did that a lot just to avoid contact with him. I'd clean house till two o'clock in the morning and hope to God he'd be asleep when I went in. Sometimes he was, but then he'd wake up and it didn't do me any good anyway.

We were the best of friends for a long time after we divorced. But that ended as time went on. Up until six months ago, he was still saying, "I'm a different person now, let's try again." I tried to tell him, "You might be a different person—and I hope to God you are a different person—but I can't forget what I went through. The love that I had for you, if it ever was love, died. I love you for being the father you are to

143

Jill, but I look at you and just think how could I have been with you?'' I finally had to say to him, ''The thought of making love to you physically makes me sick at my stomach.'' I know that sounds harsh, but I said it. I think he finally realized that it was over. He has a lot of regrets. I do, too. I wasn't perfect, for God's sake, but I'd be nuts by now if I still had to live that way.

M̶y Mexican grandmother was my grandfather's second wife. She married him when she was fourteen. He was thirty-five. She died at thirty-six, having given birth to thirteen children. My dad was the thirteenth.

My dad knew what his mother's situation had been and pretty soon all his sisters were married early and had a bunch of kids and husbands who mistreated them and they were stuck with these people. His line to my sister and me was, ''I want you to grow up, go to college, get a career, and make enough money so when you marry a jerk—not if, *when—when* you marry a jerk, then you can tell him to go hit the road, because you're not dependent on him.''

My sister was in a relationship awhile ago and she called me up crying. They'd bought a condo together and he was in one bedroom and she was in the other. She was saying, ''I can't stand it here. He's being verbally abusive. I don't know what I'm going to do.''

''Get your toothbrush,'' I told her. ''Go get in your Thunderbird. Go check into the best hotel in town. Take a long hot bath and order up dinner. Put it all on your credit card. This is what Dad always said, 'You don't have to stay there and take this shit.' Just go.''

144

She didn't go. But later she said, "Just knowing that allowed me to stay there."

Men don't want to be trapped. Guess what? Neither do we.

So she and I say to my father, "You got what you wanted. You don't have any grandchildren, but you got two daughters who are real independent."

I did okay as a lawyer. I worked as a public defender. I had an 80 percent win rate and a real large caseload. I just didn't handle myself well on other levels. I was new in town. I didn't know anybody. Didn't make any friends. I worked in a hostile office. There was one other woman attorney there. She liked being the only woman attorney in the office. Plus I had a secretary who just hated my guts. That can make life really bad.

I did a dumb thing. I started dating a guy who worked there who unbeknownst to me had everybody in the office in love with him. I wasn't picking up on these things. So when we started dating, I automatically made these other girls angry. They're all welcome to him now.

It just happened. I had dated some other people, mistakes, too. I always seem to lapse into that when I get someplace where I'm real insecure. I'll go out with anything. It sounds really bad, but I do that, and I start drinking too much. I was going to bars a lot. I wasn't like picking up men in bars, but I was dating men I probably shouldn't have gone out with. Not clients, but men that I knew better than to go out with. Then he and I started seeing each other.

First, our relationship was a big secret, because he worked in our other office and we thought it would be smarter to keep it under wraps. It became public knowledge in a weird episode—the weirdest thing that's ever happened to me. I was in a bar one night. I had been seeing him for about two months. He lived about an hour away. He was coming into town that weekend to this bar. A friend of ours was flying in from someplace and I was going to meet the two of them there. I arrived with a bunch of people from work. All these people are leaving after a few drinks to go to another bar. I was in the ladies' room combing my hair. This girl comes in and she says, "We're going to such and such, do you want to go?"

"No," I said, "I'm going to stay here for a little while. I'm waiting for somebody."

"Who're you waiting for?"

"Just a friend of mine. You don't know him." I knew damn well she knew him, but I was all caught up in this Mata Hari crap.

"I wonder," she says, "if you're waiting for the same person I'm waiting for?" Now this is the guy I'm crazy about. No, don't say this.

"I doubt it," I say. "Who're you waiting for?" Then she said his name. I looked at her and she said, "I'm supposed to be meeting him."

"I'm not really supposed to be meeting him, but I knew he was going to be here, so I was going to wait for a little while. We were all going out to dinner afterward. We'd talked about it."

"Well, I went out with him last weekend."

"That's nice."

"What are you going to do?"

"I guess I'll go home."

"You're not going to stay here?"

"No, I think I'll go home."

"I think you ought to stay here."

Now this is getting too weird. I said, "Why?"

"Because," she said, "I think we ought to make him choose when he gets here."

146

Oh, my God. The next thing this girl is going to slap my face. I just looked at her. Nothing like this has ever happened to me. For her, this is Joan Collins and Linda Evans. I just looked at her. I said, "I like him. I'm not going to do that. Why would you do that?"

"That son of a bitch, he told me he wasn't dating anybody."

"Why? What happened?" I said.

"I went to bed with him."

"What do you want me to do?"

"He told me he wasn't dating anybody."

"Maybe he doesn't think he is. It's no big deal." I was real tolerant back in those days. I don't know what was wrong with me. "This is kind of a secret. We haven't told anybody that we're seeing each other. Maybe that's why he said that. Plus, it's not exclusive. We're not in love or engaged or anything."

"He should have at least told me he was dating somebody," she says.

"Well, you know men. He probably meant, 'I'm not dating anybody seriously.' "

"He went to bed with me!" And she just kept going on and on and on.

So, I'm leaving. I'm walking out. This is not quiet conversation back in the bathroom. She's screaming and I'm standing there looking at her like I've seen this someplace, but I can't remember the movie that it came from. Before I could get out, somebody had already heard it and told everybody back at the table. I can't believe I'm here. One of those situations where you wish you could snap your fingers and leave. I couldn't because I'd left my purse and stuff back at the table, so I had to go get it. I had to have my car keys.

So I walk back to the table. People there are taking sides. This is now a nightmare. I have people walking up to me and telling me, "You ought to stay here. She's just a slut. He won't leave with her." As if I were really concerned about who he was going to leave with anyway. My position at this point was that I really liked him, but I'd never been in a catfight and I'm not going to get in a catfight. I have never challenged a man to choose between me and somebody else, with her right there. I'd never been the floor show in a public lounge. I kept thinking over and over again. "This girl is going to smack me. No, no."

And all these damn people are going to me, "I think you ought to stay."

"I think you ought to leave."

"Oh, stay and see what happens."

"I don't really give a damn. Give me my purse and let me get out of here." Then one of my so-called friends is standing there with my purse behind his back saying, "I'm not going to let you leave until we get this thing straight."

"Get what straight? We're going to get down on the floor and fight? Should I pull her hair? I'm leaving. I don't care what happens."

In the meantime, someone has called and had him paged at the airport, so he wouldn't come there into the middle of this horrible scene. For the first time in my entire life, I felt totally innocent. I had done nothing wrong. The only thing I'd done stupid was to say that I was waiting for someone, but it never occurred to me that this would happen. It should have, but it didn't.

So I left. I don't know what they all did. The next day I knew where he would be and I went to find him. I wanted to straighten this out. First of all, I really did like him and I didn't want him to think I was doing this stuff. All that kept running through my mind was, "White trash. White trash. Oh, my God."

We had a long talk. I made him promise me—I didn't care who he went out with—but since he lived in another town, could he just do it over there. I told him if he ever went out with her again, I'd kill him. I didn't mean I'd kill him, I just said, "That's it. It'll be over and I'll hate you forever."

So we went from there. This went on for another six or eight months. He's alcoholic. I'm sure he's not aware of it. He thinks that he's functioning just fine. We both just drank like fish for the better part of the year. That's all we did. Drank and played cards and went to parties and drove around drunk. It was miserable, just a nightmare.

It went from this casual thing to where he was my total existence. Probably the competitiveness in me made it worse. If I'd never found out about this girl, it might not have gone as far as it did, but I just lived for him.

I had nothing else. I spent all my time living for him. If he didn't call me, I cried. If I couldn't see him, I didn't have anything worthwhile to do. It got really sick. I don't think he was aware that it was that sick at the time, but he knew later. He knew there was something wrong and he didn't discourage it. So he was equally wrong.

He kept telling me he didn't want to get involved. He didn't want to get married. He didn't want to do anything, and yet he spent every minute with me. I kept thinking, "He's saying this, but he doesn't really mean it. Otherwise, he wouldn't be practically living with me, right?" Now I listen to what people say as well as what they do.

I had one male friend then who was actually my only friend there at the time. He kept saying to me, "You've got to do things to make yourself feel better. Take a class, do something. You can't live and die for this guy."

"Why not?" I kept thinking. "Why can't I live and die for this guy? He's wonderful."

He is wonderful. He's brilliant, absolutely brilliant. He taught me so much about just stupid things. I'd never read Hemingway. He bought me books. He taught me how to survive in the wilderness on all these horrible camping trips where we almost died every time. We did stuff I never would have done. But he also taught me how to drink more than I'd ever drank in my whole life.

He was the only person I ever knew who got up and had a shot of Wild Turkey at seven o'clock on a Sunday morning, followed by beer and as many joints as he could roll. And he functions. I don't know if he's still doing this, but at the time he was a brilliant trial lawyer. He was wonderful in court. I've often wondered how he could get up in the morning and do that.

He taught me how screwed up you can be and still carry on a normal life. I would be up and really be sick, but I'd get to work. I was pretty bad off, too, but I was still going to work every day. Didn't miss a single day at work. Still winning all my cases and functioning. None of my clients thought that I was doing anything horrible. I didn't have any complaints out of that period. It was bizarre.

The funniest thing is the way it all ended. We were at a party on Halloween. He still denies that this happened. He went out to the car with this same woman from the bar incident and had sex with her in the car. Everybody I knew was at the party, and everybody came back in and told me.

I don't understand. He still says he didn't do that, but I know nobody would make up something that outrageous, especially more than one person. All these people kept coming up to me and telling me. I stopped drinking after that for a year. I was so drunk. If it had happened normally, I would have been upset, but I was so drunk that I couldn't handle it at all. I didn't know what to do. I couldn't dial the phone to get a cab. I couldn't do anything. I just couldn't function. Probably if it had happened when I was sober, I would have slapped him or done something constructive. I would have left somehow.

When he came back into the party, he told me he "wouldn't have any of these jealous, bullshit scenes," blah, blah, blah. At that point, I thought I was justified to have a jealous, bullshit scene. Gee, I don't know why. I guess it was the alcohol talking.

As it turned out, I eventually got a ride home from somebody else, but I went and hid in the woods first, because he was insisting on taking me home. I didn't want him anywhere near me. It was real sick.

I thought about killing myself that night. I honestly think today that if I could have loaded a gun I had at my house—I couldn't because I was just too drunk—I might have done it. Of course, if I wasn't that drunk, I probably would have been madder at him than I was at me.

The worst part of the whole thing is—and I'm leaving this out probably because it's so demeaning—the next day I called him up and begged him to forgive *me*. "I'm really sorry. You're free to do what you want. You've been free all along. It was really wrong of me." God! I should have killed myself after I said that. What shit!

And he had the audacity to look a gift horse in the mouth. "No," he said, "I don't want to see you anymore." He had a doormat. He should have kept me. He was stupid. I would have forgiven this guy anything if I'd have forgiven him that. I was real insecure. I needed somebody. He was perfect. He was brilliant. He was well liked. I had entrée into things with him that I didn't have by myself.

It changed my whole life. I never trusted anybody the way I trusted him, and I never will, because it was so mean. He did the one thing he really could have done to hurt me. I think the reason he did that was because he couldn't deal with his feelings for me. He couldn't deal with his growing dependence on me and my dependence on him.

Jules was so reserved that you had to read his fiction to get an idea what he might actually be thinking. Jules really didn't write that much, but his stories were the only place where you might get an inkling.

Here was Mr. Reserved. His first letter he wrote to me, my girlfriend came running over to me with it. I thought, "Oooh, maybe he could write something that he couldn't say."

The letter opened, "This is a business letter . . ." It was about what kind of sleeping bag to buy because he'd done some research and thought I might like to know.

I went out West with Jules. The first stop on the way was Jules's parents' house. Jules introduced me to these people who didn't even know me by saying. "Hi, this is Wendy. She's my date to go out West."

"Wendy Weinstein," his mother said. "Oh, you come from a family a lot like ours." Which translated means, "She's Jewish. It's okay. She's a good Jewish girl . . . well, she's a Jewish girl, at least."

We ended up in a small resort town in the Rocky Mountains. Jules bought this book called *Back to Eden*. It was our health-food bible. We were going to change our lives and go back to nature and live where you could be a hippie and not eat meat. We had all these herbal cures and we weren't going to go to doctors.

We became strict vegetarians. We lived in this incredibly cold climate where you need as much fuel as possible and we were strict vegetarians. We were crazy. But we were very adamant about it, except that I used to sneak off and drink chocolate milk shakes when Jules wasn't around.

Jules was a ski lift operator—little, skinny Jules, in this bitter cold. We only had enough money for one down jacket, so we bought it for him, since he had to stay outside to work. I had some hand-me-down ski jacket which had thin places that were kind of cold. We'd get up at six in the morning and hitchhike twelve miles to work. We'd always get a ride with the fire chief into town and then we'd get a ride the next six miles with whoever would give us one.

But it was lonely there. Everybody in town liked to get real drunk and climb up ten- or twelve-foot-high rock fireplaces for fun. We stayed home and read a lot and listened to the one station that we could get on our FM radio, which was actually a television station —TV on the radio. We didn't have enough money to pay for the heat in all the rooms of the cabin, so we just shut off all the rooms except the living room and slept in there. We used the electric blanket, because the landlord paid the electricity. It was really a Spartan existence, to say the least.

Here I am, my first Christmas away from home and Jules hates Christmas. He wouldn't let me have a Christmas tree. Dad loved Christmas. He'd get these trees that were way too big and have to cut them off so they looked like they went through the ceiling. They were as wide at the top as they were at the bottom.

The rabbi used to call up and want to visit my grandma and grandpa at our house where we had this giant eight-foot Christmas tree. We would always lie and make excuses because we couldn't imagine sitting around this tree in the living room with the rabbi.

"Jews shouldn't have Christmas," Jules said, "because it's betraying their faith." Christmas Day, he worked and I was home all by myself. I called my mother and sister and cried on the phone. He didn't give me a Christmas present. It was just awful. For the seven years I was with him, I went home every Christmas and left him, because he wouldn't let me have a tree and he wouldn't celebrate it.

We moved to California. We had no money, so we had to get jobs. I started selling donuts. Jules worked at Taco Bell—the vegetarian, mixing pounds and pounds of beef and he wasn't even eating it. We had a little garden and grew beautiful strawberries.

We had no car. I had to ride my bike all the way into town for the donut job. I didn't get off until ten o'clock at night. Every night, Jules would pedal his bike to meet me and ride me home, so that I didn't get murdered on my bicycle. He wasn't so chilly after all.

Whenever I'd get sick, he was wonderful. So I wound up getting sick a lot, because he was a real good nurse. That was when he'd be his most tender. I realized I was getting sick, because that was the way I could get this stuff from him. It was weird.

He actually gave me my first birthday present after we'd lived together for three years. He celebrated my birthday by buying me a plant and a Hostess cupcake. So maybe birthday presents are okay.

Then I started wanting something else besides this chilly Jules. He *was* pretty chilly and intellectual. I felt like I was living in the desert. It was real numbing, though he meant well. So I told him I want to be able to see other people, while we were still living together.

I saw this man who turned out to be an amazing jerk. I didn't love this other person. I just wanted to see what else there was. I didn't want to stay with just one person forever and ever. I'd been with Jules for four years. It seemed like a lot.

Jules quickly found him somebody to have an affair with. We pulled back on that and decided that wasn't a very good way to be. It was really hard. You can't do that.

Then Jules went back to school and became an obsessive student who never wanted to do anything but study. I got lonely again. When he finished school, we moved to town. I had a job and I wanted to separate. So we separated, but still dated each other.

Then he met somebody and started dating her. I met somebody. He was very affectionate, real sexually satisfying. That was attractive. He was very competitive on an intellectual level. I liked that, too. He had a great mind and I was stimulated.

But Jules started to like this woman he was seeing. I didn't like that. I was afraid I was going to lose him. So we made a deal to break up with these other people and get back together. I broke up with the man I was seeing and Jules broke up with the woman he was seeing.

For the first time in my life, I was ready to make a commitment. I would have gotten married. I was completely ready. I'd thought I would never get to that point. I always envisioned myself going from one rocky affair to another. Just sort of saying, "Whoops, I'm going to go take a date with somebody else now." Okay, Jules, let's just get married. That's what we should do.

But Jules *really* liked this other woman that he was with, or he thought he did. He couldn't get her out of his mind. So he went to her and said, "I want to still see you."

"It's either her or me," she said. "You can't do both."

"All right," he said, "then I'll take you." He went off with her and left me.

Meanwhile, I really didn't like the other man anymore, so I was left for the first time. It was really terrible. I was crushed, miserable. Aching, sick inside. I'd wake up and I'd have forgotten. Like when somebody dies: You go to sleep and when you wake up in the morning, something is bothering you and you can't remember what it is. Suddenly it comes to you: "Oh, God. That's right. He's dead." That was what it was like. I'd wake up in the morning and think, "Oh, God. That's right. It's over."

Didn't have a very salable profession. I didn't have a roommate, I didn't have a job, I didn't have school, I didn't have any money, and I didn't have Jules. I didn't have anything. Things were real bad.

I took this job in a bookstore. Here I am with a master's degree and I'm still working in fucking bookstores and donut places. Plus I became a real good runner. I used to run eight miles a day. I'd work and then I'd go run.

I really think that women when they have something that bothers them, they let it worry them and it eats you up, it eats you up, and it eats you up. Even though I thought, "Oh, that'll make me happy. It'll get this pain out." It didn't work.

I was by myself in every sense of the word. I started going on dates and having terrible times, doing my high-school thing: I'd get a headache, be sick, and go home in the middle of the date. They'd come here and yell at me. I just couldn't wait till I could get home to my little bed and read. I did that for a while.

Then Jules broke up with that woman. But I'd started to see David. He was warm and affectionate. Jules was never very affectionate. So I didn't want to get back with Jules by then, but Jules really wanted to get back with me. The feeling was gone. I didn't want to do that anymore. It was like a past life, and it had taken me a long time to get over it.

It was terrible for Jules: Then, he got to do the hurting.

I had also discovered that people could be warm and talk to you about their feelings. As it turned out David talked to me about his feelings, but he could never quite commit to me. He was a nice Jewish guy who couldn't bring himself to make a commitment. I was too kind to him, too motherly.

It's like you leave one for someone who'll do what the other one didn't do. Then you leave that one because he isn't doing something that the next one can do for you.

I used to think I could never have a child, because I couldn't find a man that I'd want to be with long enough to want him to be the father of my child. Once you have the child, you're stuck with the father, even if you're not married to him. He's invested in this kid, so he's forever part of your baggage. I couldn't imagine having anybody around like that.

I wound up with David's best friend who was 100 percent willing to like me all the way and did. Bob was warm and he wanted to love me. We're married now and have a two-year-old son.

But all these guys have been younger than me—chronologically younger and developmentally younger—so I was always sort of raising them. Bob is eight years younger than I am. He doesn't look it. I'm glad he's bald, because people won't notice that he's younger than me. I'm getting older in a hurry. We're really in different developmental places, which is okay, until the day you have responsibilities and a kid. Then it doesn't work out too well, because suddenly you're the mother of *two* children, and one of them is growing up but the other one isn't.

Even when I was very young, I never wanted anyone to take care of me. But now I really would like for somebody to take care of me sometimes—just once in a while. You know, it just didn't work out that way. Ultimately Bob's like Jules in that he's got the white Anglo-Saxon Protestant chilliness when it comes to talking about problems. I think a lot of men are like that. They just can't discuss it. They *harumph*. They go, "Yeah, yeah." Or else they want to jump in and fix it. Jumping in and fixing it aren't all right. I want to discuss it. I just want to be treated like an equal. I want to be treated like I have brains to figure this out, so let's talk about it. Maybe you have a good idea, too. Men either want to treat you like you're their little girl or they want you to be their mother. They don't get how you can be on par, equal in every sense. It's hard to find that.

I was always moving so fast. I met some wonderful people in my life, but for some reason, no one was ever a basis for staying anywhere. Now with the feeling of my mortality, I'd like to stay somewhere. I need commitment, but I don't know how.

I keep getting involved with younger and younger men. I like the hopefulness they have that I don't have anymore. It's not the direction I expected to be going in. I'm involved with a man—and that's a strong word—who is twenty-seven years old. In some ways, he is very much a man, but in other ways he is such a kid. He's very loving. I do love him. He's brought love into my life. But it's a very impractical relationship. All my life I've always had people telling me whom I ought to be with. Sometimes I think that people will never tell you that the relationship you have is a good one. They just do it to fuck with you. Nobody was ever good enough. I don't ask anymore what people think. I've been hearing that this one isn't good for me either. Okay, okay.

In relationships with men, I don't like to end up the stronger person all the time. I'm not really all that strong. I've taken on too much of it as it is. I'm looking for a vacation.

There have been times when I say, "Oh, no, we're not going to make it another six months." Then I wonder if maybe this is how *everybody* is dealing with it. Maybe the people next door and the people across the street are feeling the same way. The few women friends that I talk to on that level tell me that it's going on for them.

WOMEN

There is no Ozzie and Harriet and 2.2 kids, but that's what we grew up watching as kids and hearing about. My parents projected that. I'd never seen my parents relating very much. My father wasn't a very affectionate person. I never saw my parents fight. I know they had arguments, but that was all behind closed doors. Affection was behind closed doors, too. The *whole thing* was behind closed doors. I felt like I'd never had any models. So I had to learn it all for myself.

I don't feel like I've sacrificed my personal life to my job, because it was what I was most interested in at the time. It wasn't like I left anybody or anything to go pursue a career. I was only in love twice and I don't do it easily. It doesn't come naturally to me.

Women like me are supposed to marry a guy who has a *better* career and makes *more* money. That pool is so small that we have to stop looking in that direction, start looking at more normal human beings and saying, "Let's do that. That'll be okay."

I said to my sister a couple of months ago, "You know, I bet if we spent as much energy and time and thought on finding somebody we really wanted to be married to as we do on our careers, it would probably happen in about three or four months." She agreed but we said, "Yeah, but is that really what you want to be doing?"

Let's say I took off a couple of months and found this person, I achieved it. Then the next day and the next five years, I'd have to live with somebody. Then I'd have to compromise. That looks more like sacrifice to me. Obviously, if you're in love with the person

159

and you're building a life together, you're sacrificing some other things: decisions you might make differently if that person wasn't involved day to day. Working at it, too, that seems like a sacrifice. Inevitably somebody's feelings get hurt, yours or his, and then you have to *deal* with it. I get home, I don't have to deal with anybody's feelings but mine. I think that's part of aging. You get more selfish. If you don't get married earlier you forget how to do it.

So far it's not that much of a big deal. If it happens, it happens. I don't want to be old and alone, but then who does? The way things are going I can always wait for the second round of divorces. Maybe I'll meet somebody at fifty and we can retire together.

Before I was involved with somebody—and this is probably the longest steady relationship I've ever had —I thought the worst thing that could happen to me is that I'd be forty years old and sitting in the singles bar. Of course, that age is hyped up all the time. It used to be twenty-five and sitting in a singles bar, then thirty and then thirty-five. Now, of course, it's forty. I don't know if being by yourself is the worst thing in the world. Maybe I don't remember right now.

I guess the worst thing that could happen would be losing hope, which a lot of my female friends have done, and they're not even thirty yet. I know a lot of women who have just given up on men. Life too sometimes, but men mostly.

That's stupid. There's a lot of men out there and nobody thinks there are. All these women just walk around using the male-shortage magazine articles as a crutch. "There's no men out there anyway, so I'm not going to try anymore." You can't say all men suck, just like you can't say all women suck. You just can't do it. It's not true.

If you get to that point—I've been close, but never to that point—there's nothing left. It's a basic instinct that you seek out male companionship or some type of sexual companionship. When you stop doing that, everything else suffers, your whole life suffers. Not that you necessarily have to be with somebody, but when you cut that off, you cut off most of your life.

I know women who won't even be friends with men, because they just think men suck. "That's it. They suck. They're awful and I don't want to have anything to do with them."

I don't see how you get that bad. Most of these women have not suffered horribly. It's not like they've been beaten. They don't have a rational basis for it. They haven't been abused in any way that's worse than anybody else I know.

Some of them haven't even given a man a chance. One woman I can think of in particular has never even really dated anybody. She's just picked up men here and there. That would give you a bad attitude, but she's never been involved in an actual relationship. She hates men. For the sake of it.

It's fear. She thinks that if she had a relationship it would just turn into a disaster, so it's better to just walk around talking about how men suck.

I don't understand it in men either. I see men who act that way toward women. Relationships are difficult. It's awful now, because there's no rules. You don't know what you're supposed to do. But just because it's difficult doesn't mean it's not worth doing.

I met Bryan and we walked around and around each other for about six months. We were both seeing other people and I was scared to death. I knew not long after I met him that I really liked him, but I didn't want to let anybody else get close again. I didn't want to get hurt anymore. And he seemed kind of mean. I'd always gone for men who were mean to me. They'd hit me and done mean things to me, taken my money. I didn't want to get involved with someone like that again. I wasn't sure that he wasn't like that, because he was so brash. I wasn't sure, but maybe that was what attracted me to him.

He would come over at ten-thirty at night for twenty minutes and leave. I didn't know how to cope with that behavior.

"You mean you don't want to have sex?" I didn't understand, because that's how everybody else treated me. They'd come over at ten-thirty and leave at twelve, but they'd get their rocks off. He'd talk for a while and then leave. I was really perplexed. I was convinced that he had something up his sleeve. That he was trying to pull something over on me. But he wasn't.

I announced to him one day that I was leaving, that I was quitting my job, going to Europe for a month, and then going back to grad school in another city. He said, "Oh, you are?"

From then on we just got tighter. He became my boyfriend. He was real attentive. We got closer and closer. He proved that he cared about me. And he still cares for me and I'm still scared.

It's not Bryan. It's being left over and over. I'm getting past a lot of that. I'm realizing that I can't think that's always going to happen, because if I think that way, I set it up to happen that way, too. Your behavior starts to reflect that belief.

Bryan is not like the others. I've seen what a good

friend he is to me. He really supports me in what I want to do and he's not just giving me mouth music with it either. He seriously means it. He actually gets involved. "Go for it," he says. "You've got all this wonderful potential and I love you."

"Nah, you just want me to cook dinner for you tonight." But no, he does the cooking, too. I've never known anybody to be such a good friend, and if we were over tomorrow, I'd know that he has been that to me. That's meant more than any kind of incredible sexual thing. The sex is great and important, but it's not what's really the most important to me. I never thought life could be on this level with a guy, where I wasn't playing cutesy-coy games and manipulating him and all that stuff that everyone does to everyone else.

I fell in love with someone who was what I needed. But he wasn't what my mother would have expected. I had a moment of panic just before we got married, because I had to deal with all these expectations. "Okay, Mom, is this okay? Is he all right?" I wanted to have her permission. My mother had wanted a lot of things for me, but she also would have wanted me to be happy, so she probably would have approved. She would have loved his laugh and all the puns he makes. She would have loved everything about him, but he wasn't a doctor. He *is* an incredibly nice man. You don't meet many men like him. I hadn't.

I have a perfect example of why I fell in love with him. It's a simple thing. We were leaving his house one morning right in the beginning of the relationship. I had to go one way and he had to go the other. He wanted to walk with me to the bus stop. I said, "But it's out of your way."

"Yeah," he answered, "but I want to be with you." I could have burst into tears at that moment. I still could. It was so different than what I was used to. There was no game playing. There was no, "If I do this, what's she going to think next or expect of me?" It was, "I want to be with you." Who knew what would happen next? I'd never met anybody who was so genuine. Lucky.

As my friends started slowly getting married, I realized that I didn't envy any of them. I really liked the life I had. I was involved with different men. I always had this image that I was going to be one of those women you see in some magazines. *Leggy,* leggy was the operative term. I was going to be limousined to the theater and the opera by some fantastic guy.

Of course, my life was never that. My life was going to dinner with somebody, offering to pay half, and that person accepting. We're talking about in some little Italian place downtown, not a four-star restaurant. I never seemed to be a high-powered, high-octane dater. There are people who are.

I had a lot of independence. A lot of men didn't like going out with me, because I was away all the time researching a book or giving a speech or being on a TV show. I like going on vacation alone. Even in the thick of a relationship, I'd go away by myself. Partially, it was because of interviewing maybe as many as ten people in a day on an ordinary day or being interviewed by other people. There was just too much Me, Me, Me. I needed to be alone and not talk to people. I've stayed in hotels for a weekend just not to be around people. It can be a little scary by Sunday when I realize I haven't said anything but, "Put the tray here," but I really like being alone.

Being married is great. I don't understand now what I had against it. I just couldn't think about it until I met the person I could marry. If you said to me, "Pick five words to describe yourself," I'm sure *married* wouldn't be one of the top five. I'm sure it wouldn't be one of the top ten. But that's the great part about it. I finally realized that I didn't have to change to be married. That there was somebody who liked all that nonsense that is me and that I could still be alone and have time to myself. That's the biggest thing.

Most people think it's women who want to get married. That's the picture, that's what's out there on the street in the whole dating game. That's how men *and* women see it, except for those of us who have been there. We know better. It's men who want to get married and women who have to accept that in order to not end up alone. That's the big fear. Many women want to get married when they are young, because they are afraid that they will *never* get married if they don't do it then. But the business of getting married and settling down is more and more a male thing as time goes by. Men are afraid they're going to continue to fool around, and marriage is a kind of control, a self-limiting sort of thing.

The interesting thing I've learned about men is that they want to be home more than I do. Once they settle down, they *really* settle down. Women often want to get out, and the men want to be home. That's a real shocker, when we find out that in the end each of us wants just the opposite of what we thought we wanted.

Adapting to that is really difficult. He really wants to be there at home, just *be* there and *have* you there. You want to be taken out or to go out or have him go out and leave you for a while. Getting to know that about each other, accepting it, and not taking it personally is a real struggle that goes on, back and forth, for years in relationships.

One of the keys to survival in a relationship between a man and a woman in my experience has been space, private space, a way to get away. It's good for a man to go away on a couple of trips, to stay out a few evenings, and not come home on time.

What women want from men is to pay some attention. Men don't understand when women make a big deal about now and then a bunch of flowers or that when a man buys a gift it should be personal and not something that's being pushed in a wrapped box at the department store, that the gift makes clear the man really knows the person that he is giving the gift to. Valentine cards and all those sentimental, sloppy, stupid things are a big deal to women in lasting relationships.

I feel very strongly that I don't want to ever get married again. A relationship is safer longer, it's better without that legal, formal thing which in itself doesn't guarantee anything. People do better with each other when the struggle is there. It's good for people. The idea of and the feeling of commitment, the way you live, is more real than these paper promises that more often than not are broken these days anyway.

Women and women have an easier time making a relationship. They take each other as they are, and if they don't like each other, they drift apart. If they like each other, they get closer and continue to get closer always. We don't have to be something we're not.

A man and a woman commit to one another in an intimate relationship that they expect to be ongoing. Now they are going to start sharing each other's life. They start to expect things from one another. There are these tests that go on. If you pass A, B, and C, and you do it in the appropriate amount of time, you pass. They are unfair tests, but are part of the struggle to maintain a relationship and part of the struggle to end it that's going on all the time between men and women. It goes on if you are married or not.

Once a couple are married, especially men, but women too, become complacent and think they don't need to be as present for one another. They're wrong. It's that loss of presence of the centrality of that person in your life that is the great destroyer of primary relationships between men and women.

Real romantic love is very important. The flirtation period passes. You have that tantalizing excitement of not knowing what the other one is feeling and all that goes on at the beginning of a relationship that all of us love, but then it changes into a deeper more abiding love, an all-enveloping feeling.

It's really hard to maneuver in those waters; they really are treacherous for a woman. It's threatening to give yourself to another person and be in the power of that kind of a relationship, because at the same time you fear you may drown in it and be lost as a separate, independent person. There's that real pull toward giving up your friends, giving up your other interests. It's like alcoholism. You isolate yourself within that world. Everything else is secondary to it.

So this fear creates another force that is trying to push that person out of your life, so you can be by yourself. It's a struggle to hold onto love and to hold onto your own self and your independence. The feeling of security in a relationship comes from independence not dependence. I can take care of myself.

I want a relationship. I do want to be pregnant. I'm at the point that that's what I want, not because of any time clock, but because I think it would be wonderful. This whole past year, I went looking. I'd never looked before. I never wanted a relationship since my divorce.

I'd jump in, date one guy, think I was falling in love, because when you're looking, you want to fall in love. Then the person would be a schmuck or I would be a schmuck. It's devastating.

I did that for a solid year and I must have dated ten guys. I was involved sexually with some of them, others not. Just went running from one to the next to the next. Not like a woman in heat. You know, I was cool. I'd check it out, but then you jump in.

I didn't have the skills to communicate, to say what I wanted, to say what I needed and to be honest. I think I was totally dishonest. I was playing a game to see who would want me the most and then I'd gyrate toward that person. Then you play a guessing game. I was too insecure and unsure of myself with men to say, "I think you're wonderful," or "I don't want to go out with you." I would just play it out. I didn't know how to be up front, to be assertive, to be hard.

Then you go through withdrawals, the wondering and the anxiety. What did I do? What did I say? Did I do this wrong or that wrong? It can be very harmful. The reverberations of this type of thing can hit you later on, too, because then the anger comes out. You may not display it at the moment, but it builds up. We are emotional animals. We're human, we can't help it.

I was terribly hurt. I was frantic all week. Why am I this hurt, if I'm just having a fling? Why be with someone, if you're just having a fling? I don't understand that. How can you be with someone for a month all the time and be having an affair? It was a relationship.

I see it happening too much, just too much. I love my friends and I don't like to see myself or anyone else getting hurt. We all need to be loved. We need it so much. I see this whole momentum rushing on like something on high speed, fast forward. It's the neurotic, unstable, erratic energy of people hunting and looking and trying to put everything together very quickly.

Sometimes I get scared. I'm thirty-seven. I've accomplished a lot. I feel quite good. I've got my head screwed on fairly well. There's a lot of alteration, a little altercation, as I make adjustments once in a while. I really would like a relationship. I find most men feel the same way. They want a relationship, too. They want to fall in love. They want romance very much. They bring flowers and champagne. They wine and dine you. However, they're frightened. They say, "It's not the right time," or "I don't know what's going to happen with my career right now." It's an excuse and I wish men would grow beyond it. All this is Old World stuff.

They don't understand that you should go through hard times together *and* wonderful times together. It doesn't have to be perfect. The reason why you're with someone is because you need support, you need tenderness, you need love. You need a comrade, a partner.

Women don't really give a damn if a man's having trouble with his business. They don't care. Women are rescuers, they want to help. They have to be careful not to rescue too much, but they want to be supportive. It's an instinct. An adult woman can be supportive and comforting without hanging all over a man, clinging too much. And men would really grow from it. It would be good for them; they wouldn't have to take it all out on themselves.

Love is an addiction. It's a fantasy. We start building up our expectations and that's when you really get hurt. Women are really great at expectations. A woman figures out what she wants in life and she's got this whole fantasy about what's going to happen ten years down the line. Women are very calculating. They size everything up. They have their little checklists. A woman's been thinking on the first date what it would be like to make babies with this man—truly —even if she doesn't want to have kids, she'll still do it. It's a flash thing, it's in our brains, in our programming. Genetically, we can't help it.

New Year's Eve, I introduced one of my dearest friends to a man I know. She's a doll, he's attractive. They're sitting there at dinner, drinking champagne, getting really high, and having a wonderful time. He becomes more attracted to her as the night goes on, because she's with me, she knew my date, and we were all laughing, so it was family and familiar. He wasn't frightened. He starts to move on her. She's playing hard to get. No, she's not going to sit there, making out with him.

He calls her a couple of days later and they go out. He kisses her on the cheek good night and she's a little bit reserved. He thinks something's wrong. She didn't jump him. I mean, is a woman supposed to jump a man? What's been going on? Women have been so aggressive that men expect it. If you don't jump them, they think something's wrong. I had to reassure him that she was interested.

So they started dating. On one of the first dates when they were just friends talking, he told her, "I'm just getting out of a divorce. I don't want any involvement. There's this woman down South where I have some business interests who I see sometimes. I really just want to play the field. I don't want a relationship. I don't want to have kids."

She sizes him up in her head: "He's a 'No' on the checklist, but I'll go out with him, because he's cute. Whether or not I sleep with him, it doesn't matter. He's a cute 'No' and let's just leave it at that."

What does he do? He's stupid. He's not planning properly. I can see it coming. He's calling her every day, sending flowers, crazy about her, loves being with her. He's imprinting on her. She's out of town on business right now. He says, "Call me as soon as you get back." He has her car in the garage at his place. He's moving in.

She's starting to imprint on him. Last time I talked to her about it, she said, "I don't know, but this might go someplace." She hasn't told me this, but I can see it in her head as she's checking off the vital statistics on the list. Will he make nice-looking babies? Does he have money? Do we have the same tastes? Yes, we both wear the same type of clothes. And on and on, this thing women do.

But he's "just having an affair." He loves calling and doing all these things. He's going to get tied up on her, but the bottom line is that he doesn't want a relationship.

She's late thirties, she wants a relationship. She wants to get pregnant. She wants to get married and have kids. A month down the line, she's going to start putting out little demands. "Well, am I going to see you this weekend?" Women do that. It's ingrained in us.

He'll move away. He already knows that. She will get hurt. He will get angry. "What happened to her? We were having such a great time. We were having a wonderful affair."

Then she'll get pissed off, because she'll feel like a whore and say, "No, I'm not the type who has an affair. You were the one calling me all the time."

"I told you from the beginning, I didn't want a relationship."

The thing is, why did he have to move so fast? Why did he have to wine and dine her and set her up? Men have to capture, to charm. Plus men are terrible romantics, more than women. They get off on it, they love it.

If you don't want a relationship, then don't play around with it. If you want to send flowers, send them to your mother. There's got to be a way to do it, because it's not fair play the way things are now. There's so much emotional abuse in this dating game. You might as well just kill each other.

It's hard not to rush in, especially if you have passion. Who wants to put passion on the back burner? I certainly don't. When I feel passion, I'm going to go for it 100 percent. It's so great to be naughty, to have this incredible chemistry and to just go for it. That's what it's all about. So what do you do?

If we're going to be smart about this, people are going to have to learn a new etiquette. There've always been parameters and rules in the past. Now we're moving so fast that we have to write our own rules. Usually, there was a generation ahead that would create the rules, then their children would follow those rules and maybe shift them about a little bit.

But this is like a time warp. We've been the generation ahead of ourselves. We are the parents and the kids at the same time. We made all the radical changes, and now we're trying to figure out the rules to deal with the changes we made.

Our practical side, our very human and tactile side, is saying, "Reproduce, have love, have family and neighborhood." The other radical side is trying to figure out how to maintain independence, stay your own person. Each one of us has to be both. We have to still be radical enough to develop new rules, as well as practical enough to play by the rules.

I have to develop my own rules. I have to learn about taking care of my emotions. Being sweet and loving to men, and if they don't love me, to love them anyway, to let them be free, to be friends. That's the reason why you're together. I don't want to be angry at anyone for not being in love with me. How foolish! The anger between women and men hurts me deeply. I see so many women getting angry with men. So what if a man doesn't want to marry her? So what if he doesn't want to have kids? Big deal. You can't get angry. It's just the wrong man.

What I'm practicing is, if I see that it's not going to work, I let go before I get really pissed off. Breakup is too difficult. Breaking away is okay. You can break away if you plan carefully, before you get too heavily imprinted.

If men don't want to play by the rules, the best thing is to take them at their word. If they say they don't want a relationship, then I will take them at their word and I will make the rules about how fast it will go.

It could be that if a woman used that instinctive quality that she has, that beautiful focus, and just played fair with the man, she would say, "I know you want an affair. Go to someone else. I'll be your friend. I'll date you. I'll even sleep with you. But this is not going to be an affair. Don't call me every day or send me flowers, because if you do, what's going to happen is trouble. I like you, but I am looking for a relationship. I'll be with you in the interim. Know that I'm going to be dating other people. Let's just see it logically." If I was a man, that type of a woman would turn me on and I might even change my ways.

Women have been little girls, little Cinderellas. High emotion, naughty, bitchy, off-the-handle, attack-dog type of behavior. We act cruel and sophisticated, yet inside we're all going, "Oh, God damn it, son of a bitch, why doesn't he love me?"

The most beautiful women are women who are calm inside and who have vision. Women will have to become more and more patient. More adult. Women are going to have to learn how to handle their emotions very well, how to quit having expectations, and how to be thankful for what is. That's love.

When women are calm and clear and confident, they see what's going on, they know the type of man they want, and they won't feel rushed and impulsive. Once women do that, they will develop even more self-respect.

My parents have such a good marriage that I think that's just the way life is supposed to be. You're supposed to have somebody to share things with and to go through life with. I want that, too. It's very hard, though, to find somebody to marry. It's difficult to plan it. I don't know how to do it, so I don't. I think about what I should do instead of actually doing it.

Sometimes I'm lonely. There's more to life than reading books on a Saturday night. There just is. There's something that I'm missing. I don't want to go through life without it. As soon as I figure out how to get it, I will.

For the past four years, I've been averaging one date a year, which usually happens in the spring between March and May. So I'm hopeful about this year's date. I can't wait to see who turns up this year.

So it's pretty much chance, isn't it? There must be something you can do. I guess people are going to bars. I'm not a bar person. It used to be health clubs and I belonged to a health club for a while, but I never met anybody. Maybe it's video stores. They have The Social Safeway here, the local grocery store pickup scene. That's where I shop. But I must shop at all the wrong times, because I never met anybody. What do you say in a grocery store to start a conversation? "So, the romaine looks good, huh?" Do you follow them around with your little cart? Come up from the other direction and run into them? Will that have an effect on them? Will they assume you want to meet them?

I'm twenty-six and a half. I'm absolutely convinced that everything is going to turn out like a Rodgers and Hammerstein movie musical for me. I have to think that way. Otherwise, life is just so dull. I have a really good imagination and a great fantasy life. I make up stories and keep myself entertained about how wonderful my life is going to be. I don't think it's weird. I hope most people have their lives in their heads, inside themselves, the way you want life to be. That's the only way that you can try to make any change. You have to be able to imagine it to make it happen in reality. I can imagine it real well. It's hard to make it happen.

My ideal man is funny, smart, ambitious . . . and taller than me. Do you think that's too much, that one physical characteristic? Someone who has goals. I don't have a lot of goals in life. I just kind of hang out. I admire people who have goals and work toward them and achieve them—that's a biggy too—achieving the goals. Somebody who's fun to be with, who talks more than I do. Somebody who likes kids. I'd like to have a family. That's really about it, except he should love me back. It happens to other people. I'm not discouraged about it. Well, sometimes, but not really.

4. Never Done

I'm not a person who you're going to see out there screaming for women's equality and that sort of thing. I don't care how you look at us, we're not the same. I could be just as good a brain surgeon as any man, but if a man and I went out there to stack those bales of hay, a man'd beat me every time. I can't stack the bales like a man can."

It was mid-August, near the end of the haying season in the valley. As far as the eye could see all around the house, new-mown fields stretched away to the foot of the mountains. The woman speaking had spent every day for weeks driving the mowers, the balers, and the pickup truck that collected the bales through the fields that belonged to her and her husband. It is bone-jarring, dangerous work that lasts from first light until darkness. The hay has to be brought in while the weather is dry, so if there's a threat of rain, the couple might work well into the night, the roar of the diesel engines drowning out the chirping crickets, the headlights on the machinery startling rabbits and gophers.

"I can go out there on my machinery and I know exactly how to fix it. I know this piece has to come off, so I can put this new piece on it. I know how to set the thing, but I can't get the nuts off of it. I always

177

have to get my husband to help me. Yes, there's some women who can probably get out there and get those bolts and nuts off the machinery, too, but they're a minority.

"Everybody should be respected for what they can do. If it was intricate brain surgery, I'm sure I could stack them with the best of them. If I was a brain surgeon, I should be able to get the same wages as a male brain surgeon. It's not fair that you get paid less just because you're a woman. But at the same time, I know women who've gone down and worked in the mines not far from here who think they should be paid the same as a man. They can't produce the same as a man in the mine, most of them. There's always one with an extra chromosome or something who can outdo some of the men who are there. If they can produce as much ore out of the mine, they should be paid the same, but they should have to prove it. If they don't like it, too bad. Find a different job.

"But this, 'Hire me because I'm a woman,' I hate that. You should be hired not because of what color you are or what your religion is or because you're a man or a woman, but whether or not you can do the job and are qualified. That junk drives me nuts."

If not the majority, then many American women would express a similar opinion on "that junk." Yet in my travels across the country, I did not interview one woman who had not suffered some form of sexual discrimination or harassment on the job. Twenty-five years after the landmark Civil Rights Act, most jobs are still gender segregated. There is women's work and men's work. The women I interviewed expressed anger over this, but not the level of outrage I would have expected considering the pervasiveness of the problem.

Somehow a few network TV anchorwomen seem in the public consciousness to balance the hundreds of thousands of drudges providing the backbone of the national economy at wages only 60 percent as high on average as men receive in comparable jobs. Women at the bottom of the income scale are too busy scraping by to express much of anything but fatigue. They work where they do because they have no other choice. Women in the middle range of salaries try to believe that plenty of hard work will soon erase the huge disparities in opportunity and salary between them and their male coworkers. They strive to make themselves indispensable to their bosses, or they simply resign themselves to subservience. The result in either case is about the same.

And when these women go home at the end of the working day, they don't pop open a can of beer, prop up their feet, and watch the evening news. They go back to work at their other full-time job—mother, housekeeper, laundress, cook.

The women at the top expend much of their energy consolidating their limited power and fending off contenders, female and male. The women who seem to exercise the most control over disbursement of funds, their staff, and programs are those who work in nonprofit corporate America—charitable institutions, museums, educational institutions. The equivalent position in for-profit companies of approximately the same size and worth would command at least double these women's salaries, provide extraordinary prestige, and ninety-nine times out of a hundred be held by men.

Those few women who have reached positions of authority in American business play by the male rules, but they pay a price. As one woman put it, "I've reached very near the top of my profession, and I still have a hard time being assertive in business, because that means you're a ball-buster. It's all right for a man to do it. Do you think a man is warped or sick if he acts aggressively in business? No. But if I do it, I'm just a bitch.

"The fact that I'm an emotional person has not helped me in business. I've cried a couple of times in business situations. I don't think anybody saw me, but people who worked for me knew. This is a major no-no. God forbid that you should show your weakness."

The most successful women I talked to avoid direct confrontation. They know they are unlikely to be heard above the din of big-gorilla chest-beating many men resort to in a crisis. Women prefer other methods of gaining the upper hand, as the executive officer of a multimillion-dollar nonprofit institution explains:

"In business, half of it is your manipulation of your environment and the other people you're doing business with. Women, always being at the mercy of men, learn to read people really well. You learn to be perceptive. That intuition that they talk about women having is really just a survival skill, so that you can be where you need to be in case *he* makes the next move. You're constantly in response. You learn to figure out, 'Where the hell are these guys?' If you can manipulate that information, you can win.

"I sit around meetings and look at men and say to myself, 'They don't know what the hell's going on in this meeting. They're not aware that the president is upset about the whole subject, that the VP is trying to make himself look better, and the treasurer is trying to position himself with the majority at any cost.' With that kind of information, you can say, 'Okay, now how do I want to be around all of this?'

"I'm not above using whatever skills I've got to get what I want in business—other than sexual skills. That's not what I'm talking about. When I say that I play up to men, I mean I do whatever I need to do to get my program across.

"My board president, he's not a real bright guy. That's okay. I like him. I don't mind him exactly the way he is. But I don't confront him. I don't go up against him. I say, 'Well, I was sort of thinking it would be best if we did this.' Then he gets to make a decision. 'Okay, good,' and off I go. It's a little bit disrespectful, but it's also just easier.

"I grew up around my father's sisters, watching and being trained in how to manipulate men without them thinking that they're being manipulated. My mother never did that; she refused to do it. So I was given both the skills to do it and the disdain for doing it. Manipulating a man for me means that I can't have any respect for him. Men that I want to maintain respect for I have to address directly. Now, if they can't handle the directness, that's another question. But let's try, because otherwise it's a wash."

Contradictory and discouraging as it can be, the business world has presented women with a relatively new and fascinating challenge. A career offers independence, self-esteem, and equality with men unavailable in the past. More intriguing opportunities open each year, and young women are pursuing their prospects in the marketplace with a kind of sportive joy.

But the danger of playing hardball with the boys is in becoming "one of the boys." Like men, more women now define themselves almost exclusively in terms of what they do for a living. Like men, some women are becoming obsessed with their work to the exclusion of all other aspects of their lives. This is how a successful businesswoman in her late thirties expresses the feeling: "After ten years of very hard work, I am that executive woman I wanted to become. I am exactly that image I would look to when I started and say, 'Wow, if only I could be like that.'

"But I've realized that by being this woman that I aspired to be, I'm a single-faceted success. I'm very successful in what I do. I'm not as successful in what I am. Somewhere along the line I got confused. I began to believe that what I do *is* who I am.

"I went to work when I was twelve years old and I

always worked a lot. It was a grand escape. Continues to be so. You can write off a lot in terms of work. A lot of women have made their lives disappear by working. I see it so much all around me.''

I hate it. I do it, but I hate it. Guido's Italian-American Restaurant. The place is huge—there's four kitchens—and old Guido just keeps adding on to it. It's one big restaurant, but it's got two sides. One side they call the Italian side. All the dishes on the menu are Italian. The other side is the American side which is like steaks, seafood, and a lot of Italian dishes. The place is all dark inside and there's brick walls everywhere like a maze. The brick walls on the American side are decorated with those big, enamel commemorative decanters the liquor companies put out. You got your Dutch shoes. You got your Mexican guys with donkeys. You got your Elvis. In the Italian room, it's Chianti bottles all shaped weird and swirly and stuff. The waitresses have two different outfits that you wear depending on which side you work that night.

The host is Juan. He's got fuzzball hair standing straight up on his head and he's dark. When he laughs, it's hysterically high. He goes around and picks up all the girls' dresses, just like high school. The cashiers wear dresses, too, and where they stand is also a walkway between the two sides of the restaurants. He goes by and picks their dresses up, looks at their panty hose and everything. Nobody ever turns around and smacks him. He's quick. He walks around and pinches and tweaks things, if he's in a good mood. If he's in a bad mood, he won't talk to you and he won't seat anybody at your tables.

Usually, I like working with him on the American

side, because I make money with him over there. He will load me up. He'll give me four tables at one time. They all put their butts on their chairs simultaneously and look around for their waitress. They're very demanding. They want a two-hour sitting. They want to take their time, smoke their cigars, eat their appetizers. They'll all order oysters Rockefeller which takes fifteen minutes, and then sit there and look at me like, "Did you get lost? Did you have to go to Maine to get them oysters yourself?" Oh, brother, it irritates me when they say that shit.

You take their orders and then you run to the four kitchens. There's a pizza and pasta kitchen, a kitchen for the Italian side, a kitchen for the American side, and a kitchen for the specials. You have to time everything. Pizza takes ten minutes, lasagna takes seven, prime rib takes three. So you have to put the orders in at different times so that everything comes out at the same time.

I'm carrying this big old tray; I can hardly lift the thing. The skinnier girls walk kind of crooked after a while carrying that tray. I do. I sway to the right, because I carry it on my left shoulder. You run around while the other girls are running in the opposite direction, kicking the swinging doors—make sure you don't hit the busboy in the hallway and kill him— "Order in! Order in!" is echoing through the building. Then you run back around to all the kitchens and pick everything up and get it out there before the people leave.

"All I ordered was the fish sandwich, for Christ's sake."

"Yeah, all you ordered was the fish sandwich, but the bitch next to you ordered stuffed lobster and an appetizer from the other kitchen."

Everything is different on the Italian side except that the same guy comes by and lifts your skirt up. Juan is hot on All-You-Can-Eat Spaghetti night, because all the old ladies love him. He knows them all by name. They come in their wheelchairs and walkers and he ties their lobster bibs on them, even if they're not having lobster.

Here they come. There's eight of them and they all plop down—Flap! Separate checks. Little old ladies and little old men, too, but they all look alike, white hair and glasses. So I label them, A, B, C, D, E. "Okay, you're F. Don't forget." When it comes to giving out checks, how am I supposed to know?

In the kitchen, we're in lines to get this stuff. The All-You-Can-Eat guy just stands there with all these big steaming tubs of pasta cooking around him and a colander big as a fish net in front of him. He throws this stuff on the plates and shoves them at us. Everything is happening so fast that the plates are boiling hot coming from the dishwasher. You can't even pick them up, they're so hot. You're screaming.

It's easy now that I got the hang of it. You get into being a little robot and just doing it, not talking or breathing or going to the bathroom for the whole night. Then you can make some money. Throw it at them and get them out of there. That's what makes them happy, not this small talk about the weather and their snotty grandkids from out West, that chitchat stuff. They want to eat and get the hell out of there, so they've come to appreciate me, because I'm quick. I'm starting to get more than a nickel from some of them. A dollar sometimes.

The place drives me nuts. Its never-ending bitchiness all the time. Everybody's on everybody's case.

"You got in my way."

"Hey, you got my order."

"What do you think you're doing with my table?"

You never know what your status is there. You never know if Juan is going to help you or hurt you. You never know if the owner is trying to date you or your best friend. You never know if you're going to go in and make money or not. You hope. I made thirty-one dollars Tuesday night.

I feel sorry for everybody who works there. I like them. They're going through the same thing I am. Sometimes worse, because they haven't been there as long as I have, so they're not used to it yet. It's real hard work. I didn't think I was going to make it.

I get up at six A.M. During the whole day, I don't ever really stop. It's a frustrating job being a mother and a housewife. Running a corporation is the way my husband describes what I do. I pay the bills and I do the grocery shopping. I've got to drive one kid to basketball practice and another kid to the hospital for volunteer work. Take the youngest back with me to the basketball game and kill an hour trying to entertain her coloring and writing and watching the game and then go pick everybody up.

I figure out Christmas. Not just the gifts, but orchestrate the whole thing. All the fun. Fun of the month. I do Easter, the scavenger hunts, the birthday parties. I've set such a standard for myself and now I can't get away from it. I don't think my husband, my children, or my parents ever really think about how it all happens.

I'm on the phone for this one and have a hand in the dishwater here and cooking dinner and invariably my husband will call on his car phone. He's on his way home and he's bored. I'm trying to cook dinner for this group of kids and serve it in order to get everyone fed so that the youngest can go to bed and the others can do their homework. He calls at six every night. I said, "Jerry, don't call me anymore. I'll talk to you when you get home in two hours."

Then he's home. I've gotten everyone settled, dinner's over, dishes are cleaned up. I'm exhausted. I've still got to make sure everything's done and everybody's in bed, make sure all the security blankets are zipped up real tight. But he wants his dinner and to talk about his day. Tell me all the things that are happening with investments and taxes . . . And then fool around!

At eleven at night, I get into bed and I'm in a huff. He's thinking, "What's wrong with you?" I can't remember when I really stopped today. Everything got done, but, gosh, I've got to get up at six o'clock in the morning and do the same thing over again. It's like housecleaning: It never gets done and it's never exciting. You never have openings and grand luncheons. It can be fun and challenging. But, still, it's work, just like going to a job nine to five. But it's every day for the whole lives of your children and your family. The everyday routine, 365 days a year. The only satisfaction I get is what I can draw from it myself. It's a good thing I'm real secure.

Mothers worry a lot. Much more than husbands. We wake up in the middle of the night. I have four children and the youngest is six. Until this year, I have been awake every night of the year. I hear noises. If it's not babies needing you to change diapers, you've got kids getting up to go to the bathroom. Or there's a sick child or you've got one out on a date who's not home yet.

Who lies awake at night? Me. I'll go to sleep and then I'll wake up and the clock says two in the morning. I wonder, "Did he come home while I was asleep? Should I get out of bed and look? It's cold. I don't really want to. But I've got to be sure." Husband is over there snoring away having a wonderful sleep.

This is a curse. It never ends. That takes a toll on you. I don't think I'll ever feel like I've had enough rest. I wake up in the morning and I'm tired. But somehow I get through the day again. No one ever told me when I got married and had children how difficult it was going to be. You don't know until you get into it.

I really love to cook, and I would really rather be the one to do the dishes, although I have to fight for that sometimes. I like to run the water. It blocks out other sound and it keeps my hands warm. I like cleaning. I love mindless work, because it's comforting and it has an ending to it and you can see what you've done. It's not like the work I do during the day which seems to have no end to it and never is done and I'm swallowed up by it. I like doing all that stuff that liberated women are not supposed to like doing anymore. Unless I'm feeling rotten, I only share that work when my arm's twisted to do it.

I realized how good I was. It scared the shit out of me. It was the heyday of abstract expressionism and I was talking to the leaders of that movement. I was either visiting their studios or sitting on the beach in the Hamptons talking to them. Living art up to the armpits. It was heady. I thought I could be a sculptor.

187

I was a woman, so I knew I had to be better than any of them. But I knew if I devoted the time, if I really did it, I could be an artist.

I also discovered that I had some inflated view of myself. If I was going to be a sculptor, I would be shown by a class A gallery and hung in the Museum of Modern Art and the Whitney. I took myself very seriously, maybe too seriously.

Something happened in the course of hanging out with really great painters and of thinking of myself as a sculptor. I didn't really know what art was about until this point in my life although I had been studying art all my life. Suddenly something very special opened for me and came together and I was overwhelmed by it. And very frightened.

I thought I would explode. I don't know how else to say that. I'm revealing a great part of myself that I don't want to reveal, but I was frightened by that prospect. So frightened that I turned my back on it. I knew that commitment would be more than I could deal with and remain a mother.

At work on a project, I would be totally, unequivocally absorbed. When I was sculpting, I was so involved that I just didn't hear, and when I realized what happened, I was shocked. I said, "My little daughter could have died in a fire and been lost and I wouldn't have known it." That was scary, so I stopped sculpting from that time. I really couldn't bear to deal with my art and deal with motherhood. There was guilt that went along with that. "I'm not entitled to work this way. Women shouldn't feel this way about their children. Women should not want to kill their children because the child asked a question when Mom is into making an aesthetic decision."

My ego and my sense of what it was to be a woman was involved with being a good mother and a whole lot of other things. It was okay to be talented or a working woman, but frankly sculpting made me resent my child, made me resent all the things I was brought up to believe that a woman was supposed to do. Nothing else frightened me. As far as I was concerned a woman could do manual work, could use power tools —I had learned to be a welder—could do all those things. But that my child who I loved very much made me be sorry that I was her mother, sorry that I had anybody in my life, was too much for me.

When I was sculpting and into it and things were going right, I didn't want to have to make dinner for anybody. And I resented all the things that otherwise gave me pleasure, not just pleasure but my sense of ego, who I was. Those things changed. That was very scary. I realized that I couldn't compromise with it. Just couldn't seem to. Other artists led lives and had families, but I couldn't do that.

I said to myself, "There's a time for everything in life and this has to be put off until another time. I can't make a compromise. I can't be a Sunday sculptor." That's what I did. I postponed that part of my life.

When I got this apartment before I remarried, I thought this room we are sitting in would someday be my studio. Once I got married, the whole thing overtook me again, this square life. Some of the '50s came back. I was a wife and a mother and we should have a living room.

There's a piece of me that's always been the bohemian flower child, the artist who wants to fly and do her own thing and live her own way. Another piece of me is the middle-class girl who does the "right thing," who should be a good wife and mother. And they aren't at war anymore. It's just that one goes to sleep. Sleeping Beauty is out there. One day, someday, the Prince is going to kiss her and she's going to give wings to that other person.

I was going to be a college counselor. That's what I went to graduate school for. My first and only job out of graduate school was at an exclusive women's college as a dorm director. Part of the job was ordering enough toilet paper and part of the job was to counsel these girls. I couldn't believe that these little people thought they needed therapy for the problem of living away from home. Most of their problems were so petty and stupid to me that I had to reevaluate whether I wanted to do this or not.

I had this fantasy of living in Greenwich Village. It was one of my only fantasies that I realized that wasn't a letdown. I loved it. When my mother saw the first apartment I had there, she burst into tears. Which was fine with me, because then she would never come to visit.

I got a job with a straight publishing company. I worked in the promotion department. But I was not really ready to have an office job. I couldn't take the responsibility seriously. I would disappear for hours out of the day. I'd just walk around Madison Avenue. I discovered a branch of the public library and I would stay in there for a couple of hours. But they refused to fire me. They kept giving me more money.

I had a moonlighting job two nights a week and on Sundays at a café as a waitress. That job I really liked. The place was filled with writers and artists and musicians. Even though I wasn't doing any of those things, I loved being around those people very, very much.

At the time I was reading *The Village Voice*, which has gotten me into a tremendous amount of trouble in more ways than one. The first ad I answered was to be a lingerie model. At the time, I had the right figure for lingerie—skinny every place else, but big boobs. I knew that for runway work you didn't have to be five foot eight. So I actually did that for two weeks.

It was really strange, because most of the other girls

who were working there should have been in live
porno shows—that's where their inclinations were at.
The guy running this place was one of these big fat
Jews with a big cigar. He couldn't figure me out, because I was the only Jewish girl who was walking
around his place in a slip and a bra. He kept thinking,
"She must be a real oddball, because I wouldn't let
my daughter do this."

After two weeks, he started talking to me about how
you really increase your paycheck, by "being nice"
to some of the buyers. So I said to him, "What does
'being nice' entail?"

He told me. I said, "That sounds like being a call
girl." He stuttered and was mincing words. I told him,
"If I'm going to do that, I'm not going to do it for you.
I'm going to do it on my own and make more money.
Forget it."

That was it, but it was interesting, because a certain
amount of sexual exploitation has always been in my
life. I got into trouble in seventh grade for writing a
short story. Now I can see that it was just erotic, but
they thought it was dirty. I wrote it and turned it in as
part of an assignment. It seemed like Harold Robbins
to me and he was making a lot of money. I couldn't
understand what all the fuss was about. They called in
the school psychologist and a really big deal was made
out of it. My mother was sure that I was doomed to a
sordid life, which turned out to be pretty true. That's
what happened.

Once again, I turned to *The Village Voice*. There
was this blind ad for somebody to write erotic stories.
I figured I'd already been in trouble for writing erotic
stories years ago, so I wrote another one. A girlfriend
had told me some sexual experience she had, so I
fictionalized it—I actually toned it down from the
things she was telling me—and I sent it in. I thought
it might just be a pervert collecting stuff—Anaïs Nin
sort of thing.

I get a phone call about a week later from a men's magazine with a name that made me think it was *Town & Country*. I had no idea what this woman on the line was talking about. "You know, that was a really great story. Have you had a lot of experience doing it?"

"No, this is only the second one I've written."

"We're always looking for new free-lancers, but you seem to have such a talent for this, why don't you come in and talk to me about a full-time job?" she said.

So I went up to their offices. They weren't sleazy or anything. They kind of looked like the inside of a toaster oven. The walls were foil and everything was shiny. It didn't look like a straight office. I met this woman who was a famous porno star who parlayed this into being a magazine publisher. But she made no impression on me; I had no idea who she was; her name didn't mean anything to me.

They hired me. But I had no idea what I was supposed to do. The first week she sent me to cover a porno event. It was a transsexual show and circus with trapezes and everything. It was a real zoo. My eyes were bugging out of my head. That was my introduction to this stuff. I loved it. It was the greatest thing in the world. It never occurred to me that it was a sleazy job. Not at all. I was never embarrassed about it and frankly nobody else seemed to be either. It was before porn really started to get a bad name. They were also much tamer in those days. It was just tits and ass, no big deal.

Then I got hired at a major men's magazine letters' digest. That was like *Reader's Digest*, it was so tame. It never bothered me at all, except when it was boring which was quite a bit of the time.

I even produced those phone sex things and it never bothered me. It was just a business and it was fun business. If you have to work you should at least have fun, and this was fun. Some of the nicest and most interesting people I've ever met have been through "X." In terms of baby presents, my husband and I got the nicest stuff from the people who are allegedly in porn. And it paid more than most publishing jobs.

When I was with a very upscale men's magazine, a friend of mine got me an interview with Condé Nast. Everything went really well at the job interview until we got down to what they were going to pay. At the time, I was making eighteen thousand and they wanted to pay me eleven-five.

"Listen," I said, "the people in this office are much better dressed than I am. You can't tell me that they dress like this and pay rent in this city on eleven-five."

"No," the personnel woman said to me, "all these girls are subsidized by their parents until they get further up on the ladder."

"Well, I'm not subsidized. I can't afford to work here."

The bottom line was, they also got upset that I worked at this men's magazine—I didn't even put some of the other publications on my résumé. It's ironic because they run sexually oriented articles very heavily, but they don't want to hear from a person who really knows about this stuff. It's the biggest double standard. Most fashion magazines are more erotic than any sex magazine I ever worked on. Just look at the Victoria's Secret catalog. That's the direction that a lot of porn publishers are going now. They're putting out lingerie and swimwear catalogs because that's what they can get on the newsstand. But a love of cheesecake is not going to go away just because the country is going through a time when they have a problem with it.

One thing people would always ask me at parties in a high whiny voice would be, "How can you work in a field that is so degrading to women?" I never felt that it was degrading to women. Nobody was roping these girls in off the streets. Instead, I was turning them away. I just felt that your average woman totally misunderstood what was going on with porn actresses and porn models.

I didn't do anything for a while. But unfortunately it is a way to earn money and I'm good at it. I still review X-rated movies. I keep saying that I'm not going to do it anymore, but when I'm getting a hundred dollars for each one and it takes me ten minutes to write it, it's extremely hard to stop.

Being a mother now, I noticed that my eighteen-month-old was watching them as I was reviewing the movies on the videotape machine. I turned the baby seat around so that he wasn't facing the screen. He started hollering. I don't think he knows that it's a porn movie, he just likes the moving images. But it did come as a shock.

The guy who cuts my hair is an old friend of ours and he didn't believe that I would have the nerve to go ahead and be a mother having been a porno person. This guy has known me for years, and now that I'm a mother it's an issue to him and I'm sure it is to other people. It's tricky.

My husband used to write X-rated movies before there were all these schlock videos, when the producers were going through a phase where they thought it was real art and mainstream. He never gets any money for that. He was lucky to get anything at all in the first place. Now he writes adventure films. He's really nervous that anybody we would meet now would know he had been in "X."

"X" is one of those strange things. Everybody watches it. When we lived out in the country, we didn't pay cash to get anything done on our house. People just wanted porno tapes in exchange. When our place was burglarized, the burglars took some really expensive video equipment, but all the police were interested in was the porno collection in our cellar. They could have cared less about catching the criminals.

"X" is this source of amusement and major guilt for me from my whole life. It was such a part of my life for ten years. I also think it is a part of my life in my blood. If I had it to do all over again, I would avoid it like the plague.

Would I want my son to be in this? No. We don't even know what to do with tapes that we have. We're worried that sometime in the future we'll be out, the kid'll have friends over, and they'll discover them. His friends will go home and say, "Know what we did over at Stevie's house today, Mommy?" I'm afraid I'll get kicked off the PTA before I'll get a chance to show them what I can do.

When I was operations manager for a truck terminal, I learned a lot about working with men. I learned, first of all, very quickly, that you never ask the man to do anything for you.

A line driver is somebody who drives from point to point, usually at night. Then you have local men who take the freight that comes into town with a line driver, load it on their trucks and deliver it locally. It was my job to do all the bills of lading, to take in all the freight, to make sure that everything was routed properly, and to dispatch the men when they were on the road.

If a line driver came in during the day and there was what they call a "hot load in the nose"—a very important shipment in the front of the trailer that had forty thousand pounds of freight loaded behind it—

then everybody got out there in the morning at seven o'clock, because some guy is waiting for his shipment, and you unloaded freight like everybody else.

I'm five three. I'd get out there in my blue jeans and I'd wheel my dolly up there. They'd pile it with stuff and I would have to jump up and down on the dolly to have the leverage to tip it back so I could move it around. But you never complained or said, "This is too heavy." You never said, "I can't do this." You just did it and then went home and cried and took eighteen aspirin to make your muscles quit hurting and hope that you could get up the next morning.

Line drivers would come in, and if there was nobody on the dock to unload, then they would sit on your clock until somebody came in to unload the trailer. If you asked them, "Could you please unload this, because there is nobody here right now?" they would sit back with their boots and their T-shirts with the cigarettes in the sleeve and they would say, "Lady, I'm paid to drive line. I'm not a swamper. I don't unload freight."

So what you did was you got in and you started unloading their freight. That wouldn't do. Then they would say, "Little lady, why don't you go back in the office and do whatever it is that you do, and I'll unload the freight."

One time a shipment of six-foot tractor-trailer tires came in. It was a new line driver, so I got out there, rolled up my sleeves, got behind this tire, and started pushing on it. The guy just chuckled and said, "I'll do it." I never had to unload a trailer. They always got unloaded; you just had to know how to do it.

I drove a forklift. I did all that stuff and I loved it. I had a great time. I'd probably still be in it, but one of the drivers came up with an eye test that was 20/500 and was not correctable, so they found him another job. They gave him mine.

If you were a woman, when I was in high school and college, there were three things you could be: a secretary, a nurse, or a teacher. I don't remember any of my friends wanting to be mechanical engineers. In high school I was not interested in home economics, but I was really interested in ranching. They had vocational agriculture courses, so I went to the principal when I was a sophomore and said, "I'd like to take Vo-Ag."

"No girls have ever taken it," he said.

"I don't see why I couldn't."

"Go talk to the teacher," he told me, so I did.

"Mr. Jerkins, I would like to enroll in your Vo-Ag class."

He was a man who talked out of the side of his mouth. "I'm not having any girls in my Vo-Ag class." That was the end of it. Now those classes are primarily girls. Future Farmers of America has girls as national officers, but at that time they wouldn't allow it. I sometimes feel bitter about some of that.

After high school, I went to one of the state universities and majored in biology, but I picked up a secondary education option at that time. There were no teaching jobs when I graduated in 1969, especially in biology, especially if you were a woman. The men coached and taught biology in this state. There were no women's sports then, so even though I had a PE minor with my biology major, there were no coaching jobs available. There were just boys' sports.

So I came home and worked on the ranch with my grandmother. I pastured cows here on the ranch, ran a contract hay crew to put up the hay, and sold the hay. My grandmother and I were running the ranch. We enjoyed it. If the men in the valley laughed at what we did, we didn't know it, so we were fine. Then one summer, we got the haying done, so I went to work for the forest service for a while piling brush and that kind of thing.

That winter a member of the school board called and asked if I'd teach first grade in a town just up the road about thirty miles. My grandmother said, "Oh, do it. It would be a good way to spend the winter, and you'll be free in the summer to get the hay in."

I'd known Randolph since high school. He lived and worked for his dad on his ranch near the school I was teaching in. He asked me to go on a date and I said, "Well, all right." We ended up getting married. If it wasn't for schoolteachers in these small towns, these poor guys would never get married.

Then my grandmother said, "I think you should rent the ranch from me and make the living here." I was kind of leery of it, because Randy's the oldest son and family is very important to him and his dad. You can get that old scenario of swipe that oldest son away from the ranch and take him somewhere else to work. That was not a popular thing to do, although it was his choice.

Randy had some cows and he brought them down. We rented the ranch for about five years. Then my grandma said, "This is stupid. I don't think you should rent the ranch anymore; the payments should go toward buying the ranch." The government won't allow her to give the land to us outright. So that was what we did ten years ago. We went in debt.

There's good years and bad years. We're still here and still in debt and probably will be until we're seventy. Isn't that something to look forward to? We'll have the ranch paid for then.

We've never had a vacation, never been away from the place, because there's always the animals to take care of or the sprinkler pipes to change while you're irrigating in the spring. In the summer there's the haying. You have to do it then. It's the only time. The fall comes and school starts and we get the cows in from summer pasture and bring them home.

We're starting to hear, "Oh, are there any cattle buyers?" That's always kind of spooky, because that's your yearly income once a year when you sell your calves. "What are prices going to be?" You live with that uncertainty.

Then there's winter feeding and the cows have to be fed every day. That bumps right into early spring which is lambing and calving.

If the weather is bad during calving, you have to be out there with those babies. If there's wind on a new calf, they get chilled quickly. You've got to put them in or dry them off and get milk into them or they'll just die real fast.

At night, when Randy gets so tired he can't see, I go check them, so he can get some rest. We deliver calves all night long and we have to see if there's any problems. We have to pull calves, if they're coming out backwards or feet back. Sometimes we have to do cesarean, if we can't get them naturally. Randy and I do the operations ourselves.

We just live on what I make teaching. Every penny that the cattle and sheep bring in goes back into the cattle, the machinery, the mortgage payments, and the vet bill. The medicine bill alone on this little place is $5,000 a year. It takes $10,000 worth of gas to run this place. Parts—a good year of repairs is $8,000. That's not bad. It takes a lot of calves at $450 apiece to pay some of these bills, and we just have three hundred cows. So it's nip and tuck all the time. We've watched a lot of people go broke and that always hangs over your head. There but by the grace of God go I. You're really careful, you don't go anyplace, you don't spend money, you don't do anything. Yet some of those people that lost their ranches through this crisis did the same thing.

These ranches should be a place where a family

could live, and you could survive on what you make. But most of them have somebody working someplace else in town. The joke around here is that every successful ranch has a wife that's teaching school.

And here we are. It's a circle. Constant. I love our life here. But quite frankly, there's times when I ask, "Why are we doing this?"

At my job, I was doing the computer thing in the basement of the building. I couldn't stand it, it drove me nuts. That man we worked for, I *hated* him. I *hated* him. One day at lunchtime, I was walking outside and I couldn't take it no more. One of the bosses was getting into this big red car and he said, "Where you going?"

"I'm gone. This is *it*. I can't take it no more! The click-click-click in the basement is driving me *crazy!* What's his name, I can't stand him! That's it! I'm gone! Forget it!"

I got in the Steam Room massage parlor through this Ann girl. She knew the owner real, real well. His name was Melvin. He *loved* her. She was his little queen. She took me there and introduced me. It was summertime and I always had a tan. I was dark, I had my hair curly—one of those frizzes people had, a short permanent. Melvin thought I was black. I wasn't that dark, but he was an alcoholic. He was in one of his stupors. He went into a frenzy, "Oodle-oodle-oodle, hire no black girls, loodle-oodle-oo!"

"What?" I thought. "This guy's crazy."

Ann said, "Well, we'll just come back later when he's not drunk." So that's what we did. We came back later when he was sober. This man was like day and night. When he was drunk, he was completely different from when he was sober. Even his face changed. He *looked* different. He was all business when he was sober: "Ruh, ruh, ruh, this is what you do, this is how much." He just laid down the rules on me. It was like ten or fifteen dollars to get into the place to use the "facilities." Then after that anything else was up to us girls. He just took the entrance fee.

There were no rules. No one said to me, "Well, you lay down here, you do this, then you do that." I was like, "Whaddaya do? Whaddaya do? What is all these rooms? What's this thing here?"

"They actually do have a little steam room and a shower in here," Something Ann said. "And then there are the rooms. The guy can use the facilities if he wants to. You try to get them to take a shower first, then take them to whatever room you want."

There were buzzers; the whole thing was electrical, so if you walked down the hall a buzzer went off in the office. You could tell where everybody was. You couldn't tell *who* was in which room, but they told you. "I'm going to be in Room 8." You couldn't see anything, like TV security, but a little light would go off in the office so you could keep track of things if you weren't drunk on your butt, or drugged out on your ass, too.

There was a little raised table there next to a cot. It had all these things on it, baby oil, powder, Kleenex, and cotton balls, really goofy. We had to keep all the rooms stocked.

It was dark. The building had windows, but they were all bricked in or shuttered up or boarded up. It wasn't very gorgeous. There were no mirrors on the ceiling, no velvet drapes, just regular curtains and indoor-outdoor carpeting. There was mirrors on the backs of doors, I think, because sometimes I remember doing something and I'd catch my reflection.

I'd look and see myself and go, "Oh, God, this is hilarious."

I can't remember what the first person looked like, but I thought it was fruity doing that back-rub thing. But I did it, you know. I did it. I was horrible, I know I was. Later on I got into it when I saw what was going on, but at first I was really rough: RUB-RUB-RUB-RUB-RUB, "Okay. What now?"

I didn't know what to say. You learn. They tell you that. More girls come and you got nothing to do in between people. They talk and they tell you stuff. Some of them were real *workers,* real hard core. I mean, the Steam Room was a piece of cake for them. They had been out on the streets in California and other places. They were young girls, too. They all had different, weird work names. Like I was Ursula.

Us Steam Room girls, I guess we weren't serious. It wasn't a real job for us. Raquel and I, we did more drugs in the Steam Room than we ever did at any rock concert. We had the little Chinese delivery boy from the restaurant bringing us stuff. We started getting to know him and he would bring us downs. We were doing reds and Nembutals and Tuinals then.

Melvin didn't know what the hell was going on. He had a tiny room right off the office. It was nothing but a bed and bottles. Oh, he was obnoxious when he was drunk, but he was more likeable. You could get away with murder when he was drunk. He didn't run anything. If we happened to feel generous that night, we'd put some money in his little bag. Maybe twenty guys would come in. Ten dollars a guy, what's that? Two hundred dollars. If he got fifty of it, he was lucky. The next morning, "Whazit like last night, girls?"

"Oh, it was dead. Nobody came in." He wouldn't know. I gave tours through the place on a drunk night. I'd bring everybody down from the bar I hung out in. "Come on down to the Steam Room. You never seen anything like it." I'd have troops of people going through there, you know, looking at the place like a sight-seeing group. Melvin's in there drunk. He don't know what's going on.

Usually the customers were like guys who just got off a construction job in blue jeans and work shirts. All of a sudden, a rock 'n' roll band I knew would walk in. Melvin couldn't tell. He'd wave them on in, all fifteen of them. "Go on, go on. Raga-raga. Have a good time, boys."

We would stray from it once in a while, go do something else for a couple of weeks or go do nothing. He never knew if we were there or not there. He never knew. He'd think you were a new girl. You'd be working there forever and then come in one day and he didn't know who you were. Unless you took care of him, like put him to bed, talked to him a lot. I became his favorite person there for a while. He was in love with me, only because I picked him up off the floor and put him in bed. He'd come stumbling out them doors and go Bonk! Fall down on the desk, crack his head open. People would just leave him laying there. I'd pick him up and put him back in his room, clean him off, and talk to him a whole bunch. He'd know you for a while. But then other girls would become that way with him, too.

It was sad when he died. He was funny. I always felt sorry for him. Poor thing. I mean, he was a goofball. I don't know how he got into that business. He had a son who was straight as an arrow. His son would come there to "check up on the property."

"What?" I'd say. "Well, the property's laying in his bed now, half smashed out of his head and we're running the place, so get out of here."

I brought a black girl, Lefty, who was a friend of mine, to work there and wait till you hear this: Melvin thought she was a wetback. When I got her into the Steam Room, Melvin asked her if she swam across the Rio Grande to get there.

"What is he talking about?" She's looking at me.

"Never mind. Just say, 'Sí.' He doesn't hire black women, but he hired me, even though he thought I was black. It's a trip."

It wasn't big money, but it *was* easy. It was so easy. I didn't have to perform that many acts, unless I wanted to. No one was standing over me going, "You have to do this and you have to do that." Nobody. I'm sure the other girls were making money. They had to make money.

The Steam Room was a lot easier than being on the street. Like, I found that the easiest thing to do was specialty items, to stick guys with pins and stuff. People came in there and wanted to be stuck with pins. But it was easy. I'd just go, "Eeeek!" and jab 'em. I didn't leave the pins in there or nothing.

Lefty and I got to be the aficionados of pin sticking. I talked her into doing it, too, and sometimes we would do it together. We couldn't look at each other. I'd keep saying out of the side of my mouth, "Don't look at me. Don't you look at me." Because I'd break up laughing.

She got some big, old high heels and tried to walk on this guy's back and kept falling off. There was these water pipes overhead, because the Steam Room was in the basement kind of, so she was hanging onto them so she could stay on this guy's back. I'm in the corner going, "I can't watch this. It's too funny. It is." But he loved it. There was another guy who wanted to be treated like a dog. We had to put a collar on him and walk him around the room on a leash.

I met some guy who wanted to be peed on. I hated him. It was easy. He was a creepy little guy. Oh, how I hated him. I'd pee on him gladly. Ooooooh!

I had ripped him off, the pee-er. He wanted to see me outside the Steam Room. I went over to his house. He lived in a nice house and stuff. Then he wanted to be stuck with pins, but he wanted me to do big pins and be *mean* and stuff, you know. I couldn't. I'd just go, "Eeeek!" and jab 'em and laugh. I just couldn't do it. He made me mad. He wanted me to like nail him to the table or something with pins. I'd been to his house a couple of times before, just pissing on him, and I knew where he kept his money, so I took it. Went home in a cab. No sooner walked in the door and here's the phone ring ing. I said, "I'm not answering it." Ring-ring-ring-ring-ring. "Oh, I better answer it."

I pick up the phone and it's him, furious. "Rah-rah-rah-rah-rah."

"Prove it," I told him. "Prove it. I was nowhere near your money. Drop dead." He wanted to be hurt and I hurt him where it gets him the most. I never thought of telling him that.

I did finally work for a pimp, but he was different, too. Everybody knew him. Drove a big, old white Mercedes-Benz, a classic. He was real neat, always dressed to a T.

I didn't work for him for long and I never fell in love with him. I never fell in love with anybody. That's what they wanted. They thought I was just the weirdest girl, weird. Didn't know what the hell to do with me. I wasn't always there going, "Oh, let me stay with you. Let me love you." I wanted to make my money and get the hell out. He would have to talk me into sleeping with him. I never wanted to. If I did, I did. If I didn't, I didn't. But his other girls were begging, "Please, take me, take me."

He was nice to me. He bought me things. I used to hide my money. I'm not trying to come off like I was the smart hooker who got over, but I would hide some of it. I'd give him the rest.

He didn't want me in the Steam Room. I wasn't making enough money there. I guess not—I was having a good time, partying with my girlfriends, bringing my friends down, giving guided tours.

He put me in a new place that opened way out by the airport in the middle of nowhere. It got kind of rough in there. There were some rough people who came in there.

I told one boyfriend I used to work. Big mistake. The only reason I told him was because he was talking about how he thought it was neat or something. "Oh, you do? Well, guess what?" I'm not making that mistake again. I don't care how neat they think it is. He wouldn't understand. You had to be there.

It was something I made myself do. Men do it naturally in the job market, but women don't. A man will accept a job even if he isn't sure that he can do it, because he'll say, "I can learn this while I'm doing it." Maybe it's just women's inexperience in the job market, but a woman feels that she has to know how to do a job before she accepts the offer. It may be changing for younger women, but from women of my ilk I still hear it over and over again, "I can't take that job. I don't know how to do that." I didn't know how to be a marketing manager. But I didn't care. I knew part of it, so I figured I'd fake the rest until I got a handle on it. In a year, I was promoted to senior marketing manager with a big jump in salary.

When I graduated college, I didn't know what to do with myself. So I hung out and had a series of junk jobs, secretary, things like that. It was all pretty boring, so I quit and went home.

At this point my parents had moved to San Clemente. They owned a motel there. Through my whole life there were always periods when I'd bag it and go home. You've had it with life, you can't deal with it, you go home. Within two weeks, two months, four months, you get sort of regenerated. I never got any flak about coming home or when was I leaving or "Why don't you get a job?" That never happened.

At the time, it seemed normal, but in retrospect it was pretty amazing. I was twenty-three years old and I came home. I had no plans. I'd sleep until noon or one o'clock, hang around at the beach all day. I was extremely depressed, not knowing what I wanted to do and with no place for anything to happen. I didn't even know how to start.

If Prince Charming had come in on his horse, well, okay. But I was real picky about that, too. I didn't want to marry my psychiatrist. I didn't want to marry some guy who was going to have a good job and come home at five o'clock. The normal stuff just did not do it for me.

What I actually did was sleep twelve hours a day and watch TV. Watergate happened, so I'd get up and watch the hearings on TV. It was all-consuming. It was fun to be in San Clemente, because that was Nixon's western White House. When he and Brezhnev had summit talks in California, the motel was full of Russians. When he would come to San Clemente, the Secret Service would stay at our motel, so we were sort of hooked into things. I knew his butler. So that was great fun, and then he got kicked out and that was wonderful.

Then Vietnam fell and I watched that on TV and it was real interesting. They were sending all the refugees to Camp Pendleton. These people from volunteer agencies came to process the refugees and they stayed at the motel.

One afternoon, I'm asleep and my mother wakes me

up. She says, "Do you want to work at the refugee camp?"

"No," I said.

"I made an appointment for you to have an interview at lunchtime, so you better get up and go," she tells me.

I'm furious. What does she think she's doing interfering in my life, such as it is? She woke me up an *hour* early. My mother never did anything like this in all the time I came home. But now she's done it and I can't make my mother look bad, so I get up and shower and put on some clothes and meet these people for lunch.

At the interview, I'm saying, "I'm really not into this job. I don't want this job. I'm here because my mother sent me."

"Did you go to college?"

"Yes." Answers like that.

At the end of lunch, they said, "You're hired."

Shit! How did this happen? I said, "Well, when does it start?"

"How about right now? We're going back to the camp."

I don't get two weeks to think about this? Figure a way to get out of it or whatever? So we get in the car and we go over to the refugee camp at Pendleton.

That was an amazing moment in my life. Here I am, sullen and all these other things, we drive up and suddenly there are tens of thousands of Vietnamese, just like the movies, just like television. Not all of them, but some of them are in their little black pajamas, the hats, you know? There's so many of them and that alone is mind-boggling. They're living in tents and lining up for lunch. This whole scene is going on just behind the mountain from where I've been sleeping all day.

It really got me. All of a sudden, it was *Wham!* Wow, this is real. Not just something that I watched on television. These people, in the space of forty-eight hours, had been picked up out of their world and dropped into ours. That is unbelievable. *This* is the residue of war. This is the real thing. This is life.

So I started working, working fourteen- and fifteen-hour days at four dollars an hour. I loved it. I loved every single bit of it. What I was doing was interviewing refugees and then calling up churches affiliated with this relief agency, talking to ministers and basically selling them families. They'd already indicated that they wanted to sponsor a family and I'd say, "We have a family of six here. Or there's a very nice family of four who have a newborn," et cetera.

I had a couple of Vietnamese friends, but for the most part, because I didn't speak their language and was always working through interpreters, they viewed me and everybody else as bureaucrats. Sometimes we'd be talking them into going to places they didn't really want to go, like Oshkosh, Wisconsin—"It's not really so cold there." So there was some conflict. But they could have been Martians for all I cared. They were people who were displaced and I could do something about placing them. That was the service, that was something concrete. And this was history, and I was involved in it whatever my little part was.

The office grew to about twenty people and I was like the second-in-command. I felt good about what we were doing. Plus it was so finite. There were X amount of people in Guam and they were being flown in planeloads to Camp Pendleton and we were moving them out, dispersing them around the country. It was going to end.

It did end in December of 1975. Mission accomplished. A nice little package.

I also met these people from New York, people who were Europeans, who had suffered through the Holocaust or helped people escape from Nazi Germany, people who reconstructed Europe after the war. That was history. I'd sit around with these sixty-five-year-old guys while they drank me under the table, listening to some of their stories, and I would think, "Now this is something worthwhile doing. It's pure. What you're doing is saving people from circumstance. And you can do that. It works."

I decided I wanted to become one of those people I met there who were flying out to the camp and drinking me under the table, who worked for these different agencies and flew all around the world. I wanted to be where the center of power was, where those kinds of decisions were made, where I worked with people who had dedicated their lives to something that really mattered.

That was what I wanted. Now, how do I get there?

I had an inside track, but that's just because my mother woke me up a few days early. Plus I was smart and I made myself indispensable.

My dad always says, "I told you that in order to get a job and the career that you wanted, you got to get up early, get out on the street, talk to people, don't be shy. But all you had to do was lie by the pool."

In Thailand, things were heating up. There are lots of refugees coming into that country from Laos and Cambodia and Vietnam—boat people mostly. I wanted to go, because I knew that the people in New York had all done time overseas, working with different refugee situations. This was the one that was hot and I wanted to go pay my dues. And I wanted to see where these folks that I'd been looking at for the last few years came from and what their story was.

I got a job with a sister organization out there. I packed everything up, got on a plane, and went to Thailand. I was twenty-seven. It was kind of scary. Wow, a whole other world and not a place where I ever wanted to go. I didn't know anything about it. Somebody gave me a little tour guidebook before I left and I didn't even look at it.

210

I didn't do the traveling I should have done and I'm not a shopper. I lived in a Western-style apartment and had a maid. I went to work in the morning. We worked *long* hours. Then we'd go have dinner someplace. I'd come home, watch TV, and go to sleep. Then do it again the next day.

For my traveling I went to refugee camps. The first time I went to one, it was a bad camp in the south. It was very, very crowded, all lean-to bamboo housing. This is really bad Third World stuff. Looking around, I figured, "I didn't get these people on a boat. They got themselves on a boat. They made the choice to come here. To get out of this camp, they need some help. What can I do? I know how to process them the hell out of here. That's what I do best." So with some blinders on, I went in and started working, interviewing refugees, filling out forms and going back to the office to get it all ready for the immigration officers. Then I'd take the officers out to the camp and present cases to them. I ended up in charge of the boat people section for Thailand for two years.

Yeah, this is history. This is fun. I used to love going out with the immigration officers to present cases. These guys are high school graduates with four years on the border. Not very bright for the most part. Then they'd be flown out to Asia for temporary duty to interview refugees and decide which ones were going to go to the U.S. These are the people who look at your passport at the airport back home. The State Department ran the program, the organization I represented did the work, and Immigration would come in and make the final decision about who was going and who wasn't going.

Talk about setups. I used to set these guys up all the time. We'd have what we call "walk-on-water cases." These people were so good, nobody could turn them down. They were really qualified to come to the U.S. I'd get three of those and then I'd get one that I knew

211

they were going to reject—for good reasons—but I'd included it so that he could think he was making a decision. So I'd have three good cases and he's saying, "Yes, yes, yes." Then he'd see the fourth one and he'd go, "No, these people cannot go."

"Oh, really? Oh, all right," I'd say, knowing full well that they weren't supposed to go.

I'd play the little ingenue role, like I was this ditsy broad that didn't really understand all this stuff, but was doing the best I could to help them make their decisions. I acted in an appeasing way, like I knew they really had this power and I was just asking all the time maybe they could do this and maybe they could do that. I made sure they always got cold beers and that they were as comfortable as we could make them under the circumstances. I was young enough that I could play daughter with some of them. I'd play sister with some of them. I'd do this role playing stuff and they would just follow through. It was a riot. I didn't have any respect for them, but that's the price you pay.

I didn't mind selling my soul that way for them to approve the people I wanted them to approve. I thought that was more important than getting into their faces about things and asserting myself as an equal. I could do that and it was easy for me. I thought it was worth it and I still do.

We'd also go out to the Cambodian border camps and do what we called "Atrocity Runs." Nobody was paying any attention to what was happening in Cambodia under the Khmer Rouge. We knew it, but there was no international media about it. Nobody gave a shit. I was furious at my peers back here. They were all out marching on the Vietnam War and talking about how terrible we were over there and then here we have this holocaust going on and nobody gives a shit. What happened to caring about little brown people who get killed? Come on, guys. Does it matter who kills them? Is it okay if one of their own kills them? We'd go out to the borders and instead of processing refugees, we'd get stories from people about what was happening in Cambodia, then come back to Bangkok and try to give the stories to anybody who would pay attention.

You're not talking to people about where they want to go in the U.S. You're asking questions like, "Okay, how many members of your family have died? How did they die?" Talking to little eight-year-old boys who've seen their whole families clubbed to death in front of them. This is tough stuff.

We worked with the State Department guys a lot—what I call the "Undiplomatic Corps." Most of them were jerks. They knew a lot about the history of Southeast Asia, but they didn't know how to deal with people. They were making three times as much money as we were and they knew nothing. We would have to train them and then they would tell us what to do. It was real irritating.

I used to set them up, too, to be real honest about it. They would do something stupid and I wouldn't be part of that. Ultimately, they kept transferring them out someplace. The careers of their career-path officers were going down the tubes if they came through my office. Until finally I went to the boss and said, "Look, I don't need these guys. They're superfluous." He agreed, so I reported directly to the high-muckety-muck State Department guy. He was brilliant. He was committed to what we were doing, so we didn't have any problems.

After I'd been in Asia two and a half years, I decided that I'd done my time. I'd proved myself. How do I get to New York from here? It was time for me to go home, so I resigned and gave a month's notice. Then another organization called up. They were setting up a similar office in Singapore for the bunch of refugees in Indonesia. I agreed to do it, but I said,

"It's going to cost you. I know you are under a direct cost reimbursable contract to the State Department to do this. They always send out these macho bimbos at three times my price, so you'll have to pay three times what I'm making now." Considering how little I was making, my demands were not that great, looking back on it now.

I'm there by myself setting this thing up, and after three weeks we find out that it's not about fifteen thousand refugees in these islands. It's fifty thousand refugees on the islands and about 150 indigenous people living there. The island is supplied once a week by a supply boat. There's fifty thousand hungry people out there. We need a helicopter, we need a heli-barge. We need boats. We need ten times as much stuff.

Then I get a call. The president has decided to let in a hundred and sixty-six thousand refugees that year which is an increase from thirty thousand. We'd been picking and choosing between refugees which was very tough and heartrending just to tell them, "No, you're not going." All of a sudden, everybody can go. It's Santa Claus time.

The head guy assigned to the project didn't know anything about refugee processing; nobody knew anything about it. I was the only one. We ended up with 50 Americans on staff and 150 local staff, a helicopter, two boats, and a heli-barge. I had four different teams floating around these islands doing all these things and coming back to process the stuff. It was an amazing operation and I was in charge of it, no question.

Ultimately we had to get rid of the boss, because he freaked out, had a breakdown. So then the head guy from New York in charge of the whole deal came out. It was the first time I had ever met him. I said, "Now that you're getting rid of this guy, I want to take that job."

"No, you're not old enough, you're not seasoned enough. I need a pinstripe suit type." I allowed as how

I could never really wear a pinstripe suit, but thought that I knew what I was doing. We argued for four hours about it and I told him he was a real jerk. All bets were off. I'd made a one-year commitment and as far as I was concerned I could leave anytime I wanted, but I'd stay on to see who they sent out. I really wanted to stay.

He agreed with that. He sent out a guy who was even more of a mess than the guy we got rid of. I decided I was leaving anyway, because it was clear to me that I can't keep knocking off my bosses. After a while, it begins to look real bad. I said to myself, "Give this one up; they're not going to do anything about this." So I left and there was a big tearful good-bye.

I went to San Clemente by the pool. I didn't know what I was going to do, but I had lots of money, so I wasn't worried.

I was literally in the pool when I got this call from Washington. I went to the phone dripping on my mother's carpet. It was the beginning of the Cuban refugee crisis and they wanted me to go to Costa Rica and set up a refugee processing center. "When do you want me there?"

"Day after tomorrow."

I hung up the phone and said, "Where the hell is Costa Rica?" I take a plane to Central America, I'm hanging around the embassy, setting up the office. We're in a bar someplace late at night and a guy comes in and says, "The first boatload arrived in Miami. So guess what? Castro's shafting us. This program isn't happening."

I called up the agency in New York that I'd thrown this State Department business to from Costa Rica and said, "I'd like to come into New York before I go home, since this is the end of it." I flew up to New York and proceeded to tell them I would be interested in a job there. They offered me one. "Okay," I said, "but I still haven't had my vacation yet; I've got two months coming." Real uppity. The reason I can be real uppity is that I have this home that I can go to. If I don't like what I'm doing I can just say, "Bye," and go to the pool. Life is rough, right? I started to realize that I knew a lot of people in this business and I could always get a job. I was absolutely worth it. That was nice to know.

I'd been trying to get to New York for years. I'd made the right career moves wherever I was. I moved on and rose above it. Cream rises to the top and all that crap.

When I got to the top, I realized that these people didn't do what I thought they did. They didn't sit around and decide big questions of a refugee situation, how we were going to move governments to make sure they do the right thing to protect these people and get them to where they need to be. They just sat around and talked about budgets. They talked about how they were going to compromise with the government. They bickered. Half the time was totally unproductive, arguing over territory and money.

I was really disillusioned. Most of the people I respected from the older generation had retired or died. It was corporate nonprofit America.

People used to say to me, "It's so wonderful what you're doing."

"Wait a minute," I said. "What I've done is make a lot of money, traveling around the world, doing what I wanted to do, and having some power to do it. Yeah, I think I've helped some folks along the way, but this is not an altruistic exercise. I didn't give up anything to do this, except sitting by the pool."

The woman who retired from the job I hold now called me up and said, "They are recruiting to replace me. Would you be interested in the job?" I told her, "Sure," and I went through the series of interviews.

There were forty-three people who applied for this job. Three of them were women. I figured, "This place has 150 employees, $4.7 million annual budget, four major divisions. It's been going on for seventy-four years. It's one of the top fifty jobs in social services in terms of community organizations in the country—Big Jobs. I'll never get it."

It got narrowed down to three people and I knew the other two were men. I was sure I wasn't going to get it. The last thing to do was to interview with the entire board of directors and I decided to just go in and be myself. I didn't want to give any false impressions or expectations, like I was a serious person or anything. I'm a very serious person, but I like to have a good time while I'm doing it. The guy in the pinstripe suit is not me. When they told me I'd gotten the job, I was pretty blown away.

I came in here and it took me about three weeks before I could tell what the hell I was doing, in the sense that I really was in charge of this great big place. I thought I was just going to be "working." Suddenly I had to make these amazing decisions.

The place was a mess and seriously in debt. Three days after I got here, the board voted on a new pension plan, and a week later I found that at least one of them and possibly three of the board members were going to get kickbacks from this decision. In other words, I found out that basically my board is corrupt. I found out that this place inadvertently defrauded the state out of sixty thousand dollars. I'm meeting with attorneys right and left. I had one major division director who wouldn't acknowledge that I was her boss. All this stuff during the first six months was totally insane.

I was driving to work contemplating what the concept of failure was and the Peter Principle. I had no experience to know that maybe this wasn't normal, that maybe what I was doing was not what the job was like all the time. "Maybe things are always going to be like this." I was scrambling like crazy to get things fixed up and make some sense.

The board thought I was a silly dumb broad, that they could manipulate me. That became very clear within a few months. That was a fascinating realization. "So that's why you hired me instead of these other guys. You thought I'd be easy."

I was driving home and I said to myself, "I don't want you to tell your family about all these problems, because they worry about you. So just walk in and act like you're normal, even though you're not."

I walk in and sit down. My mother goes, "How are you?" I burst into tears. It wasn't anything specific, just the enormity of it all. "Wait a minute, wait a minute," my mother said. "Is anybody going to die because of you and this job?"

"No."

"All right. Then it isn't important." She was right. And I *was* having the time of my life, because as sort of a natural gambler there was a side of me who said, "Who cares?"

I actually said to my staff, "If we go under, do you think it'll be in the history books? No. So who gives a shit? Let's do the best we can, and if it goes under, if I fail—whatever that means—to hell with it." So we ended up having a good time even as we were going insane. It was good for the esprit de corps.

This place has radically changed since I've been here. My strength is that I tell the truth, because it's not worth it to me not to tell the truth. I don't care what it is. I'm sure I lie as much as anybody else, but when it comes down to the workings of a major organization, no, I'm not going to lie. If you can't take it, fire me. You guys on the board are now going to have to learn about what is happening in this organization that you are responsible for. I'm going to tell you what I'm willing to do, then if you don't want me to do that, I'm gone.

I didn't put it that way at all. Again I went into my ingenue act and I say, "Hi, wow, this is what's happening and my recommendation is . . ." But of course it did get to a couple of points where I had to draw the line a lot more plainly than that.

We went through six months of crisis management stuff and got the major problems solved, and then for a month I walked around the office going, "I'm bored." Now it's great, because we can do things that we want to do. It's great fun.

Two years ago, I was just not happy at my job. I was dying for my husband to say to me when he watched me clawing my cornflakes about the bowl, "Honey, if you're so unhappy, why don't you quit?" After all, we had been married fifteen years. Every one of those fifteen years, I had brought in a salary that was similar to his. I was an active participant in the household and I wanted him to say, "Relax, take the time off. Don't take this shit if it's making you crazy."

He didn't. Truly, he treats me like a partner. I had been married before to a man who was childish enough to be my son, and then I had a seven-year-long affair with a domineering man who made all the decisions for me. It had been nice to have a knight in shining armor, but when I got ready to get married again, I married a man my own age, whose intellect I could respect at a time in my life when I respected my own a lot more than I ever had before. I really have a partnership marriage, now. It never occurred to him to say, "Quit." As far as he was concerned, if I wanted to stop working, I would simply declare that I was going to stop working.

I thought about it for a long time. I finally screwed up my courage and said, "If I quit my job, could we get along without my salary for a year?"

"Normally, that would scare me," he said, "but I'm doing pretty well. Yeah. What do you have in mind?"

"Going into business. And I'll tell you what," I was very quick to add, "I think I will break even the first year. If I don't have the chance of making at least half of my present salary, I will quit the second year and look for a job."

"Go for it," was what he said.

So I went for it. Indeed, I just broke even the first year. There was no family money in the business. I got my investment back out of it, had enough clients to do that. Decided to go for the second year.

Now I have to tell you a very wonderful thing about the man in my life. At the end of this first year, I was feeling horribly guilty. I didn't buy any clothes during that first year. This was the first time in my whole life when I was not financially contributing. The first time since I was seventeen when I did not contribute to my own support and someone else's support as well.

Just when I was feeling most terrible, this wonderful guy said to me one day, "You know, you've worked ever since we've been married and I've never had to be the sole support of the entire household before. By doing this, you've given me the opportunity to find out that I can do it and it feels very good." It was the greatest thing he could have said to me, because it sort of liberated me from those guilt feelings. It gave me permission to go for it again which was just extraordinarily important.

Although I didn't know it, my salary in my new job was much higher than the other women managers were making. I mean, *a lot* higher. For some ungodly reason, they had put the salary in the classified advertisement in the newspaper. The other women managers saw this unbeknownst to me.

My first day on the job, I'm sitting in my new office and this woman who had been in the company for nine years comes in and says, "I want you to know that we all know your salary and we all hate you." Honest to God, these are the first words out of her mouth.

"That's unfortunate and I'm sorry," I told her. "If I were you, I'd go talk to the powers that be. It's not my fault you're not making money. I busted my butt to make what I'm making."

Many women who are grossly underpaid are grossly underpaid because they've stayed in one company for many years, so they just get small incremental salary adjustments. If that's what you want, then do it. But I knew—and men know—that the only way to really jump your salary is to change companies and ask for a lot more money.

The whole area of asking for raises, asking for more money, is a tremendously more problematic subject for women than for men. I really think it has something to do with putting a price tag on yourself. Women see that as a real negative, something really shameful. Whereas men see it as something to be really proud of. I've talked to so many women who agonize over whether to ask for a raise and then don't ask for what they deserve. It's a shame. They are their own worst enemies.

Women are also frightened of being turned down. Women have said to me, "What if I ask for it and I don't get it? What then?"

"So what? You don't get it. So? Big deal," I tell them. "They're bound to give you something or they're going to fire you anyway. You might as well know if that's going to be the scenario."

When I first got this job, I went to a meeting in Washington and there were all these guys there—the suits —who two years before might say hello to me and then move on to somebody more powerful and more important or a woman who was prettier and they were interested in. Now, suddenly, they all want to talk to me. And I'm thinking, "Assholes, you never talked to me before."

I had internalized it before: "Well, I'm not in such a high position and that's why they really didn't want to talk to me." The field I'm in is mostly women until you rise to the top. Then it's all these men. I just took it for granted that that's the way it was. Then it became so clear to me at the meeting in Washington. When I came in, people got up and walked across the room to come talk to me, treated me like they'd spent hours talking to me before, when they'd always been rather impolite, in fact.

I was real irritated. I never respected people who don't treat everybody like human beings. I treat the janitor like a human being. I don't have to be any less nice to that person than I do my board president, and I treat them almost the same. It doesn't take anything from me to treat people well.

It's not easy for the suits, because I don't act like I think an executive is supposed to act. You can see I don't dress like it. In most corporations all the women wear navy blue suits. I decided a long time ago I wasn't going to wear suits. I'd look like a tank in a suit. The right hairdo? This is the hairdo I wore in college. My father used to call it the Halloween hairdo, because it used to look a little worse when I was trying to look like Jimi Hendrix. But, it's basically the same hairdo.

I used to go through this crisis thing about maybe I should act differently. So I had to go buy a bunch of clothes and at least look somewhat legit, but I like bright colors and that's the way it is, too bad. But I can see the guys going through all kinds of stuff about it. They are more comfortable with a woman who is maybe more severe or something. I don't think I'd know how to do it even if I wanted to. First of all, acting that way is no fun, so why do it?

My associate executive director is this big guy in a suit and we get along real well. My comptroller is always impeccably dressed in a suit. He looks just like a comptroller is supposed to look. You want the man keeping the books to look like that. Then there's me. It's really a weird crowd.

We meet with guys and you can see them looking around the room. They understand that I'm the boss, and yet they still sort of talk to the guys, hoping that somehow they are going to be able to communicate with me. I kind of like to watch people do this. I'm not angry about it. It's real easy for me to say, "Okay, this is the way it's going to be," because they're pretty careful about stepping on my toes. If I want to assert myself, I just do and the suits get it. But they're not sure, they really don't take you seriously. I worry that this has become like reverse racism.

The guy is a little too close when he leans over your typewriter. His shoulder is a little close. He puts his hands on you. After fifteen years on the job market— and the first ten they didn't even have rules against this stuff—it's not difficult to spot. It makes you angry. You just want to grab somebody by the cheeks, fill the sink up with hot water, and shove them in.

You do the best you can. You get around it. You try to make as few enemies as possible. Sometimes it works and sometimes it doesn't.

At the same time, it's not enough to make me get up in the morning and not put my makeup on, so that I won't be as attractive. Obviously that's a price I've been willing to pay, because I'm *not* willing to be my normal self and scare small children when I walk to work. I do the face and the hair and the whole shot.

It's people that think you don't have a brain because of the way you look that is the most insulting. The, "Well, honey, what do you really think now?" when you're talking to somebody about a sixty-thousand-dollar computer system and they're talking to your chest for an hour and a half.

I don't know if it's ever going to end. I don't think it's much different now than it was twenty years ago. Men are just more subtle with it. They're better at it on the job. They've got their lawyers and they know what they can get away with and what they can't get away with. It's Darwinian evolutionary theory in the mental market. They've thrown out all the obvious stuff. Now there are different reasons why you don't get hired, or why you don't get promoted, or why you don't get this or that. It's the same old base reason, it's just got a new name. They really want a prettier secretary, or someone who is more pliable and submissive. But the story they give you is, they need someone who more fits the corporate image, someone with more executive experience, someone with fresher ideas. Whatever. You name it, they'll come up with it, but it's the same thing.

At least they're not looking straight at you and telling you that they're not going to pay you as much as the guy next to you because he's got a family to support. They'll find another reason, but it won't be that one.

I just outsold all the men every month. I worked in a men's clothing store so it wasn't too hard. I specialized in all these little old men, and I had them going. I'd call them and say, "I've got some new ties, you better come in to pick out one for your new suit."

I had a good time doing it. Then I got pregnant, so I knew I wasn't going to be working. I just became a housewife and mother and whatever.

I really enjoy that, just being at home. I said, "These women who want to go to work and have to have a career, they can have it." I enjoy staying home. I don't mind cleaning. I don't mind doing the wash. Let him go to work. Let him worry about it. Just give me the paycheck and I'll take care of the bills, have a little spending money on the side. Nobody's telling me what time to be home. I got news for you, he has to beg me for money. Did you see him when he left? He said, "Honey, I'm taking the credit card," real meek. I've got things well under control now, let me tell you.

The first time I got pregnant, Frank was in law school. About a third of his class were women. There's nothing worse than a female law student.

225

They're all with their noses in the air. Since they're women, so they have to prove themselves twice—in the classroom and then with their peers—so they're very aggressive. They said to me, "What are you going to do? How are you going to go to work?"

"Are you kidding?" I said. "When I have this baby, I'm retiring. I put him through college and law school. That's enough."

"You mean you don't want to do anything with your life?" they said.

"You mean to tell me having a baby and raising it is not doing something with your life?"

I admire those women with big jobs. I have a friend I admire more than anybody. She's got a baby who's just a year old and a career. She's thrown herself into her work and she really is going to be successful. She's a go-getter.

I'm not bragging, but I admire women like myself, too, who have said, "I don't need that crap. I'm happy doing what I'm doing. This is my station in life and I'm not going to be intimidated by somebody and go off and get a job that I'm not happy with."

Do you realize how hard those women work? They're working ten hours a day and then they got to come home and take care of kids and the house. Some men do pitch in, but they're working just as hard. They don't feel like coming home and taking care of a house any more than she does. I'm sorry, but wouldn't life just be so much easier if one decided she would go to work and he would stay home, or he would go to work and she would stay home? Wouldn't that make more sense than everybody bashing their heads together trying to fulfill themselves while they're making themselves miserable? They're so worn out, nine times out of ten, they don't even have time for the kids.

When I was pregnant with my fourth, I knew this girl who had just had a baby. Although she had another child at home, she had worked all through the pregnancy. When her baby was six weeks old she went back to work. That was okay with me. I could care less. But she comes up to me and she goes, "How do you stand being home all day? With those kids?"

I said, "How do you stand being away from your baby all day?" and I walked away.

I'm applying for a second job. I lie awake at night trying to figure out how to get us out of our hole. Not just out of it, but into a school district I like. We want to have bambino No. 2. I'm getting up there in age, so it really is a "now or never" situation, but how can we pay double for child care?

On top of that, I want to be with my kids. I'd love to have this time with them. I don't want to pay someone to raise them.

Every morning, my son watches me get dressed. If I put on a dress—which I never wear unless I'm going to work—he says, "No work, Mama. Stay home. Play here." Then after I take him to the baby-sitter, I get to drive away waving to my little crying boy in the window. Nice start on the day, huh? It makes me crazy.

This have it all—work-and-motherhood—stuff is a lie. Everything you do is diminished. Work is diminished and so is the feeling of motherhood. The satisfaction is diluted in both arenas.

Of course, I didn't get a penny from this guy when we got divorced. I was totally self-supporting the family. This was tough. It also made me work harder than I might have if I didn't have two kids to support. I knew I was going to have to support them until they were out on their own. I wasn't going to be out of control again.

I do carry around some guilt and some sadness that I had to work as hard as I did when they were small. God damn it, I wish I could have been here at three o'clock when they came home from school. I wish I could have been a PTA mother. I wish I could have been a Boy Scout troop leader. I wish I could have been involved more in their lives.

I feel bad that I missed a lot because of working. I have guilt for when I came home too tired to play with them. But it's not overriding guilt. The fact of the matter was I was supporting the family. I had to. Nobody else was going to do it for me.

The other sales managers wouldn't give me the time of day if they didn't have to. To make my point, I really had to shake them. But I didn't try to confront them. I worked my tail off and let the work speak for me. I was a very compulsive worker, and while it wasn't always good for me personally, it was great for the company. I'd work like a maniac. I'd turn out reports and analyses and anything I could think of. I'd go home at night and be with my kids, feed them dinner, and put them to bed. Then I'd work until one o'clock in the morning. Part of that was my obsessive need to prove myself. But it was also necessary for me to beat these guys to get any attention at all.

I worked very hard on the governor's campaign. When he was elected, I asked to be appointed to the museum board of directors. He said okay and appointed me. I was the only woman. If you sit on the museum board, you become a stadium commissioner, which basically means you get great football tickets. I didn't care about football.

There were eight guys on the board and myself. At first, they really ignored me. Then slowly I worked in. I became chairman of the finance committee, then chairman of the budget committee and the administration committee. If you do the work, they make you chairman of the board. You just take them out to lunch and say, "How wonderful you are." Give them your football tickets.

But I had no idea of what to do when I wanted to accomplish something. These eight guys taught me how to play the game. They would say to me, "You can't please everyone. You just need the majority of the votes. You need four votes every time you want to do something. You have to find a common need for both parties in order to move anything." Men don't react out of the goodness of their hearts. They are into, "What's in it for me?"

When I went to the guys on my board of directors and said, "We need a new museum," and gave them all the women's viewpoint, the yin and the yang, it was like, "Yeah, okay. So what?"

But when I said, "We need a new museum. You can have my tickets—eight tickets a game, in the press box," I found out the information source went open. But there was more to it than the football tickets. I'd say, "I'll give you the tickets."

"More important than the tickets," they'd say, "are the parking passes, so we don't have to walk eight miles." I discovered I could keep the tickets and give them the parking passes. Then I found out there were two kinds of parking passes. There was valet parking—which none of the guys had bothered to tell me about—and then there was just a place to park. I had to give a guy the tickets to the games for him to tell me that. Once you learn that you have this common interest, you just keep moving.

So what happened is, I got my block of four votes. I was a Democrat, they were all Republicans. I gave all the football tickets to these guys, and as long as I touched base with these people, I did anything I wanted. I hired staff, I fired staff. I met with who I wanted to meet with, I gave interviews with who I wanted to. The guys loved it. They were totally supportive.

They trusted me. I always called them before I did something. They'd take my phone calls. I'd say, "Listen, I'm going to ask TRW for a couple of hundred grand to fund this program. Can I count on you guys?"

"Sure, just make it as easy as possible." They were doing something else. They were heads of corporations, corporate giants. So I would get the staff to put together the whole gig, I'd go down to TRW and I'd say, "This is what we're going to do."

"Is your board supportive of you?" they'd ask.

"Absolutely." Then I'd call the guys back and they'd say, "Okay, we'll call our friends on their board and we'll get it through."

We were all in the news. One guy told me, "Never say, 'I did it.' Make sure you say 'We.' "

"What do you mean 'We'? You guys aren't doing anything."

"It's the game," he said. "You always have to say *we* did it because that makes us look good and we'll do what you want to do after that." I was busting my ass and these guys weren't doing anything. But I always said, "*We* raised $41 million."

Once it clicked, I had the opportunity to have all this power. I was running the museum, that was the corporation I was running. They wanted to run their corporations and be on the stadium board and not do anything. So they were quite happy to have someone else do the work, especially since I kept checking in with them. No end runs.

It was the first time that I have ever worked with men in a collaborative way. I could see certain things that they couldn't see and they could see certain things that I couldn't see. I could see that we needed the museum. They could see that we had one of the best football teams in the nation at the time and we personally had fabulous tickets. I couldn't see the purpose of those. Once we agreed on respecting each other's interests, each other's turf, it was just smooth sailing.

I have three bosses at three levels above me and they are all women. My office is female-dominated. I have never worked for a man. It would be very interesting. I'm sure that I would learn completely different things than what I'm learning from these women. Somebody was very offended recently when I said, "I wish that I had a man to work for just to see what it would be like."

Men do things without the guilt. In a difficult situation at work, a woman, out of total frustration, will start to cry—I've seen it. A man would never do that. He would never be so overcome with that type of emotion. He would cut right through that. Men just get angry.

The senior vice president, the person we all ultimately report to, is the head of a major entertainment division of this company and is very, very successful at it. I don't know if she meant it as a joke or not, but one day at a meeting she said, "I always wear one article of men's clothing every day." Maybe she meant the hanky in her suit pocket. Hopefully, it's not a jockstrap.

It's probably true that women get too emotional about things. I think we let go better. My boss has temper fits in the office. I can't think of any other way to put it. He screams, he yells, he curses. He pulls telephones out of the wall. He takes them off the hook for hours on end.

I cry and it pisses him off. Then he has a temper fit, because I'm crying. This is the way I get rid of that emotion. When I was younger, I used to throw things, and I still do on occasion, but I can't in the office. I'm in a weird situation there. I don't have an office where I can shut the door and throw things. I'm in the law library. I can't throw the books around in there.

So I'll start crying. I don't think that's necessarily bad. It's a good bit healthier to cry than to hold it in. I don't like to cry in front of people either, but sometimes it happens and I can't control it. I don't do it to manipulate. I'm not doing it on purpose. My God, if I could control it, I'd never cry.

I've cried once in a real courtroom, during my closing arguments. I didn't mean to. The funny part is that the prosecutor came up and congratulated me on what a great trick I'd pulled during my speech. I didn't do it on purpose. It just happened and I didn't cry a whole lot. I didn't start sobbing and fall down on the floor. I just started crying. It was a very emotional case.

When I got in a position of power in corporate America with all its task forces and committees, I found out that when something really had to be done, a lot of the guys would promise to do it, but the women would do everything. That's a sexist thing to say. I think it has something to do with cultural expectations. Women are expected to solve problems, whether they're solving problems at home or at work or anyplace else. Growing up as a little girl, you're expected to make people happy, to solve their problems. Most little girls of my generation didn't question the assignment or the authority's right to give you the assignment. You just did it.

That's in part what explains the fact that women tend to dig in their heels, roll up their sleeves, and get to the task at hand. Generalizing again—not with all men, but with many men—men seem to spend an amount of time equal to the time it would take to do the work finding ways to delegate the task to someone else.

One day early on in my career, I was approached by a woman who said, "We're starting a women's group to focus mainly on our work. Are you interested?" So I went to this group meeting of seven or eight women. We established some guidelines—confidentiality, a commitment to attend the meetings which would be every other week, and limit our focus to career and job problems and goals. Eight years later this group is still meeting. It has turned out to be tremendously helpful in my career.

Part of it was just luck that it was the right mix of women. We have the same level of sophistication about who we are and where we're going. What developed was a real caring for each other. So while we may tell each other at meetings that we're full of shit and that's garbage, there's a lot of love there, too. We've exchanged a lot of information about being in business, and these women are there for me when I've had a job crisis.

Men have a natural network. The Old Boys' Network is very real. They share names and give advice and trade tips. They talk business.

Women are very much behind in how we do this. When women get together, what do they talk about? Their husbands, their kids, their cooking. Women hate for me to say this, but I think it's true, men naturally talk about business and women don't naturally talk about business. So setting up this network for this particular purpose really made it happen for us. Once every two weeks, I am forced to focus on what's happening to me in my job and am I going where I want to go. If I'm in a state of crisis, I get some help. If I'm faced with something I've never done before, there's someone there who knows someone who has done it before. She'll give you the number and say, "Look, this is my friend, Connie. She'll tell you how to do that."

234

The group has evolved so that we are not competitive with each other. There's no backbiting. We're all about equal on the success quotient. We're on an equal footing and we've dared to open up and talk about our real feelings. Some women are too competitive to do this. You have to be willing to put that aside.

Although men are competitive in their own way, women are often negative in their competition with one another. For some women competition means putting down another woman rather than just getting ahead yourself. Men learn competition in sports, as the old adage goes, so they learn to be competitive on a team. Women don't have that experience. Men can let it drop better than women do. Some of us don't know how to turn it off. Women who do this are fools because they're prohibiting the development of the natural kind of network that men have. Instead of widening their contacts, they're boxing themselves in. I'm not saying there aren't men who are cutthroat and who'll do you in in the blink of an eye. This we know for a fact. But there may be more women who will do that to other women because of the competition among our gender.

I don't feel like I'm on a crusade for women in general. I believe in the tenets of feminism and try to make sure that they happen. I've been accused of being sexist. On my executive staff there are four people, me and three men. I've thought about that and said, "That's kind of weird, Marilyn. Maybe you should be looking at bringing up more women into those kinds of positions.'' But I get along easier with men in a business setting. And to me, most men are more interesting than women to a certain extent.

My fantasy when I was a little girl was sort of the knight-in-shining-armor fantasy. My fantasy was to ride to work with my husband every day. It was down Park Avenue in Manhattan. I was clearly going to work. I wasn't dropping him off and then going shopping.

I don't know where this comes from since I didn't have immediate role models for this fantasy in my family. Maybe I felt guilty for being given so much. Maybe I thought I owed somebody something. But to me, it all comes down to work and feeling accomplished. Not feeling that my work is supplemental to a boyfriend or a husband, not to anybody. I always thought that my work was what made me special.

I haven't told my husband yet that I'm going back to work. If I just go out and do it, then he can't stop me. But see, if I tell him first, he'll try and sit and talk me out of it. I'll listen to him and he's a good talker. I'm ready to get back in the work field. I'm bored with staying home and I don't want to be on welfare the rest of my life. I've been on it for seven years and that's seven years too long. I tried to get them to put me on a work program, but they won't do it because my kids are under six years of age. I'm going to do it on my own; I don't care how much trouble it is. I'm going to do it because I want something out of life and you can't get it sitting at home.

My advice to women is to get up off of their butts and do something about it. You can't sit complaining. You got to go out there and make it. It's going to be a long hard fight, but you got to do it. Fight it to the finish and you'll see when you come out on top that it was worth it.

5. Rape

If you read at an average speed, every fifth page you turn in this book another woman has been raped somewhere in America. A woman is raped in this country every six minutes, according to the FBI. The odds are one in ten that a woman will be raped in her lifetime. These statistics are based only on the rapes reported to law enforcement agencies. There are some estimates that nearly twice as many rapes occur than are officially reported.

Although rape involves a sexual act, it is not a crime of passion. In fact, it is only superficially a sexual act. Rape is male sexual violence intended to dominate and degrade a woman. It takes a very small leap to recognize that *all* violence aimed at dehumanizing the victim can be characterized by that one small word, *rape*.

Three women out of the one hundred I spoke with told me about being physically abused by a parent. The stories would come in quick bursts, and then disappear just as suddenly, like this one: "Being thrown across the room is my first memory. It is not all that conscious, more a frightening sensation. I don't remember being hurt, just the sense of not being in contact with anything. My father was a violent man."

Three other women told me about incestuous betrayal in their childhoods either by a father or a brother. Extrapolate that 3 percent from this small but random sampling of American women to the population as a whole and the numbers are harrowing enough. But since incest is so taboo, there is a good possibility other women among my interviewees simply did not mention their own encounters. As one woman who told me part of her story said, "I don't talk about it easily. I am still very ashamed of it. Although I know now intellectually that I had nothing to do with it, I'm still embarrassed.

"A couple of weekends ago I was with friends in a country house. There was an article in the newspaper about a horrendous sex abuse scandal in this rich boys' school. So we got into this whole conversation. I could sit there and talk about how it fucks people up, if not for their entire lifetimes, it sure interferes with their functioning for a long time, and how horrible it is to keep someone like that around and not to prosecute him. But I couldn't sit there and tell people that I'd been a victim of it. I still feel connected to it. How can you walk around saying, 'My father sexually abused me'? It's hard to say that and it's hard to own up to it."

Most amazing to me was the number of stories I heard about men who resorted to physical violence with women—whether out of anger, frustration, plain meanness, or fear of somehow compromising their masculinity. These were not always stories of terrible beatings, although there were more than enough of those—two women were even attacked with knives, one by a husband and the other by a lover. Instead, there were isolated slaps, shoves, and punches, being banged against the wall, momentarily choked or held so tightly by the wrist that his fingers left bruises. Some women had objects thrown at them: drinking glasses (with and without drinks), a book that hit a woman in the shoulder and cracked her collarbone, a key ring that struck a woman in the face and drew blood. I did interview one woman in her mid-fifties who had recently left a physically abusive relationship in which she had been struck, threatened, and humiliated by her female lover. She had also been married to an abusive man earlier in her life. But my conservative estimate is that 75 percent of the women I interviewed had experienced some level of physical violence from men.

And then there are the women who endured psychological abuse from men. A few women suffered under a distorted image of themselves imposed by a spouse or boyfriend or pimp. Many of them had grown up with a browbeating father. Not entirely uncommon were mothers who tried to usurp their daughters' identities or retard their emotional growth. Some women had been humiliated by a boss, or terrorized by a callous doctor or an unbalanced psychiatrist. Others were menaced by rejected suitors or roughly used by false lovers.

If all these forms of abuse are added together, the percentage of women I interviewed who have been literally or more figuratively raped by men comes alarmingly close to 100 percent. I had not expected such a thorough indictment of my gender.

In a violent sexual rape, a woman may acquiesce to her rapist to save her life. It is harder to understand women who remain in physically or psychologically abusive relationships, often for many years. One woman explained it this way: "People say when women get hit that they like it and that's why they stay there. But that's not true. Sometimes you don't think you're any better than that, anyway. So what? That's what you deserve. Anyone else would treat you that way, too. You're so afraid that you don't understand that you have an option. It's really horrible. I know that now, but when he was hitting me, I just didn't think I was worth much more."

The women who speak in this chapter are survivors. Disturbing, vicious things have happened to them, but they have lived to tell the story. A few of them are facing the future with an optimism based on the discovery of their own inner strength. One of them, as you will read, is hanging on to existence by a tenuous thread. I don't know whether their experiences hold some answers and a little hope for women in similar circumstances. But I do know that there are victims who didn't survive for me to talk to.

I'm trying to build up to this, but I don't know how. It was the beginning of a pattern. The first time I was betrayed in a sexual way was by my brother, I was around six or seven; he was twelve or thirteen. He started coming into my room late at night after my parents were asleep. He would wake me up and hold me and touch me.

At the time, I really didn't know what he was doing. I was too young. I was so young that when he asked me if I had any questions to ask him, I was asking things like, "What is fire, Carl? What's water made of?" I clearly remember that, because those were the things on my mind at that time. Not, "Tell me about sex, Carl," which he was obviously beginning to experiment with.

What I've pieced together and found out since that point is that our next-door neighbor was involved with his half sister. He was six or eight years older than her, too. He suggested to Carl, "You've got sisters. Why don't you try fooling around with them?" And that's what Carl did.

He told me not to tell Mommy and Daddy, but eventually I got so tired of being woken up at night that I did say, "Mom, Carl's waking me up at night." So that stopped.

I don't know how much of a big deal it would have been if it hadn't happened again at a later date. I'm sure I could have remembered it—it's a betrayal any way you look at it—but it's more significant if you look at it as a problem that was never dealt with and a situation that just got worse.

As a child I was always aware of how sad I was in some respects; then right before all this shit went down for the second time, I developed some really bizarre behavior. I started to throw incredible fits, screaming, just losing control.

I contemplated suicide when I was eleven years old. I told Mommy that if I really was that crazy I was going to eat mothballs. That was the only thing I knew that was poisonous. They were underneath the bathroom sink. Talk about Twilight Zone time. The psychs said I was a spoiled child and needed to be disciplined.

I was very sick and I wasn't responsible for that, but I was really misbehaving when I was sick. It was very difficult for my mother to feel love toward me. I was acting out all over the place and it was understood that this was not what you do in our family. You don't throw yourself on the floor screaming in public. Both my brothers would tease me until the frustration would push me over the edge. I would get into such a frenzy that I was completely out of control. My parents had been told by the psychologists to ignore me. I felt more and more abandoned. Here I am losing my mind and they're acting like nothing's wrong, because they think that's going to help me stop this behavior. My brothers are attacking me and laughing hysterically.

In reality, my body was wacko. Luckily, it was discovered when I went to my annual checkup with the pediatrician. My reflexes were through the ceiling and my pulse was way out of whack. I was losing weight. Everything was going haywire, so they took me to a special clinic.

I had an unusual type of hyperactive thyroid. This made it even worse, because a lot of doctors were interested in me. The place was full of doctors who wanted to look me over. They were pulling my hair. The symptoms are that you lose hair and your hands become real shaky. I bit my nails and they asked me did I always bite them. I was very confused.

Once they put me through all these tests and took a tremendous amount of blood, they prescribed a medication. I got better. I was a fairly serious child anyway, but there were some really, really sick kids in that hospital. There were seriously deformed and dying children. To have to be around them made me see things a little differently. To be confronted with death at that age was weird.

Something that stuck with me from that whole experience is fear of authority. I have a serious fear of not being in control, of having my view of reality questioned. I was losing it and people around me were trying to ignore it so that it would go away. The house was burning down and everybody acted like it wasn't.

Also I was in a family where I was sexually abused and no one knew it. On the surface, everything was fine. My three closest friends come from divorced families. To them my situation looked ideal. To come from a nuclear family that was actually dysfunctional and to have it look like everything was okay made me very sensitive. If there is something wrong with this picture, I want somebody to say something about it, not just go, "Oh, tra-la-la-la, everything's fine now."

So I went through being a weirdo, strange kid. All the time, I was looking toward my brother as the symbol of what I wanted to be like, as a model for my boyfriend in the future. In my eyes he was a cool guy. He was definitely an unhappy kid with a lot of problems, but you have a different perspective when you're a kid looking up to an older kid.

Around the time I was twelve or thirteen, on the brink of puberty—not quite, since I hadn't gotten my period yet—my brother became interested in me sexually, again.

I felt this reverence for my brother, so any chance I got, I would be around him. A lot of the time he'd say, "Go fuck off. Get away. I don't want you around." But one day, he didn't. I was in his bedroom and I was sitting against the wall. He was reading and I was looking at something. It just sort of hit him. I remember him saying, "You really love me, don't you?"

"Yeah," I said.

He asked me to come sit on the bed. He showed me this psychedelic painting of this woman who was half naked and had all this shit going on around her. He questioned me on it. "What do you think about this?"

"I don't know," I said. I knew that something was going to happen. I got this weird, prickly, sick feeling that something was going to happen, but I didn't know what. He started to kiss me. From that point on—I don't remember how many times it happened—but when we were alone in the house, he would approach me, he would come to me. We never actually had intercourse, but there were a lot of other things that happened that were a complete betrayal of my innocence at that time.

At one point he put his finger up inside of me and broke my hymen. Later on, the first time I went to a gynecologist, the doctor didn't believe I was a virgin because of what had happened to me. How could I possibly tell him, "No, no, I haven't had intercourse with anyone, but my brother does things to me"? There was a tremendous amount of self-hatred that evolved out of that.

I did what a lot of abused children do. I thought I was protecting my parents and didn't want them to know, because they would never be able to live with it. It would hurt them too much. By simply not knowing that it happened, they allowed it to happen. On a real integral level, they weren't able to take care of me, to protect me, in the way that I needed to be.

I was so incredibly needy that I was willing to accept any kind of affection from Carl, no matter what, even if it felt wrong, even if it was wrong. I was astounded that he actually wanted to be with me and in that respect it felt good, but the actual physical fact of being with him was frightening and made me feel sick. Eventually, I said no. I don't know what would have happened if I hadn't. Maybe it would have continued to the point where we were actually having intercourse. I don't know. I was just so young.

It took me many years to understand that I was a child at that point, that I wasn't in control of the situation. As I grew older, that part of me petrified. In my mind, in that part of myself, I was that same twelve- and thirteen-year-old. It was only three or four years ago when I was talking to a friend and I told her what had happened to me. She said, "Maybe you should go into therapy about this. It might help you to feel better."

Then I began to understand the depth of what had happened to me, and to understand how old I was then and what it meant to be that age and to have the first person who ever kissed me be my brother. There was always so much shame from being involved in that.

It was even more complicated. On top of everything else, back then he was dating the woman who is now his wife. She was everything else I wanted to be, only the female version. She was also one of the first people I'd ever been around who was kind to me. But when Gail was around, Carl wanted me *away*. He didn't want to have any evidence of me. He would be very cruel and Gail couldn't understand why he was being so mean to me.

Within a year's time of going into therapy, I decided that I was going to tell my parents and confront Carl, for whatever it's worth. On some levels, I'd like for it all to just go away. I'm the one who wants it to go away the most. I can understand that response. At the same time, I had to recognize that my needs were not met then, they weren't being met now. I had to try and rectify the situation for myself in the best way I could. For me, it was just to say, "I've been carrying this around with me for twenty years. Here, you can have some now. It's been killing me."

It was a major upheaval in Carl's and Gail's lives to be confronted with this. They still haven't dealt with it in a way that would make me happy. Carl went to therapy for a little bit. I have very little contact with them now, which makes me really sad. I would rather that it was different. There's no way that wounds will heal from not seeing each other for years and years, but it looks like that's what's going to happen. For a while, I was trying to take care of him. I would call them and contact them. But I'm not going to do it anymore. It's sad.

The situation is far from perfect with my family now. I'm still struggling to accept them as they are and to accept whatever it is that they are able to give me. But this past Christmas I was thrown back into my nuclear family and saw them in a clear way without any of the distractions of my life. I look forward to the day when I can be around them and feel some kind of love for them and accept what they are giving me without feeling this tremendous sense of loss and lack of love in my life.

There was a time when there was so much pain welling up inside of me that I didn't think it was ever going to stop. It was a chasm. I remember sobbing, sobbing, sobbing. It was very old pain for something I had buried and I had to let it come out, let it come to the surface.

By the time I did confront it, I was so eager. "Yes, please, let's just open up the windows. I want to feel clean again. I don't want to be carrying this garbage around with me."

I feel that I've been victorious with the help of my therapist and my friends and through my own willingness to change myself. I have risen above what has happened to me and learned from it. The pain did pass. If I'd tried to keep it locked away, it would still be inside me now. It has really abated in an incredible way.

When I was in the middle of it, when I was really starting to look at all this stuff and confronted my family, I can't find words to describe the profound sense of abandonment I felt. Like a child who knows she is completely alone and unloved, that she's not being taken care of, that she is not safe. I had buried those feelings under denial. My family was the perfect family. I was taken care of. I was loved. All those beliefs had to be thrown out the window for me to have compassion for that little kid who was me.

I used to be depressed all the time, on a daily basis, suicidal half the time. I wanted to kill myself, and I don't say that in a flippant way. "Well, if I jump out the window, will I just break my legs or will it really work?" I'd go into the logistics. Would I shoot myself in the head or would I take poison? But I think I really love life too much, love my body too much, and that thread held me together when I was considering the Big S.

I still have my bouts with self-hatred or anger or sadness, but it's not like that constant hum that was always there before. I have a much greater understanding of who I am, a much better capacity to express myself, a better understanding of what I need. I am very lucky that I see it at this point in my life, when I'm not too old and too bitter to do anything about it. I feel like I've been given a major second chance. I have a chance to have a relationship with someone that could be really wonderful. I could have a family. That makes me very, very happy. If to change any of the pain or the experiences, I had to give up some of the knowledge I've gained, I would not do it. Simply because this knowledge is very precious to me and very hard won. I really have a lot of hope for myself.

M<small>Y</small> mother was beating the shit out of me is what was really happening. In those days, the school system turned a deaf ear and a blind eye to bruises and things on kids. Like all battered children, I never would have told them that she did it anyway.

She never did stop hitting me. I just got really good at dodging it. She had terrible aim, but she would throw lamps—whatever was in her hand.

I couldn't wait to get out of the house. Going to college when I was seventeen was the biggest relief to me. From that time on, I was never home for more than forty-eight hours in one stretch. She was still wilder than wild. That never stopped until literally two weeks before she died when she threw a cup of hot tea in my face. That was the way she was.

I was one of these kids who belong to a gang. I hung around with tough guys who wore leather jackets. We drank beer in the park. All the neighbors around thought we were really bad kids and their kids should stay away from us. We were pussycats. We didn't carry weapons, we didn't threaten people, we didn't get into fistfights, we didn't have any drugs. We were just tough-*looking* kids. My nickname was Ginger and I painted it on my garrison belt with nail polish and then put gold sparkles on it so the name really stood out.

I felt like I had to be tough, that I had to be part of this gang. But really, inside, I was feeling very empty, like if I didn't attach on the outside, somehow I was losing myself. I didn't have any real identity. I didn't know what I wanted to belong to. I didn't know what my value system was.

These were the days of early rock 'n' roll. I was an Elvis Presley freak. I went to see *Love Me Tender* six times and would stand in the balcony screaming my head off. At the same time, my oldest brother, the egghead, was into opera. We'd have battles. Upstairs, my brother would be playing his records and down-stairs I would be playing my rock 'n' roll. I'd hate his music and scream at him. I went to all the rock 'n' roll shows. That was what I believed in. That was where my vitality came from.

Then almost overnight, I was transformed into this opera freak. I can't even tell you how it happened. While I was working and going to college, two or three nights a week I'd be a standee at the opera house. I became a real snob about that. I followed singers. If Joan Sutherland sang in a neighboring city, I'd take a train to hear her sing some esoteric thing. I stood in line for a weekend to get tickets for a Maria Callas performance.

Opera became an area of socialization for me. What it did for me was fulfill a need for friends. I would befriend people standing on line at the opera house. I was a person in those days that you could call a fag hag. Most of my friends were gay. I got an enormous amount of love, support, and tenderness from them and felt accepted by them. It was very convenient. They were all standing on line for the opera, too. When the opera wasn't there, there was the Paris Ballet or the Kirov, or whatever came to town.

A lot of my gay friends had rented this house at a beach resort one summer and I went out to visit them for a week. It was in the days when I was looking more like Joan Baez. I had long hair. I was making beads and smoking dope. We were opera buffs, so we would put on Callas records from way back when or Tebaldi. They'd perform in costume. It was fabulous fun and we had a great time.

In college, I majored in psychology, because on some level I was pretty confused and mixed up about who I was or what I was or what I wanted to be. All the papers I wrote had something to do with homosexuality. All the research I did was on the legal status of homosexuals and what made them tick, but it didn't have to do with me. It was all about them.

They were so comfortable and secure for me. I was hanging out with gay men because they were safe. Then at some point, I realized this was crazy. There was a part of me that was dysfunctional. I wasn't dating. I knew there had to be something else in my life. There was a yearning in me. It was a very painful period for me because I knew I couldn't continue to surround myself with men in this way.

I couldn't handle straight men. My thinking in those days was that any straight man was after me for my body. There were no ifs, ands or buts about it. For years I wondered why I wasn't gay and wished I were, but I'm not. I had to accept that.

I had everything I wanted except what in those days would have been called a boyfriend. There was this window dresser at the store I worked in who was gorgeous and bisexual. I chose him as the first man I was ever going to have a sexual experience with. I was kind of grandiose at that point and felt, "He's bisexual, but he won't be after he sleeps with me." That was all total naiveté and craziness.

He didn't mind it. We had a brief, but weird relationship. He was wonderful, sweet, and much older than I was. I just remember spending a few nights at his apartment where we'd go to bed, and somebody would knock at the door. It was his male lover. The three of us would end up sitting there, having a meal or watching TV or talking opera, because his lover was a writer for an opera magazine. I didn't think anything of it then. I didn't know in those days what I know now about people who are bisexual. I thought they were fifty-fifty—fair on each side. That's not true at all.

At the same time that I was terrified of men, I also knew that I was *absolutely* terrified of women. More terrified of women. At least, I could be comfortable with men, as long as they didn't mention any kind of sexual stuff, as long as that wasn't a threat. I didn't know what it was about the women. I just knew I didn't have any women friends. I had gotten myself into a position where all my friends were gay men.

Eventually it got to the point where it was real scary. I had an anxiety attack, if one can call it that, that really made me dysfunctional, the closest I came to what would be considered a nervous breakdown. I sat in my room and cried for days. It scared the shit out of me. I dropped all my courses in school except Greek mythology and one on opera, because they were nonthreatening. But the psychology courses, I just let go.

I didn't know what to do about it. I went to a therapist. That worked for a little while. Then it got too threatening so I dropped out. I didn't want to hear what my problem was and what I had to work on. It was still all too traumatic for me. I was still real confused. Yet, I knew I had to seek another piece of my life.

I was sexually abused when I was ten or eleven. I went to my mother and told her what happened. She didn't believe me. She *wouldn't* believe me. From that time on, something went off in me that said, "I guess I can't trust my feelings anymore. She's telling me it didn't happen. I know it happened. I feel a lot of pain and horror and trauma about it, and yet she's saying it didn't happen." As a kid, you automatically know that something is wrong, but you don't believe it yourself when you're told it wasn't real, it didn't happen. You have to hold on by yourself to that piece that no one believes. So you put it in the back of your head somewhere. Someday it's going to come out. It's there.

Sure my mom was threatened when I told her the persons who abused me. It was her husband—my father—and my oldest brother. That's one of the reasons she didn't want to acknowledge that it happened. I mean, what would that present to her and her life?

I wished my father dead. For a long time after this happened, I didn't want to speak to him. There were times, when my father would kiss me, I'd run upstairs and wash my mouth out with soap. I didn't feel free and relaxed in the house. My mother would be off— when work was over she'd go take a writing course or she'd go to some school to teach English as a foreign language—she was not around. I felt terribly uncomfortable with my brothers. I still say to this day that if it wasn't for my middle brother, who never tried anything on me and was always loving and I could always trust and be close to, I don't know what I'd be today. He was very protective.

My father was a pretty intense, angry man. My mother would like to recall him as a loving husband and that they never argued. I remember I could not be in a group of people where there was silence, because to me that signaled rage. He was always in a rage.

We'd be in a car going somewhere, and if he was quiet, it meant that he was seething about something. He was about to explode.

I wished my father dead for a long time. But by the time I got to my therapy, there was a part of me that began to feel sorry for him. He went through a depressed state when they had to sell their business, because it was failing. He didn't have a job. He drove a taxi and got mugged a number of times. He had a slipped disk and was in a lot of pain. It was awful for him. He'd been a real hero to his immigrant family.

So when he had this fall from grace, I began to feel sorry for him, but I could never bring myself to forgive him or even talk to him. Except around superficial stuff like Adlai Stevenson. He discussed politics and was a gung-ho Democrat.

Then there was a tragedy in my family that forced me to give up two years of my life. My dream of wishing him dead came true. I was twenty-one when he was killed in a car accident with my nephew, who was three, and two cousins, also children. He had taken the kids to the beach for the day. They were involved in a horrendous automobile accident and his car caused it. It was a horror on the front page of the Sunday newspapers. They burned to a singe. They could only be identified through dental records. It was a trauma like people never want to think about being involved in.

The loss of my three-year-old nephew really slayed me. I was very close to him. In some strange way, I felt that there was finally a male in my life who was perfectly innocent that I could love freely. Obviously, he didn't want me for any other reason than for my love. Then he was taken away at the same time that my wish for my father going away came true.

On another level, my nephew and my father were very close. He loved his grandfather and vice versa. Somehow this was an indirect way for me to communicate with my father through my nephew in ways that I couldn't directly express. I buried myself in the loss of that little boy for a long time. I can't even begin to think about when I stopped feeling sorry for myself, because a part of me died with him.

That was a horrible time to live through. My aunt blamed my mother for sending them to the beach. My mother didn't know how to cope with it. The family was so destroyed there was nobody left to comfort anybody else. Then there was the reality of a court case. People suing people, getting lawyers, and all the stuff that you have to deal with—and we didn't want to deal with—because my father's car had caused the accident.

I was living at home still. My brothers were both married and living out of the house. The relationship between my mother and me became symbiotic in a way that I can't even really describe. Once we were through with the funeral and all that shit and got back to a sense of normalcy, she wouldn't go out or make plans for the nighttime until she checked with me to see if I had plans. I wouldn't go out. We both knew we'd have trouble being alone. We'd come home, turn on the TV. Watch reruns of Dick Van Dyke or whoever was on. Sit there and cry mutual tears to each other until eight or nine o'clock. Finish watching TV and go to bed.

It was horrible. When I think back on it now, I hated it. But I felt trapped. I felt totally victimized by my emotions and her emotions. I was responsible for her. She was left alone, abandoned. Feeling that she was abandoned touched off in me feelings of being abandoned by her that I wasn't even aware of at that point. At the same time that I was feeling attached to her and needed by her, I was in a rage at being part of this.

Then I was feeling guilty about my father dying. I felt so powerful. God, I could never wish anything else, because it might happen. My rage would kill. I still have problems with anger. I can feel anger on behalf of my clients. I can go out there and scream. I could scream about Vietnam, I can scream about the murders going on or somebody being raped or my clients not getting justice and their fair square deal. But when it comes to something for me, I can't do it, because I feel that my own rage is so powerful that it'll destroy.

My mother's power over me was enhanced by this. All my life she'd given me a pretty clear message that I was there to serve her, that my needs were unimportant, they were irrelevant. It wasn't tasks, it wasn't cleaning the house, it wasn't cooking, because she had no high regard for that. It was emotional. It was, "You're there because I want you to be there. You are not a child in your own right, you are there to function for me and to meet my needs. To be pretty for me. I will give you the kind of haircut I want, dress you the way I want. You'll be a showpiece for me."

I didn't realize the control that this female person had over my life until then. I always thought the sexual abuse with the men in my life was controlling me and making me dysfunctional. The fear of men was more overt. But the real trauma, the real sense of abandonment, the real sense of "you can't trust your own feelings" came from my mother, and it came way before the sexual abuse. It came from the time I was too little to remember.

I still have problems with my mother, but I'm working on that. Sometimes we walk around talking about how our environment or our parents programmed us to think in a certain way. All my life was superficial bullshit, because inside I didn't know who I was. I think it's clearly connected to how my mother programmed me. I'm learning how much control I allowed my mother to have over my life. I'm forty-some-odd years old, and somehow I'm still sitting around learning how much this woman controlled me.

He was doing very violent things to me. He was sick and I was real locked into it. I was just wandering around moping. The wife would come over and I would hide in closets so I didn't have to deal with her. That was getting pretty sick, so I knew that I was in trouble. I had to do something.

"You've got to get a grip on this," I told myself. "This guy is tearing you up and you're letting him do it."

I had the funniest dream and that's one of the things that made me get out of that situation. I had a dream that I was reaching out for help and there was my father who had committed suicide when I was still a child, standing on the beach, stirring a big caldron and putting things into it. He said, "Well, we all make our own stew, sweetheart."

I woke up with some clarity. It took me six months to get my apartment rented and to save up the money, but I did it. I got out.

I was rambunctious, in the principal's office every day, because I was like smarter than the other kids. The stuff that they were learning, I learned really fast and then I got bored.

By the time I was fifteen, I just couldn't deal with it. I was like always in trouble in school. I was really reckless. I would do anything. I did a lot of drugs. I cut school. I'd leave home, go to school late, and find my homeroom so they won't mark me absent for the whole day. Leave, go find some guys in a car. Go buy beer, drink all day. Take drugs.

I used to sneak out after my parents were asleep at

night and just go hang out. I wasn't doing anything. I mean, I didn't have a boyfriend, I wasn't having sex. I just was going out, because I wasn't allowed out. My parents were so strict. I was always baby-sitting for my brothers and sisters. Then I'd put like two diet pills on my dresser at night when I came home. When my alarm clock would go off in the morning, I'd eat them, go back to sleep, and fifteen minutes later I'd be, "Up! Good morning!" Buzzing around.

Then I started running away. I wanted to get away from my house. The first time, my friend Lane, who lived across the street and was a couple of years older than me, she was running away and I wanted to go, too. She was going out with some guy from town who was some sort of drug dealer or something. We hitch-hiked into town and went to this guy's apartment that night.

I took acid that night, the first time I took real acid —you know, LSD. I don't remember much. I just remember that the police were at the door. I went running and hid in a closet, because I knew they were after me. The others were flushing all these drugs down the toilet. The police are coming in and my parents are with the cops. Then I remember I left and went outside of this brick building. My dad just took me and slammed me into the brick wall, like my head. It seemed to go on forever and ever, because I was tripping.

My mom didn't want me to go home with them, not with my dad anyway. My mother was afraid, because my father was so furious that she didn't know what he would do. I guess she got upset when he slammed me into the brick wall. So the cops took me and my mother to my grandmother's house and we stayed there.

They never knew I took drugs that night. I thought it was pretty obvious, but maybe they just didn't want to deal with that. So that was it. We didn't talk about it. It was just over. I went home. It was like it never happened pretty much.

My mom wanted me to go to counseling. I'd go, but I wouldn't talk, and I'd be a real bitch, because I just didn't want to do it. I probably should have. I was bad. I was really bad.

If they would have just let me have a little freedom, if they'd been a little more permissive with me, I wouldn't have been so rebellious. They'd never let me go anywhere. I couldn't go out with my friends. If I went to the movies, they had to drive me there and drive me back. I was fourteen years old. It wasn't like I was ten. The more they put restrictions on me, the more I rebelled against it.

Then, I just decided I was leaving. My friend came with me, Maria. We planned it like a week in advance, packed everything, got on the interstate, and just started hitchhiking. We didn't know where we were going. We had sixteen dollars. We weren't running *to* anywhere. We were just running away.

We got picked up by some truck drivers and they took us to the next state and got us a room that night. We dyed our hair black that night so no one would recognize us. We called our parents, said, "We're okay," and hung up.

The hitchhiking wasn't too bad because I was with somebody. We were real lucky, because after these first truck drivers picked us up, we just got rides so easily. If they weren't going wherever we wanted to go, you just got to the next truck stop and he'd get on the CB and say, "There's two girls who need a ride." We wanted to go to California. But we got a ride with this truck driver who had a son in Texas who had an apartment. He said that he would take us there. Maybe we could see if the son would let us stay there and like clean the house, and, you know, do dishes.

So that's what we did. We went to Texas and stayed with these six guys in a two-room apartment. They were pot dealers, so every night there were four or five ounces of pot on the kitchen table. They'd be putting it in bags and cleaning the seeds. We were listening to The Grateful Dead. Everybody had long hair. We thought it was totally cool.

Then, of course, I liked one of the guys and Maria liked another one of them, so we started sleeping with them. Maria got pregnant.

All the guys had to move to another place, and they found out that we weren't as old as we told them we were. We'd said we were seventeen, because in Texas seventeen was legal. Maria left with her guy, and I didn't have anywhere to go. This guy, Sonny, who liked me, took pity on me and said, "Okay, you can come stay at my house for a while." So I went to stay with him.

I met different guys and lived in a few different towns. I'd fall in love and go off with some biker guy or something. I had a lot of fun, but I got homesick a lot. When one of my brothers' or sisters' birthdays would come up, I'd sit there and cry, thinking, "I want to go home." But I was afraid that if I went home, my parents would kill me for running away.

After a while, I was scared. I decided, I can't deal with this anymore. I want to go home.

I called my home and the phone was disconnected. I thought, "Oh, my God." So I called my dad at work.

"Phil, it's your daughter," his secretary said.

"What!" He gets on the phone and he can't talk.

"I want to come home," I'm crying. "I want to come home."

"Of course, where are you? Come home, please."

"But I'm not by myself."

"It's okay, I don't care. Just come home." He thought I had a baby. I had a dog.

He bought a plane ticket. I got it and flew home with my dog. I got there in time for my sixteenth birthday. I wasn't stupid.

While I was gone, my mom and dad got separated. My mother moved to another state and my dad moved into the city. He had this really tiny apartment. He was lucky to get a bed and a table in it. It was funny, because he would sleep on the floor and let me sleep on the bed, it was so small.

But I screwed up again in school. This school was even less structured than any school I'd ever been in, because it was an alternative school for really bright kids. They used resources all over the city. They'd give you a bunch of tokens to ride the bus from place to place. What my friend and I would do is take our tokens, cash them in and use the money to go out and party.

I started working again. I worked in a recording and rehearsal studio and started meeting a lot of bands and musicians. Then I started hanging out in the bars that were popular. I worked at one of them for a while. For a few months, I never saw the light of day at all.

My dad didn't want to discipline me, because he was afraid if he did I would run away again. So I was just doing whatever I wanted. My dad gave me an American Express card for my sixteenth birthday that year, and took it away when I was sixteen and a half. I'd go out to one of these bars and buy the whole bar a drink. There'd be sixty people there. I had fun, but I got my dad in a lot of debt.

When I was seventeen, I met this guy and I moved in with him. My dad was not happy about it, but what was he going to do? I'd been on my own already, so it wasn't like I'd been home all that time and they had a lot of control over me.

I was baby-sitting for this girl, Lizzy, who I met through one of my old musician boyfriends. She had been doing X-rated movies. She did a lot of them, but I didn't know what she did. I just thought it was really cool that she was an actress. They had a beautiful apartment and I thought they really had a great life. They had a little blond-haired, blue-eyed kid.

One day, she came home and said this director that she knew was looking for somebody who was really pretty and young and unknown. I was like, "Whoa, let me go see him. Yeah, I want to be an actress, all right!"

So I went to see this guy and he told me there was going to be some nudity involved and I said, "Okay, Jane Fonda did *Barbarella*. I mean, there's a lot of nudity, so what?" I did it. I have one sex scene in this movie. They saved that to the very end. They didn't exactly manipulate me into it. They misled me. I don't know. If I'd known what it was from the beginning, I might not have done it. The way they did it, they just made me feel like when it actually came down to it I was already obligated. They had already given me a certain amount of money. I got $850 for that movie. So I took a couple of Quaaludes and I just did it.

Lizzy thought she was doing me a favor. She was really into it and she had no problems with what she was doing at all. She thought she was doing a good thing for me, because that's really the way she felt. She didn't make any money off it. It didn't do her any good to bring me up to meet this guy. I never had any bad feelings toward her about it. I never really blamed anyone. If anyone, I should blame myself for being so stupid, so naive, that I believed people all the time. Even after I know better, I still trust people too much. But I'd rather be like that than be suspicious of everybody.

I figured the film would play at a few porno theaters for a few weeks and nobody would ever see this movie. Then the next thing I know it's plastered in the newspapers. It was all over the place.

My parents found out. My dad was pretty laid back by this time. One of his buddies saw the film and recognized me. He just said, "I wish you would have told me. How do you think I feel hearing it when I'm out bowling with my friends and they're talking about you?'' My mom and me, we never really talked about it. My brothers found out. I was an awful person. I couldn't deal with it and I started doing a lot of drugs.

Some guy I went out with turned me on to heroin. Then Lizzy's husband turned me on to it a couple of times.

I was a stripper for a while after the movie came out. That was really rude. We would have all these sellout crowds because the movie was so hot. Everybody knew the movie. In the movie my hair is long and blond. When I was dancing, my hair was short and brown. These guys would be yelling, ''No, that's not her!''

''Look,'' I'd yell back, ''see this scar on my knee? Go see the movie again, okay? Fuck off.''

I made a lot of money. I was bringing in a couple of thousand dollars a week while I was doing it, a lot more than I made from the movie. It was harder on me, too. I was raised so strict and so Catholic. Maybe if I hadn't been raised the way I was, I wouldn't have felt so guilty and such a Mary Magdalene, such a bad person, and maybe I wouldn't have gotten so into drugs.

I'm really shy, so I just couldn't go out there and do it. I started getting high, because I could do it if I was really high. Then I had to keep dancing to get the money for the heroin. You just get into a circle where you don't want to dance, but you're doing it because you're high, but you're dancing to get the money so you can get high, because you get addicted to heroin.

Then I had to stop, because it got to the point where I was thinking about prostitution. I said to myself, ''If I do that, then there's nothing else. You can't sink any lower. That's like the bottom. I can't do it anymore. I can't do that.''

I went into a couple of detox programs, but I'd always go right back. I'd be in detox for three weeks and the twenty-second day, I'd be out copping on the street again. I'd go through all that pain and then go back. I did it three times, too. It was stupid. It was stupid.

Then I finally got on a methadone program. I was on that for two years. That's not really good either, because they want to keep you on it. They feel that the chances of people going back to heroin are greater than the bad effects of staying on methadone, so they make it very difficult to get off it. They don't want to cut your dosage. They'll keep you there forever. It's supposed to be rehabilitation, you know? If you have someone and you see that they have a normal job and a normal life and are not your normal junkie in the street, then you should help them get out of the life all together. I had to call the State Drug and Substance Abuse Program and complain that they wouldn't let me take a cut before they would let me do it. It was really hard, really hard.

I started working at a regular job. I met my husband. He helped me get off methadone. He got disgusted with them when he saw what they were doing to me. They'd be perfectly happy if I was on it the rest of my life. He had to push me, because I probably would have procrastinated. But I wanted to have a baby, too, and I didn't want to do it on drugs. So that helped, too.

It was hard and there are times I think about doing heroin again. But I can't, not with my little daughter. She makes such a big difference in what I'll do now. I just don't want to do it with her.

I love kids. One of the things I'm saddest about right now is that I'm not having another baby. I think it really sucks to be an only child. I never intended that for my daughter, but as soon as I had her, my husband said, "Okay, let's have another one."

"What? Are you crazy?" I said.

Finally, when I was ready to have another one, we weren't getting along and it probably wasn't a good idea anyway. I'm to the point now where I'd like to have another baby, but I don't want another husband. Maybe if it was someone different, who wasn't so authoritative and condescending. He wants to run my life. I say, "Don't you understand that everybody has to have their own experiences? I'm not going to learn from what you've done. I'm going to have to do it myself and you're going to have to let me. If you can't let me, then I can't live with you." He acts like my father sometimes. He drives me crazy. I don't need a father.

I got so sick of that, so right now I just want to be alone. We're separated. I've got my apartment and I've got my work and I've got my daughter. I've never been alone in my life. I've always lived with people or had a boyfriend or a husband. I never had my own phone in my own name or anything. So this is what I should have been doing instead of getting married at twenty. I'm doing everything backward.

I'm okay. I'm doing okay. If I can just stay out of the park. It was just so weird. I was hanging out and drinking in Needle Park last night. This girl Fezzi, who's like a real psycho, she's been there forever. She's really pretty, but she just thinks she owns the park and has got a hit list a mile long of people she's going to kick the shit out of and kill eventually. She fights really dirty. She'll sneak up behind you and hit you over the head with a bottle and stuff. I never had any problem with her. We get along fine.

Just last night she started picking on a girl and for no reason. It just pissed me off. I was pretty drunk. I just held her back against the fence. I wouldn't let her go. I just went, "You're not going to do this. There's no reason for it." The girl she was picking on, I happen to like and it was stupid.

So that was that and she backed off. But later she

264

got in my face about something. I just hauled off and I hit her really hard. I think I knocked one of her teeth out. I didn't mean to do it. I just got mad. I'd never done that before. I'd had a fight in junior high school and that was it. After I did it, I was so upset, I was crying the whole night. "What am I doing? During the day, I'm this almost Yuppie and at night I go out and beat up people? This is great."

After that, I decided that I'm never going there again. It does not bring out the best in me. It's an interesting place. What you see down there, you got your skinheads, you got your punks, you got all these different rebellious groups of people. The nice thing about it is they all stick up for each other. It's like you feel like you belong to this group of people, and they don't care what you do or how you are. But they're all really fucked up. Most of them are bums and unemployed and aimless, no goals in life except to get enough money to buy another beer. So I think I've had enough of that. I think I've rebelled for the last few months, and I think it's killing me. I've got to stop. It's just nuts.

I met this guy named Flip and I fell in love with him. It turned into an on-again, off-again love affair throughout the years that I would call an abusive relationship.

While we were living together, he had other girlfriends. I was really jealous of that. He was going out nights and not coming back until the next afternoon. Of course he'd have some totally stupid excuse about what he was doing and where he was going, like I was really dumb.

I was really tied into him, to the point that I just figured, "If this is the way it is, that's okay, but I want boyfriends, too. I'm going to feel like a fool, staying home crying." I started having an affair with this guy. The first night I actually went out and spent the night at this guy's place, I came back the next afternoon and I still beat the asshole home. So Flip never knew that I was gone.

He drank a lot and I used to drink a lot trying to keep up with him. That just made everything worse. We would get into arguments, we'd both be drunk, and then there would be black eyes and stuff. It was a messy situation.

I actually did call the cops on him one night. Well, I didn't call them. The neighbors did. I had run upstairs to their place for help. He stabbed me in the hand with a kitchen knife. The guy was really going off. I was so beat up that I didn't go to work for a week and a half. My whole face was just a pulp. I was going to press charges. He started calling me on the phone. Then, like a dodo bird, I went down there and did the most sickening thing. I got him out.

For the longest time, I was really afraid to move out. I thought if I ever came in and said, "Look, this isn't working, I want to move," that would be the end of me. The week I finally moved out, after I put a down payment on the apartment and took all my money out of my savings account, I came home one night from work and told him, "Flip, we have to talk."

"Oh, yeah? What's going on?"

"I don't know how to tell you this, but I'm moving out. I already put a deposit on the place."

He was cool about it at the time, but later on he was really crushed. He tried to do everything in his power to get us back together over the next four or five months. It was going to take me longer than that just to figure out where I was at and what was going on.

I made a little artistic, poem-type book that had all

these pictures in it. In there, I wrote down all the rotten things that Flip had done to me over the years. There were a lot of them. Every time I started to feel bad for him, or feeling I shouldn't have done it, I'd get that little book and start looking at it and reading it. I'd say to myself, "Man, that guy is an asshole. How could I waste that much time with him?" From the time I met him to the time I finally moved out was a span of fourteen years. Once I was really over him, I burned the book.

I remember mostly unhappy things, because my mom and dad fought a lot. My uncles and aunts lived around us and there was always a lot of friction. Fighting, arguing, total chaos like that. They got divorced. Then my mother began moving around a lot. She was a pretty woman when she was young. She went out with a lot of guys. I never knew where I was going to go to school. I never knew what I was going to do. Just different places around town. I bet you we moved a hundred times. Like I do now.

I could probably count on one hand the number of times I saw my dad. I can only remember him bringing me two presents in my life: a doll when I was little and a ring when I was a teenager. That's about all I remember about him.

It was just me and my sister and my mom who lived at home. I didn't even find out I had a sister until I was twelve years old. She lived with her aunt, because when my mother married my dad she told him that she didn't have any kids. She had had my sister out of wedlock. When I found out I had a sister, I lost it. I was an only child and all of a sudden I had a sister and an older one, too.

The three of us, we were fighting all the time. We'd fight about anything, it didn't matter. Over clothes, over TV, over food, over who was going to sleep in which bed. I don't care what it was, we fought over it.

Then I decided I wasn't going to school anymore. My mom begged me to stay in. I promised her I would never hold it against her if she'd just let me quit, that I'd never throw it up in her face. Which I really have stuck to that. She signed the papers and I quit. I regret quitting school. Boy, did I go downhill from that point on.

I started running with these people, and I forgot about homelife. I didn't want to go home no more. Home wasn't home for me. It never was. I couldn't wait to get away from it.

Then I started going out with this guy who was in a band. He was a black guy and the first black guy I ever dated. I'd sneak around to see him. He was a twenty-eight-year-old man, married with five kids.

About this time, I met my husband—he was a white guy—just walking down the street. He was in a car, and he honked the horn at me and said, "Would you like a ride home?" I told him, no, I didn't hitchhike. So he says, "I'd like to talk to you."

He parked the car and we started talking. Then he asked me for a date. I lied about my age. I said I was older, because he was older. The next thing I know, we got married. I bet I only dated him about three months.

My mother was real happy. They were all real happy that I married him. They liked him real well. I was also saved from dating black guys. They considered it that way.

I'd just turned sixteen and he was twenty-two. We was getting along real good. He was a draftsman. He bought me a house. Then, I had my daughter exactly about nine months later.

When my baby was about a month old, all of a sudden, out of the clear blue sky, I don't know how he got my phone number, but the first guy that I dated that was black called me at home. He said would I meet him. I don't know why I did it, but I did it. I took my baby and left her with my mom. I went with him and I didn't come back. I stayed for three days.

They were looking for me everywhere. I don't know how they found me, because I was in another town, two hundred miles away in a club, dancing and having a good time. The guy that I dated was playing in the band. In comes my husband and jerks me off the dance floor.

The guy I was dating stopped the band, came down, and was fighting him. I was yelling, "No, that's my husband." The manager was in it and it was just a big brawl.

"You have a choice to make right now," my guy said. "You can either stay with me or you can go home with your husband." I chose to stay with the guy, because I always thought that I really liked him over my husband anyways.

"You can stay here with him if you want to," my husband said, "while your baby's in the hospital dying of pneumonia!"

I freaked out. I said, "Oh, my God, are you kidding?"

"No, I'm not kidding. You've got to come home or else you can just let her die."

Well, you know I was young. I wasn't quite eighteen at the time. So I did; I left and I never seen that guy ever again. I loved that guy, but I loved my baby. So I went and got in the car. My mom was in the car.

He didn't say one word to me all the way home. But my mother did. "How could you do that? How could you do that? Leave your baby, disgrace your husband, disgrace your family?'' That routine.

"Because I wanted to do it," I said. "But how's the baby? That's what I'm concerned about."

"If you were so damned concerned," they both said, "you wouldn't have left her in the first place." But I was going to do it. I don't know why. I just did it.

Then when we got back to town, we dropped off my mother at her house. He took me home and he beat me all over that house. He almost killed me. The only thing that saved my life is that my cousin and uncle and aunt lived next door. They heard me screaming. They came over and busted the door down to get into him, because he had almost killed me.

After that I didn't want anything to do with him. I was just living with him until I could get away. I didn't know what I was going to do. I didn't know where I was going to go. I didn't have a job. I was really dependent on him.

Then I got raped. I would never have sex with him. He did rape me. It was such a thing as rape, but back then it wasn't recognized. That's how I got pregnant with my second baby. I didn't want to have any more kids either.

Then I lived with him and I had the baby. By this time I really hated him. Oh, I hated him with a passion. But there was nothing I could do. I was stuck. Even though he had a good job and he tried to be good to me. He was sorry about what had happened, but I could never forgive him for it.

Then he got another job and sold the house and we moved to another town. He became a salesman and was on the road a lot. Maybe once every two or three weeks I'd see him for a day. So it was just me and the two kids. I didn't know anybody. No friends. He had me totally isolated. He swore that he would buy me a new house to make up for the one we lost. He didn't do that.

Then I found out my husband was gay. These guys were calling up on the phone and I knew they were funny. You know? It's some instinct that just tells you.

I lived there until the baby was about a year old and I said, "This is it. I can't take no more. I'm leaving." I left a note that I was gone for good. He could have everything. I didn't care, he could do whatever he wanted with it.

I had a car of my own and I drove the kids and me home to live with my mom. I left the kids with her during the day and I enrolled in beauty school. I was going to become a beautician. I was halfway through and I quit.

I got involved with another guy. This was another black guy. I met this guy in a bar. He played in a band. In a way, he kind of reminded me of the first guy that I was with. I was hiding dating this guy until my divorce was final. Then when I found out that my divorce was final, I also found out I was pregnant.

My mother had heard that I was dating a black guy again, and she turned against me. Told me to get out of her house with the kids. Then I told her I was pregnant and she said, "You won't have it, 'cause I'm going to kick it out of you." She beat me and I did almost lose it. I had to go to the hospital.

My family disowned me. Turned me down. Said they would never speak to me again and they haven't. I had nowhere to go, till I could find out what I was going to do. I was already mixed up. This just made things worse. Then I was debating whether to keep dating this guy or quit dating him. But I kept thinking, "Boy, if I let them run my life now, they're going to be running it forever and I'm not going to let them do that. I'm going to still date him."

I had my baby first and then I got married to my

second husband. He got me an apartment and I had the kids with me. His job wasn't enough to support us. His band was on and off all the time. But I wanted security, so I got on welfare. I hadn't finished school and I hadn't finished beauticians' school. I didn't have much I could do to get a job. I should have used my head then, but I didn't.

I was stuck with three kids and I was going through hell. It was the '60s, I lived in a black area and there was a racial thing going on. I was scared to death to go out of the house, because it was a time when the blacks and whites were really fighting one another. You had to hide and it was really bad.

I decided that I had to move out, so I got a job. It was in a go-go dancer bar. That was the only thing I could get. That was it, the bottom line.

Me and my husband wasn't getting along. He wasn't going for my job. I wasn't going for his job. We started fighting. He went his way and I went my way.

I started out in this club downtown as a waitress wearing this little outfit. The money wasn't so good. They kept telling me, "You'd make more money if you was a dancer. You've got a good body. You would really make the money."

I started thinking, "Boy, my kids need this and my kids need that." They were my main concern, my kids, not me. I says, "Yeah, I could really get them what they want and they wouldn't have to do without. Eventually, I could get out of this and buy a nicer place to live. I could get a car."

"Okay," I said after I thought about the money situation, "I'll start dancing." I never had danced before, but I never had waitressed before either. Watching the girls who was working in there dancing, it looked so easy. Actually, it was easy except for the mental thing about it. The next week, I put on an outfit and I got up there and danced. I made more money than I made being a waitress. I thought, "Boy, they were right. This is easy money. And I kind of like it. I like the attention that you get.''

The mental thing is having somebody look at you like that, the guys all yelling at you and saying things to you. Some guys wouldn't make cracks about you and they'd be okay. There'd be some of them who'd come in there and say, ''What's a girl like you doing in a place like this? Why are you doing this? Can't you do something better with your life?''

''I really don't think it's any of your business what I do with my life,'' I would say. ''What I do with my life is my business. I don't have any more to say to you.'' I'd get up and leave them. I was that type of person that I would just tell you how I felt right then. If you didn't like it, to hell with you.

The guys that was real nice and didn't say anything to me would want to ask me out for a date, but we weren't allowed to date. I'd just put them on hold, ''Maybe next week,'' to build up the clientele for the bar and to make them money, to make me money.

I started hooking from the dancing job, because they were telling me I could make *more* money than the dancing if I went out with guys for money. For a long time I didn't want to try it, but all of a sudden, I said, finally, ''Okay, yeah, I think I will.''

My first date was a five-hundred-dollar date. I thought, ''Gee, how easy. How easy! It's not work. It's fun.'' I started doing it after that.

Pretty soon I had enough money to buy a house. I moved into it with my kids, but I didn't like being by myself. I was used to having a man around me. A man to come home to even if we didn't get along. It was like a security thing. Plus I was lonely.

I didn't stay lonely very long. I met this other guy. He was a black guy. I never dated white guys after my first husband, never. I don't know why. I started dating him and we moved in together. He knew I was a dancer. He also knew I was a hooker. I wasn't going to get married again. I'd had enough of that, but I was going to live with him to see what it was like. In the beginning, this man was nice to me. Before long I was pregnant again.

Right before I had my baby by him, my mother wasn't going to put up with this again, when she found out that I was pregnant. I had spent the night with her and my kids at her house. That next morning, I got up and she said to me, "I want you to stay here, watch your own kids, and don't go nowheres today. I'll be right back. I have to go make an errand."

"Okay," I said, "fine." She leaves.

I bet she wasn't gone ten minutes and there was a knock on the door. A teenage girl come in. I go, "What are you doing here?"

"I come to watch the kids," she says. Behind her was two guys from the nuthouse. They had the straitjacket, everything, just like they talk about, and they put me in it.

"What are you doing?"

"We're taking you," they said. "We're taking you away." I was screaming and crying and carrying on. The kids didn't know what was going on. They put me in that wagon and they take me to the crazy place. They wouldn't answer no questions, except I said, "I want to know who put me in here and I want to know now. I have a right to know." They told me my mother did. My mother had me committed.

It was hell. The other people was in there, you would think that they was all right for a minute. They'd be talking to me and I'd be saying, "Oh, God, how can we get out of here? What are we going to do?"

"Yeah, what *are* we going to do?" they'd say. All of a sudden, they'd flip out. Be chasing birds, saying, "Get that bird. Get that bird over there."

"What bird?" I'd be going. "Gee, God, am I going to be like this? Oh, get me out of here."

Then I'd scream and try to talk to one of the nurses there. They'd say that I was nuts and to go sit down with the rest of the nuts. They wouldn't talk to nobody.

"I want to talk to a lawyer."

"You're not talking to no lawyer."

"Let me write a letter." So I wrote a letter. They threw it away.

I stayed in there for two weeks and then I had a hearing, right? The day of the hearing they said, "We have found out that you're not mentally ill and you're going to be released."

My mother was there. I went and grabbed her. I wanted to kill her. I started to fight her and they said, "You were going to get released today, but because you're acting like this you're going straight back upstairs until you can act right."

"You would want to kill your mother, too," I said, "if she had you committed. There is no way I'm going to let her get by with that."

They says, "If you don't calm down right now, you're going back upstairs." So I had to calm down. They told me I was released and I could go. They took my mom away, because they knew I was going to kill her.

Then they said, "There's two bus tickets. One to get you there and one to get you home. You have a hearing about your kids this morning. You can go and find out if you get to keep your kids or not." I thought they were kidding me, but it was for real.

I took the bus down to the juvenile court and at that time they didn't give me a chance to fight or nothing. I didn't have a lawyer or nothing. The judge, he says, "At this time, we are going to take these kids away from you, until you prove to be a stable mother, because of your incidents that we've got reports about." They told me, "You have no rights here. As far as we're concerned, you have no rights. Until you prove that you are a stable person, you cannot have these kids back and your mother gets them."

I hated her with a passion. I wanted to kill her. I mean, really kill her. Not just say it, but do it. I felt like I lost both my arms and legs when they told me that. My ex-husband was sitting there, too, the second one. He came over to me and said, "You deserve everything you got."

I clawed him to death. I just fought him and told him to get out of my face, get out of my life, and don't ever come back. I says, "I got rid of you a long time ago. Why are you back here?" I just lost it.

I couldn't find the guy I was living with. He was nowhere around when I got back to the house. There I was with nothing, all alone with nothing. I can't even explain it, how it really felt. After I cried for hours and hours and hours, I thought, "I'm going to get myself together and I'm going to get my kids back, one way or another. They're not going to win. I'm not going to let them win."

This guy I was living with wasn't a monster then. He felt sorry for me and he was going to do all he could to help me get them back. There was a case-worker coming to the house every day, talking to me and watching how I lived, how I was doing. I told her I was pregnant. I said, "You might have took the other three from me, but you will not get this one— never, if I have to leave out of town."

This lady, she really felt for me. She said, "I know what you're going through." I had told her the whole story, too. "I'll tell you what. I'm going to help you get your kids back, because you're a good mother. I can tell. I know you would never do anything to harm your kids. Your mother's wrong. Just because you're with a black man don't mean that you're a disfit mother." They had interviewed my mother, too. She said, "Actually, your mother is so prejudiced that she

276

don't need to have that next child over there with her, because she really deep down inside hates blacks."

"I know. I have been trying to tell people this for years, but nobody listens to me. I have been through the mill for years with this racial thing. I'm tired of it, but there's nothing I can do about it. Now I have this baby inside of me, and I'm going to fight for it. I'm going to keep it, and I want my other ones back. I went through hell to keep these kids and I'm going to have them back."

I had the baby and they gave me visitation rights for my other kids. My mother and me were enemies. The court told her she had to let me have them kids on the weekends. I'd bring them to my house and then take them back again.

Finally, I didn't have to take them back no more. The lady told me I could keep them. So I kept them. They knew I was living with the guy I was living with.

We were getting along real great. Then I went back to work, back to the only thing I knew. I went to dancing in a bar.

He didn't want me to do it at first, but then after a while we were having real hard times, because he didn't keep a job. He was like living on me. Then all of a sudden we started fighting like cats and dogs. Everything just started falling apart. He was a beater. He would beat the kids. My mom and me was fighting, and I'd try to get her to get the kids and take them for a while to get away from him. Then I'd miss the kids and I'd want them to come back to me.

He was a heroin addict. I never figured it out till we were through. There were times when he would be really good to me and the kids. Real good. The kids liked him those times. Then he'd flare up and I didn't know why. Then, he drank a lot, too, and mixing the two together, he was a maniac.

I had stopped hooking for a while, but he kept saying that he wanted me to work and get everything in order, because things were falling apart. He blamed it on me, so I started doing it again. Then that's how we lived after a time, my hooking alone. He didn't work. He was sitting at home, beating my butt all the time. For anything, just anything.

I was taking care of these kids. I was trying to be a good mother, which was my main objective, that was all I really cared about. I never left them with him.

I also cared about having a man around me for some reason. I just had to have a man around me. I stayed with him up and down like that for ten years.

Then one day, I just packed up the kids and I left. Left my house and everything and went to my mom's house and stayed.

He kept coming over there trying to get me to come back with him. I told him no through the door and he tried to break down the door. We had to call the police. Then he'd leave, because he'd get scared.

He called us up on the phone. He talked to my mother, but I was on the extension. He said, "I want you to hear what your bitching daughter would be getting if she were here right now." And you could hear all this, Crash! Bam! Bang!

"You are crazy," my mom said. "I'm calling the police right now."

We took the police over there with us. He'd already left. When we went into my house, we couldn't believe our eyes. The house was like a tornado hit it. He even ripped up the carpet. It was like a maniac that just lost his mind. He tore up everything. There wasn't anything you could save. He took a hammer to everything. I have pictures of it.

I was real scared then. So I left the kids at my mom's. I said, "Mom, I don't have any choice but to get out of town." I hated to leave my kids. It about killed me, but I had to do it. I knew he'd try to kill me or the kids or my mom.

"Don't worry about us," she said. "I'll take care of us."

I went to California to start over with this guy I had met. Come to find out, this guy was no good.

I get to California and I'm staying with his relatives, right? We had nowhere to live. I was working in a stripper place. All of a sudden, he becomes my pimp. I wouldn't give him my money. I said, "No, I'm not going to do that. There's no way. You're going to have to kill me first, because I don't do that. I'm going back home. If I'm going to get killed, I'm going to get killed by the first one I just left. Not by you." I was real brave and stood up to him.

"You're too brave," he said, "so I'm going to kill you right now." And he took that gun out. I thought he was going to blow my brains out. I was scared to death, but I'd already mouthed off to him. He beats me up and takes that gun and beats my face in. I mean, I'm lucky I have no scars from how bad he ripped me.

This was what he intended all along and I didn't know it. I didn't know him very well, you know. I told his relatives, his sister, and she was scared of him, too. She said, "Honey, all I can tell you is, the first chance you have to get away from him, you just do it." She says, "But it's going to be hard."

I really had nowhere to turn to. I was in a strange town, never been there before. I didn't know what to do. So I had to stay there and take that abuse for eight months with him, till I could get away from him.

I lied to him. I had my mom call me. I didn't want to tell my mother what had happened. Boy, I just got away from the other maniac, and I didn't want her to know what happened. So I didn't tell her. I just asked her to call me and tell me that there was an emergency and I had to come home for my kids. Which wasn't a lie, but who cares anyway?

He heard her on the phone, because he monitored all my calls. He said, "Okay. I'll have to let you go

279

back." That's the only way I got away from him, and I was lucky to do it. Real lucky. There were a lot of people who wouldn't and couldn't get away from people like that.

I started working in a bar again, dancing. My kids was with my mother. I knew it was a stable place for them to stay and I wasn't stable again. I was mixed up, because of the confusion I just went through. I couldn't handle it. The kids wouldn't have understood, but I knew. I go and move in with one of the girls I danced with.

Then I met Henry. He was like a god. It was like fate, because he had never been in that bar in his life. All of a sudden, he had broken up with his girlfriend. He saw this sign that said, GIRLS! GIRLS! GIRLS! He wanted to drink. He wanted to set and see girls and have a drink. I was one of the girls he saw in there.

I didn't want nothing to do with him. He was too cute. I thought, "Oh, God, here's another trouble." I was trying to go straight, do my job, and go home at night. I didn't want to be bothered. I told him so. "You, I don't want nothing to do with you."

Then he asked me out on a date. It was nice because he was like a gentleman. A *real* gentleman. I really fell head over heels. But I didn't trust him, and I told him so. "I've been through too many men. They start out to be sweet and then become devils."

Then he found out I was older than I said I was. I lied about my age. But I told him I had four kids. I never lied about the kids. The next thing you know he got me an apartment and we moved in together. Then I got the kids back and they come to live with us. It was hard for him at first to adjust to the kids. He was a lot younger than I was, but he was from a big family.

When I met his family, that's what really decided me that I could trust him. His mother was the sweetest person that I'd ever met. Sixteen brothers and sisters and they were all well-mannered gentlemen and lady-like people. I knew that I was in good hands.

From then on it was like a fairy tale. All he did was anything he could to help me and the kids. He just really worshiped me. The only problem we've had is been me finding a job. A good job. Something that could help him, because he's been the bread-giver here, working and taking care of me and these kids. From my past experience, I knew how hard it was to be the person to take care of all the responsibility. So now I've been working part-time, doing odds-and-ends jobs just to help him out. But I don't feel good about myself, because I can't get a real good job. And then I'm getting older, too.

After all this lifeline, here, I'm getting toward the end. That's how I feel. I'm in my early forties. When you get to that point in your age, you feel like there's not much more of your life to go. I finally get started and I feel like it's ending.

I went to the doctor and I had this lump in my breast. He said, "Oh, well, it's probably nothing. You're only twenty-nine."

My mother said, "Get it out. Just have them take it out."

"But, Mother, it's nothing."

"Just have them take it out." Good old Mom. So I did.

I went into the hospital. I was awake during the surgery. The doctor took the lump and dangled it over my face. "Look!" he said. You know how surgeons are, they think everything is interesting. As a kid, I saved my tonsils. I saved my teeth. I had my appendix in a jar. I didn't want my body parts in the garbage. I liked looking at them, so I collected all my body parts. But this part I didn't want to keep, much less see it. He says, "Look at that raspberry end on it. It's fine."

"Okay, okay." So he sewed me up and I went home.

I called a few days later. I said, "You know what? I want to go swimming. Can I go swimming with these stitches yet?"

"I've been trying to call you," he said.

"Yeah?"

"You have colloid carcinoma."

"What?"

"You have cancer."

"What?"

"Come to my office tomorrow and I'll explain it all to you. Here's the nurse. She'll make an appointment for you."

I'm sitting in my room and the walls are spinning, like I'm in a dream, like I'm falling. Here's this guy on the phone, very casually saying, "Oh, yeah, I've been meaning to call you. You've got cancer. Talk to the nurse." He'd sworn to me that it was nothing. "It's nothing. You don't even need to have it taken out."

I couldn't go to work the next morning. I called up and told them I was sick. I went over to my boyfriend's house and he was fairly comforting. He didn't believe it, actually. Nobody could believe it.

So I went to the hospital and I walked into the doctor's office. It was summer outside, so I had on this sundress. He stood there in front of me and he said, "Here's what we do for this. We usually just cut right around here," and he made a circle around my breast with his hand near my chest, "and we remove the breast, and we remove the nipple, and we take all the lymph nodes and you'll be fine."

The phone rang. The nurse said it was so-and-so.

He looked at me and said, "Just a minute." He picked up the phone. He just drew on me how he was going to take my breast off, then he starts talking to this guy on the phone about wines, some deal that he's got going. They're having this long conversation about vintages and wineries. This man just told me that he's going to *take my breast off*.

I waited and it seemed like an eternal conversation. Here he's talking like it's nothing to have your breast taken off. He didn't even tell me if I was going to die.

He gets off the phone and I said, "What are the other alternatives? Maybe that's what you always do, but what else is there?"

"That's what we like to do."

"Yeah, but what *else* is there? I don't know if I want that."

"We could do a thing where we take a third of the breast or we could cut around the lump and look at that and take out your lymph nodes."

"I want to go to a medical library."

"Only doctors can go there, but I'll write you a note. You sure you want to do this?"

"Yeah, I'm sure I want to do this." I went to the library in the hospital and gave them the note, and I read all about colloid carcinomas. I wanted to know what my chances were. I researched through it and found out how old you live to be with different cancers. I discovered that 50 percent of the women who got the kind of cancer I had lived to be seventy-five. Fifty percent of all women live to be seventy-five. That's average. I thought, "Oh, this is pretty good cancer, considering the kinds of cancer you can get."

I went back and told my doctor, "I want to talk to somebody else." I went down to UCLA, and my cousin takes me into the John Wayne Cancer Center —this big, black monolith. It's huge with hardly any windows and they're black, too. The only building on the entire campus that's black is the cancer center. Where do you go to die? The black building.

The coldest man in the universe was my doctor. They're famous there and they think they're wonderful. He was just really a nasty, unemotional man. I said, "Just answer these questions. Am I crazy to not have my breast removed and to do what I want to do which is to have the tissue around the lump taken out along with the lymph nodes?"

"No, you're not crazy."

"Would you do this, if you were a woman?"

"I can't answer that question."

"What would you tell your wife?"

He wouldn't answer. He refused to give me a yes, but he didn't give me a no either. I said, "I just want to know if it's completely foolish to not have a mastectomy."

"No, it's not." It was all I could do to hold back my tears, but because he was so cold and unemotional. I wasn't going to let him see me cry. I wasn't going to cry in front of him. The minute I walked out of the room, I just bawled.

I went to see a lot of people. One woman I went to worked where they do mammograms. She said, "I think you should have them both removed and have implants put in. Then you'll never get cancer."

"What?"

"That's what I would do if I were you."

"But you lose all sensation and your nipples don't have anything if they even survive, because there's no blood supply to them. Certainly they're numb. You can't breast-feed and you're just like a bionic woman." Take everything out and then you're all fine, you're just fake. I didn't like that at all.

I went back to the doctor who wanted to give me a mastectomy. I told him what I wanted to do. About a day later, the *New England Journal of Medicine* came out with an Italian study of women who had just had some tissue removed around where the lump was and their lymph nodes were checked. Then they had radiation follow-up. They had the same rate of health ten years later as the women who had a mastectomy. It was perfect timing, right in the same month that I was trying to figure all this out.

I got the article in to my doctor and he said, "I just got the *Journal* and read it. All right, let's just take out the tissue around the lump. Let's take out the lymph nodes, because I want to see what you've got in here."

My mother has to come out. I told her, "I made all the decisions. I did all the research and went to all the doctors. This is what I have and this is what I'm going to do. I don't want you to tell me that you don't think it's a good idea, because all I want around me is people who think it's a good idea." She was good. She came out here and acted like she thought it was a good idea. She understood that at twenty-nine years old you just don't want them to cut your breast off. I wanted to be able to breast-feed. I wanted to be sexual.

Between the time they told me I had cancer and I had the operation, I didn't know whether I had cancer in my lymph nodes; I didn't know anything. It was like I was a kid again. You know how the days were real long, because you don't think about the future. When you're a kid, you don't think about the future because it's too abstract. I couldn't think about the future, because I might not be there. I was in suspended animation.

I went ahead and had the surgery. The doctor came in afterward and he was just ecstatic and thrilled that he hadn't found anything else. Everything looked really good. Then I discovered what a wonderful person he was. He was turning himself inside out with joy because it looked like my chances were really good of probably not having a recurrence. He turned out to be very, very kind. He just couldn't handle delivering news like that to people. He only wanted to give people the good news.

I've known him now over the years, because I go back for checkups every year, and he is so full of enthusiasm and warmth when it's good news. But when it's bad, he didn't know what to do. So that's why he got on the phone. Now I understand him. But at the time I thought he was the biggest creep in the world to do this to me. He was older. He should have had the job down by this time. He certainly delivered that message before.

My third husband, that was a good one. That was a real good one. We were married for six years. When I got out of that one I felt like I just walked out of a war zone. My mother always told me, "Never marry a man who doesn't like his mother." I didn't listen to her, and let me tell you, "*Never* marry a man who doesn't like his mother."

If I had one word to describe Cliff, it would be *angry*. We didn't communicate, we didn't talk. To let you know the extent of his temper, he came home from a trip once and I had washed the linen. I put a fresh towel in his bathroom, but it happened to be the same color as the towel I took off the rack. When he got home it was the same color towel, so he assumed I had not washed his towel, and he was livid. That was worth about two hours of screaming and ranting and raving. You just never knew what was going to tick him off.

One night, my younger son and Cliff's fourteen-year-old boy were staying with us. Cliff had some bottle rockets that he had kept in a bathroom drawer. He opened the drawer and the rockets were gone. He immediately accused the boys of doing it and reamed them out. They were scared to death of him, because when he was angry, it wasn't just anger, it was rage. I went back into the bathroom, opened the drawer, and reached way into the back. There they were. So I called him out and said, "Look." I was half disgusted with him. There was no sense of apology or anything. I walked out of the room and I looked back at him and said, "I think you're just paranoid."

He came over, picked me up by my throat, and carried me across the room. I found myself on the bed with him over me, his hands on my throat and a look in his eye that left me with no doubt in my mind that he was perfectly capable of killing me right then and there. He wanted to. I could see it.

"This is not a good idea," I thought. So I stared him down. That was the first and last time that it happened. Unfortunately, you just don't forget. I really thought it was the pressures he was under. He had his own business and problems with his partner who was a big, big doper. Everything was always Mickey's fault. I thought if I could get him away from Mickey, maybe things would settle down. The only problem was when I got rid of Mick, then everything was my fault.

He got a new job and was on the road all the time. That's probably what kept us married the last three years, because he was very seldom home. I liked that. We were getting along. When you see each other two days a week, it's not difficult to get along.

With Cliff, I really didn't understand. I'm a fairly intelligent person, though the idea of psychological abuse really didn't strike me at all. I thought, "Things could be worse. He could be beating me." My mother thought he was the perfect husband. He was home when he was supposed to be home. He didn't drink. He didn't womanize. He didn't gamble. He could fix things. The man could hang a door with a penknife. He could do anything. Nobody could understand why I was so miserable. It was like being wrapped in cellophane. Everybody thinks you're so normal. You look okay, but you can't breathe. You simply cannot breathe.

I realized years later that I was in a clinical depression. I lost fifteen pounds. I cried all the time, but nobody knew. I was very secretive about it. He never knew that there was a problem. My husband said to me on our sixth anniversary, a few months before I left him, "We've had our moments, but all in all it's been a damn good marriage." I sat there thinking to myself, "Who the fuck have you been living with for six years? It sure wasn't me."

I spent one afternoon trying to figure out how I was going to manage to blow my brains out and fix it so that my son wouldn't come home from school and find me. That's about as close as I ever got to saying, "Okay, I check out here, this is it."

I didn't know how to get out. I felt so trapped. I never said I was going to leave. What he would say is, "If you don't like what's happening here, you can pack your fucking bags and get out."

"Okay, fine, I'll be out by Monday," I would say.

"There's no way you could make it on your own. There's no way. Without me you'd be nowhere. You can't even write a check, for Christ's sake. Who do you think you are? What makes you think that you could get out and live on your own?"

There was never a discussion. There was never a talk. It was sitting there knowing that if I said one word, he was going to come across the table and nail me to the wall. So you don't argue, you just listen. I could sit there and connect with him, make eye contact, look like I was listening, and I'd be off someplace else. I'd just pull down the blinds, fly off, and be gone. He'd be reaming me a new one and I'd say, "Yeah, you're right. I'm a fucking liar and a thief and a cheat, because once in a while I forget to put down a bank withdrawal. I am stealing.''

You can't put any logic to it. But what happens is you do get to the point where you really believe that he is right. "Maybe he's right. Maybe he's right and I am a bitch.''

I had no money. No money. I knew that if I went to the bank and drew a thousand dollars from the checking account and got out, he'd come after me. It just was an all-around bad thing. I kept thinking, "Okay, I can do this another six months. In six months, I'll be ready and I can get out. In three months, I can do this.'' You just keep pushing it off and pushing it off. Then you go through a period of time when things are relatively stable and you think, "Maybe things could work out.''

I felt guilty. I felt guilty because I didn't love him as much as I thought I should have. The point was, I'd married him because I *knew* I'd never love him so much that he would ever really hurt me.

We had an argument. By this time, I had a job with a hotel catering division. I had drinks after work with a gentleman client, because that was the only time we could get together to talk. I told Cliff I'm going to have a drink with this guy after work, but I'd be home by eight o'clock. I got home and didn't think anything more of it. At a wedding the following Saturday night, in conversation, I caught that he had counted my douches and deduced that I had used one out of sequence. He put two and two together and decided that I had slept with this guy.

I thought, "I don't need this. I really don't need this. Why am I doing this?'' So I walked in and said, "Look, I'm sorry. My girlfriend is getting a place and I'm moving in with her.''

It was like a light went on. "Okay,'' is all he said.

That was it. We parted. No more fights, no more

nothing. He thought that I was just making a point. He expected me to come back. For a year he expected me to show up at the door any moment. He didn't even tell his family that I'd been gone for three months. He would go around and put things of mine out in the house. Somebody would come over and he'd say, "Oh, you just missed her. She had to go to work," and pretended to everybody that I hadn't left.

It was a January night. I was coming home from work. It wasn't very late. I had moved into the building in April of the previous year, so I hadn't been there all that long and I didn't really know anybody. I went into the vestibule and somebody came in behind me.

"Give me your jewelry," this guy said. I used to wear a lot of costume jewelry rings at the time. But there was one ring that was worth more and I liked it more. He got the others, but he couldn't get that one off. I asked him not to take it.

He had this piece of broken bottle in his hand. He threatened to cut me if I didn't do what he said. He started to undress me. It was awful, but I didn't want to get cut.

Then he pulled out his cock and he was kind of hard. He made me go down on him, which was a horrible experience, because he hadn't washed in a long, long time. It really stank. I nearly threw up, but I figured that was not a good thing to do. I was afraid he might hurt me.

Then he tried to rape me, but he didn't really know how to do it. I was not aroused so there was no lubrication. He couldn't penetrate. He tried and it wasn't working.

Nobody was coming in or out of the building. Nobody was going by. I didn't scream. I don't know why. Screaming never occurred to me. He wanted to get inside and go upstairs with me. I told him my husband was going to be home soon, even though I didn't have a husband. I tried to talk to him calmly. He was very young, maybe eighteen or something.

Finally I convinced him to go, and the strangest thing happened. Before he left, he buttoned up my coat for me as though he was concerned about me. He was such a pitiful person.

He told me if I called the police, he would come back and kill me. The minute he left, I ran upstairs and called the police. Then I took a bath. I felt so filthy.

I called the man I was seeing at the time. He came over. The cops came and were very nice, they were very good. I went and I looked at some mug shots. Of course, he wasn't there.

I went back with Kevin to his place. It was funny about Kevin. He didn't really understand what happened. He was very sympathetic and everything, but he wanted to make love. That was the last thing I ever wanted to do. I said to myself afterward, "If I had been a person who never had any good sexual experiences, what would that have done to me?" Considering what it did do, imagine what might have happened.

All the paranoia that was ever in me—and I'm sure it was there—came out in a peculiar way. Like I would have to lock the door three times. Even though I knew I'd already locked it, I'd have to get out of bed and lock it again. I could not walk down that street at night by myself for a long time. At first, I couldn't even go out at night. If I did, I certainly could never come back home.

People said I should move to another place. But it didn't matter where I was, I would be afraid. I carried it around inside of me.

Any man who looked at me, I wished that I could kill him. The rage was incredible. Literally kill. It's lucky that I didn't have a gun, because I might have. Sometimes, when I would pass a bunch of construction workers who were yelling and whistling and the other stupid nonsense, I would fantasize that they would have this horrible pain in their genitals whenever they did this. I'd look back at them and they would feel this *terrible pain*. Of course, they wouldn't connect this with what they had just done. This was my imaginary revenge. If I couldn't kill them, at least they would be damaged in some way.

Physically, I wasn't harmed. But psychologically, it was bad. I think I've dealt with most of it now. It's been nineteen years, and that's a hell of a long time. For the first ten years, it was much more important to me than it should have been. I've resolved a lot of it. I don't get as angry. Even when people say very sexist things, I'm generally able to deal with it in a relatively calm fashion. Not always. It's kind of silly to live in a perpetual state of ignition. There are still things that haven't been totally resolved, but everybody's life has things in it that aren't resolved.

6. Four Lives

These four women's life stories illustrate the extraordinary diversity of individual experiences that I listened to. Each one is distinctive and unique, but, taken together, they show different sides of what it is to be a woman in America today—like the many facets on one gemstone.

This is by no means a "representative" cross section; these four women are not here because they are "typical." On the contrary, their stories demonstrate that there is no typical interview, no typical woman. The events in women's lives, I discovered, zig and zag unexpectedly. And the choices they make in the face of new circumstances are often unpredictable. Just when I would make the mistake of "pigeon-holing" one of my interviewees, she would unexpectedly open whole new frontiers of her humanity for me to see.

Superficially these four women are alike in many ways: All are between the ages of forty and fifty years old. Each began her young adult life in a traditional marriage. They have all experienced remarkable reversals in their lives. Their human fragility is balanced by a stubborn determination to survive, and they share an incredible stoicism in the face of frustration, intolerance, and abuse. All four of these women have been subjected to some degree of physical violence at the hands of the men. Each of them has a self-sacrificing disposition which mutes her own inner feelings and personal needs. When the circumstances in their lives required a change, their reactions were innovative and inventive, downright radical. Despite their conservative upbringings, all four women are willing to take chances.

Their stories are divided into two pairs. Ruby and Peg don't know each other, but these two women live about an hour's drive apart near a large midwestern city. Their ages are nearly identical. Both grew up in Appalachian hill country. If I were to introduce them, they would find many shared moments in their lives, they might even become friends, and yet they could hardly be more different from one another.

Sharon and Grace are from cultures and childhoods as different from one another as Ruby's and Peg's backgrounds are alike. Sharon lives in sunny southern California, Grace lives in New York City. Sharon is white, slender, blond, and rich. Her life would seem to be the stuff that the TV miniseries and celebrity novels are made of. Grace is black, a little overweight, definitely underpaid. She spent years living with her children in a run-down hotel room provided by city government as housing for the homeless. Now she has a job counseling women who find themselves homeless like she was. But Sharon's life has not been so privileged nor Grace's so bleak as one might assume.

Ruby

My earliest memory, I was four years old. My dad was driving the car, my sister and I were in the backseat. We were going to Grandma's on a Sunday afternoon. Mom said to me, "I won't have your face less than clean." So she got a hanky out, spit on it, and kept wiping at the side of my forehead. There was a birthmark there and she never even knew it.

Why her and Daddy had so many problems, I didn't ask and never did know. I figured if Daddy wanted me to know, he'd tell me.

I'm about the only one of the four kids that can remember our real mom. I can say she never hollered at any of us. She let Daddy do it. She was one of those people who said, "Wait till your father gets home." She let him do the disciplining and he did. I got my share.

Mom, she was sick. So in May of '47 after my dad got out of the service, we moved to the country for Mother's health. We really had a good summer that year. We didn't have much money, but we had the animals and the garden. We had homemade clothes, but they were decent and nobody knew any different back then. After the war, people were trying to get back on their feet.

We weren't there but a few months when Mom left. Daddy told us they just couldn't get along anymore and she wanted out. She wanted to take me and my brother with her and leave the other two children with Daddy. Daddy said, "No, if you want two, you have to take all four." So we stayed with Daddy. We didn't have no choice.

I cried. Daddy said, "You have to be strong. When she wants to, she'll come back." We kind of pulled ourselves together. I had to learn how to cook. Daddy said, "You're just going to have to do it, there's nobody else. Your sister isn't old enough. She'd rather take care of the boys than she would do the cooking."

I was ten that November. I did the cooking and Sis watched the boys which was a handful for a little girl nine years old.

At Christmastime, Mom sent us a package. Daddy

went to pick it up at the post office. On the way home he had an accident and the only thing I got out of that box that she sent us was a hairbrush and a mirror that didn't get broke. I think my sister got the same thing. There was a pair of little underpanties apiece. The boys got a T-shirt apiece and a little car. It meant a lot at the time. I was still hurt. The fact of the whole problem was that she didn't tell me she was going. I thought we were closer than that.

Not long after that we got the news. When Dad got home that day, he stood out there at the gate for a few minutes before he come into the house. I knew by the way he was standing there, holding that piece of paper, that something was wrong. When he came in, he had this strange look on his face. He sat down on the couch and called us all over to him. He told us that my mom was dead.

"No, you're lying to us," I kept telling him. "You're lying, Dad. It's not true."

"I'm sorry. It is true."

"Are you going to bring her back here?" I knew what a funeral was.

"No, I can't bring her back here. She's already cremated," he said. She had been in a fire and her body was burned almost beyond recognition.

Every other time she had left, Daddy had sent her the money to come back. I believe he loved her or he wouldn't have done that. But this time he didn't. He told her she had to come back herself. He wasn't sending her no money. So, she was picking strawberries and staying in the cheapest place she could stay in, trying to make the money to come back home.

Her room was this old boxcar they had added to the back of the house. It was off the kitchen. The old lady who owned the boardinghouse would go around and dump all the ashtrays. Apparently she didn't check them before she threw them in the trash and it caught on fire. The stove was an old gas one that probably had a leak in it. It exploded. There was no way my mother could get out. The only window in her room had a fan in it that was too heavy for her to move. When they found her body, it was under the springs of the bed. They knew it was her from the dental work.

We stayed down there in the country another year before Daddy come back to town. He just couldn't make it anymore. He only went down there for her in the first place.

We wasn't back there at Grandma's more than six or eight weeks when he took us and left us at the orphanage. Grandma couldn't take care of all of us and there wasn't room. He paid fifty dollars a week for all four of us to stay there. I lived there four years.

It wasn't a hard life. I learned a lot. I already knew how to cook. I learned how to sew. When somebody would talk about being raised in an orphanage, I couldn't understand why they didn't like it. I always felt good about it. The nuns actually loved us. We got to go to the circus. We went to the opera once. I loved that. I went to the ballet once. Went to the symphony once. Oh, it was fantastic. I've never been since. Whenever I see an opera on television it makes my husband mad, because he don't want me to watch it. He don't like that kind of stuff.

Dad started seeing this one woman, Gwendolyn. Her little five-year-old girl was at the orphanage, too. Gwendolyn was alone, like Daddy, and had never married. Her daughter was born out of wedlock. When they had known each other about six weeks, he told us they were going to get married. I was devastated. There was no way he could even think about marrying anybody else.

At first I didn't say anything, but that night when I went to bed, I cried myself to sleep. Sister Bernarda came out of her room and went around to each bed until she figured out where the crying was coming from. So she got to me. I was sixteen. She wanted to know what the problem was. I told her. She said to me, she said, "That's not for you to worry about. You're going to have a mother again."

"I don't want her as my mother." There was something about Gwendolyn that I didn't like. Just gut instinct. But I was comforted by the sister. I got to the place where I didn't ask why anymore. I just accepted it like I did a lot of things in my life, just wrote it down as experience and went on from there.

Sister Bernarda must have told Daddy that I was upset, because the next weekend when he came, he told all four of us, "You don't have to call her Mom, but I would like for you to." The expression in his voice made me think that if I don't do it I'd be displeasing him. I didn't ever want to do anything to displease him. So I called her Mom.

They got married. They did the big schmo. The next weekend we got to go from the orphanage and stay with them at Grandma's—five kids, Mamma and Daddy and Grandma in a three-bedroom home.

It wasn't so bad when we were at Grandma's, because she kind of kept a rein on all of us. The only time I remember Daddy hitting Gwendolyn was when she had cursed Grandma. She had called Grandma a son of a bitch. But that wasn't a first-time offense for her as far as her mouth was concerned. She was the most foulmouthed person I've ever met and to be a Catholic. I'd never heard anybody raise their voice till Daddy married her. Seems like she was always hollering at somebody for something. Mostly in town that was all it was, just hollering and yelling.

Then Daddy and her bought a place down in the country when I was seventeen. It was real remote, rural, just the hills. That's where I met Billy. You had to pass our house to get to his. He'd stop on the way home. Just like any other kids, most of the time we just sit around and talked. I didn't find out till later, but he kept telling this one brother that he was going to marry me. His brother kept saying, "She won't have nothing to do with you."

In November, I turned eighteen and everything seemed to come to a head. The twins had been born in October and Mom was pregnant again. By then I'd just about had my fill. She was whipping up on all the kids and treating them like they was her servants. She would make her daughter, Susan, go out in the creek and wash out the diapers. This was in the winter. That child was only ten years old. There'd be ice on the edge of the creek. It wasn't but a little ditch. They had a made a place where the water would set for a little while and then ease on out. She'd be out there doing two or three buckets of dirty diapers.

It seems like Mom was hollering at her constantly. She wet the bed. No wonder the kid wet the bed, under the tension she was under. The boys did, too. I got to the place where I could tell when they were going to wet the bed. The undercurrent was constant.

A couple of times I tried to do the diapers for Susan and I got reprimanded for it. So I'd turn around and grit my teeth. Go upstairs, sit on the bed, and let the feeling pass, the feeling to speak out and let her know how I felt.

Right before Christmas, Billy asked me to marry him. I told him, "No, I'm not ready to get married yet." He got me a Christmas present. I didn't have any money to give him anything. He said it didn't make any difference. I said, "Well, it does to me." I gave him back the present and said, "I don't want it." It was a jewelry box and a necklace which was real popular then, a thick chain with a big gold pendant thing on the end of it that looked like a lion to me.

Then me and Mom had it out. It sounds so silly now, but at the time it was real important. I had this skirt and it had like a plastic belt that went with it. I went and got the skirt to put it on and I couldn't find my belt anywhere. So I went downstairs and I said to Mom, "Have you seen my black belt?"

"Yeah," she said, "I borried it."

"Who gave you permission to borrow my belt?" I said.

"I don't have to have permission to borrow anything from you."

"That's my belt," I said. "You keep your filthy hands off it."

"You don't talk to me like that, young lady. Wait until your dad gets home," she said. She knew better than to hit me, because I think I could have floored her.

That was the last time I ever got a spanking from my dad. I was eighteen and I would not cry. He hit me with a leather belt that he used on us kids. And believe me he used it.

In February Billy asked me again. I said, "Okay." But I told him right at the start, "Billy, I don't love you. I'm not even sure if you love me. It'll have to come to me. I'm not sure what love is." I still cannot be positive what love is. After thirty years being married to the man, I can't tell you that's what it is.

He went and got me a ring. I wore it for about six weeks. Everything at home just seemed to get worse and I thought, "I've got to get out of here, I've got to get away before I do something I'm going to be sorry for." So I told Billy, "Let's get married."

My sister helped me get away from the house. Her and I both snuck downstairs about three o'clock in the morning. I had her check for him. He had told me he would wait up past the barn, so they couldn't see the taillights of the car from the house. As I was slipping out the door, Mom heard us. My sister said, "It's just me going to the bathroom."

We went on out. I kissed her good-bye and said, "I'll see you later." Billy and I went up to his mother's and picked her up. He had to have somebody vouch for how old he was. I didn't have to because I had sent away and got my birth certificate when my parents didn't know about it. His mother had to sign for him.

We went to Liberty, Indiana. At that time you didn't have to wait three days to get married in Indiana. It was just a simple thing. I wore a dress that I got for Easter the year before. It was blue with white cuffs and it had a little white fake fur jacket. I still had the little veil with a hair clip that I wore when I graduated from eighth grade in Catholic school. And I had a pink flower. I wore that.

We left there and came back home. We took his mom home, then we stopped at Mom and Dad's. Daddy was out back by the fruit cellar. I could tell he was upset. I walked up to him. I never did go into the house. I told him I was married. He said, "I know. I wished you could have waited till June when school was out."

"Well," I said, "I couldn't wait any longer."

"It's not a bed of roses."

"I know that," I kept telling him. "I know. I know." I didn't really know. I just didn't want him to know I didn't know.

"Are you going to finish school?" he asked me.

"I don't know."

"At least try to finish eleventh grade."

Later when we got over to Billy's sister's to spend the night, I asked Billy about it and he said, "Okay, you can finish school if you want to."

But, you know, when I went back to school, everything changed. The people were the same, but their attitude was different because I was married. There was this one boy I really had a crush on so bad. When we first came to that school I had seen him and said, "That's the man I want to marry." He sat in back of me in school. He reached up and tapped me on the shoulder and he said, "What was your hurry?" I just sat there and shook my head. I couldn't answer him. There was too much to tell. Everything that was happening at my home was all underground and you didn't dare talk about it back then like you can now. You didn't want anybody to know that you had a mean stepmother, beating the kids, which was just exactly what I had. Nobody knew.

In about six months, I was pregnant. I was a little upset at first when I found out I was pregnant, because I couldn't figure out how it happened. I knew it took two, but I always thought there had to be something there between them. I thought there had to be love.

I had a lot of medical problems with my daughter. Kidney problems, urea poisoning, toxemia, the works. By the time I was five months pregnant, I looked like I was ready to have the baby. It was just water. My hands and my feet would swell so big, I could hardly walk. I'd have to look down to see if my feet were stepping in the right place. I gained up to 160 pounds.

I was pregnant our first Christmas. We had this great big, humongous tree. Somebody give it to Billy. He brought that tree home and we put it up in the living room, but I didn't have no ornaments. He give me ten dollars and said, "Go to town and get some stuff." I went in a store and bought these little tiny balls and some tinsel and some rope and a string of lights. That's all I had money for.

I put all these little things on that tree. It looked so bare, so funny. But then the Christmas cards started coming and I took the ornament hooks and hung the Christmas cards on the tree. I got about thirty cards that year and that was the prettiest tree I ever saw.

In January I got to running a temperature and the doctor didn't like that. He sent me to the hospital. For the next two months they kept putting me in and out of the hospital until I finally just stopped going back.

On a Saturday afternoon I told Billy, "There's

something wrong. I don't know what it is, but there's something wrong with me or the baby.'' He called the hospital and they said to bring me up right away.

The fluid had built up so bad that I was killing her. They kept me woozy. Every time I'd start to notice anything, they'd give me another shot. I was past my due date, so they decided to induce my labor. They broke my water and I worked from seven o'clock Sunday night until five o'clock Monday morning. Every time I'd get to where the pain would start bothering me, they would give me something. But I was conscious the whole time. I knew what was going on around me, but I didn't care. I felt not involved.

They came in on Monday morning and got me back in the delivery room and they give me a spinal. I didn't feel nothing after that. I could see the clock from the table. I looked up at exactly five o'clock and I heard this screaming. Here's this kid coming out of me, all arms and legs. All I could see was this kid a-squalling and arms, big, long arms going. She was four pounds, fourteen and a half ounces, and she was twenty-one inches long, so she was nothing *but* arms and legs. She looked just like Billy, like a baby bird.

Billy and me got along pretty good. The only problem we had was with the drinking. He'd seen it all his life. He had drank since the time he was fifteen probably. His daddy and mom both drank.

Billy was a weekend drinker. He would come home on Friday night and he'd be drunk. He'd drink the rest of Friday night, most of Saturday. On Sunday he'd drink nothing, because he knew he had to get sobered up to go to work on Monday. I will give him credit for that. He did provide for us. I never had to worry where my meal was coming from, and I knew a lot of girls who married men and didn't know if they were going to eat or not.

I think Thelma was about three years old when Billy started beating on me. Everything started when I went to work. I was bored at home. Thelma was potty-trained and everything. I felt like she didn't need me anymore. We could use the money. So when the potato chip plant that he was working at needed help, I put my application in and got a job.

Every weekend it was the same thing. Billy was just plain jealous. He thought I was making out with someone at work. So he'd get drunk, come home, and accuse me of something. That's it in a nutshell.

I didn't know who to ask for help. I knew his mom and dad fought like cats and dogs. No way was she going to be able to help me. I would not ask my stepmother what to do. I couldn't go to my dad; he probably would have just wanted to go over and shoot him.

I had to take up for myself, because nobody else was going to. I started fighting back. The more I fought back, the worse the beating got, because he would get mad. Then I got to the point that I had to start walking on eggs. Every time I turned around, I had to watch what I said, watch how I looked at anybody, because he was so jealous of everybody.

I didn't have friends. As soon as I got close to a neighbor, the first thing you knew I was being accused of chasing her husband. I didn't form too many friendships and I don't today, because every time I'd get close to somebody I'd get my hand slapped. Like you do to a little child, except I got beat up. Six years, I put up with it.

That summer of '68 everything came to a head. I was going to leave Billy. He had gotten drunk early Saturday afternoon. I don't know how he knowed it, but he must have knowed something was up. He came home and he was so mad, so angry at something I had done—I can't remember what it was and neither does he at this point. I'd never seen him so drunk as this. He came in the trailer and he started in on me, hollering and calling me all kinds of names.

"What's the matter with you?" I says. He kept at

me and kept at me. Finally I got mad and I said, "I'm going to leave and there ain't a damn thing you can do about it unless you kill me."

"Well, then, *I will*," he said. He went back in the bedroom and he got the shotgun. When he come out of there with it into the living room, he started to hit me with it. I just stood there and more or less dared him to hit me. Instead of hitting me, he hit the lamp on the coffee table. He busted another one. Then he just went crazy with the gun and tore up the house.

Finally, he did hit me. First, he hit me with his fist, blacked my eye and busted my nose. Then he hit me with the gun, too. When I fell down and I was holding my face, he kicked me in my left breast so many times that it looked like chopped liver. By this time his cousin, who lived catty-corner from us, heard the ruckus. He came over and pulled Billy off of me and took him out of the trailer, got him calmed down.

The cousin came back into the trailer and said, "Are you all right?"

"No," I said, "I'm not all right. I'm leaving. I don't know what he's going to do, but I'm leaving." I called the law and the sheriff came. I said, "I'm not going to stay here tonight; I'm afraid. If he comes back, I think he will kill me."

"Where do you want to go?"

"Just take me to the police station in town." When we got there, I called to where Mom and Dad had their camping trailer at the lake. My daughter was with them for the weekend and I felt I had to get where she was.

When Daddy saw me, he cried. My daughter was nine years old then. When she seen me she just said, *"Again?"* There's this little nine-year-old kid going on thirty, saying to me, "What's wrong with you, Mom? Don't you know any better than that?"

Billy found out where I was at, and he came down. That was the first time I ever saw him cry. He sat

305

down on a picnic table and every time he looked at me he cried harder. He could not believe that he had did that to me. He kept saying, "You did it to yourself. You did it to yourself."

"There's no way," my daddy told him, "she could have done that to herself." It took all Daddy's strength not to hit him right then. He never knew how close he came to being hit.

"What are you going to do?" Billy asked me.

"In the morning, I'm going to go and file charges. You're going to be in jail."

"Well, if that's what you want to do," he said and he started to leave. He turned around and come back and he said, "Can't we try again?"

"I don't see that there's any reason to try again."

"I love you," he kept telling me.

"If a person loves you, they don't treat you like a doormat," I said.

Finally Daddy said, "Sit down and talk. Talking can't hurt."

So we sat there and talked. I don't remember exactly all we said. By that time I realized that I hadn't come to love him as much as I thought I had.

I sat there for a while. Then I got up and went for a walk. By that time it was getting dark and my daddy was wanting to leave. So I said, "Okay, I'll come back home. But I'll tell you right here in front of Mother and Dad and your daughter. If you ever lay a hand on me again, you will never see me again. You will never see your daughter again." That was in September.

The next month or so he didn't have too much to drink. But this Friday night in November, Billy come home and he'd been drinking. I could tell. He said something to me and I turned around and I said, "What did you say?" And he repeated hisself. I said, "Well, piss on you." And he reached out and he backhanded me. I turned around and said to him, "That's it. I told you if you ever put your hand on me again I would be gone.''

So I bided my time until the time was right. I picked up my check and I didn't cash it. I packed the car up with everything that I wanted, my clothes, my sewing machine, my sweeper, and my daughter and some of her toys. We went to town.

"What will you do?" Daddy said.

"I don't know, but I've got to get away." He called Susan, my younger sister, and she said I could come up there. Daddy rented a little U-haul trailer and took me to Defiance, Ohio.

I stayed there three months. I was ready to file for divorce. I had a job working and my daughter was in school. I was making a new life for myself.

I didn't know anything about this at the time, but on New Year's Day, Billy went to church. They were having what they called sunrise service to celebrate the New Year. His sister and her husband lived in a mobile home behind the church. One of her kids was sick and she wasn't going to go that morning. But her husband was in church and he sent one of their other kids to tell her to come out to the sanctuary, that Billy went up to the altar and got saved that morning.

Mom called at the end of February and asked did I care if they gave that sister-in-law my address so she could write to me. I said, "No, she and I always got along. She can have my address."

She sent me a letter and told me all about what had happened. It had been better than two months and Billy hadn't had anything to drink. He was sober. "He's not the same man he was then," she said. Between his sister and his brother's wife they wore me down. They kept writing to me and sending me pictures of their kids. I got homesick. I finally let them tell Billy where I was at.

He called me on the phone and we talked for about forty-five minutes long distance. I could tell there was something different about him, the way he talked. I finally said, "If you want to come up, go ahead."

He came up that next weekend. He tried to talk me into going back with him then, but I wouldn't do it. I said, "No, no, I don't think I want to come back now."

The following weekend he came up again and I was sick. I hadn't been able to work for a couple of days. I didn't know if we were going to have enough money to keep us till I could get back to work. I only made sixty dollars a week. That had a lot to do with my thinking. He talked me into it. I came back.

He promised me he would never hit me again. He never has until last January. That was the first time he's hit me in all those nineteen years. There are times I know he wanted to, when I would say something to him and I could watch his eyes change from the light blue that they are to a little bit of purple blue.

We'd been married seventeen years at that point. We decided the right thing to do would be to get re-married in the church. We had a big wedding and he stayed sober.

Everything was hunky-dory. He didn't treat me like an equal. He never has treated me like an equal. He has always felt that women should be seen and not heard, barefoot and pregnant, very old-fashioned ideals. He's one of these people that every time he sees something on TV about a woman being raped, he says, "You can't rape a willing soul." All he's ever listened to is other men talk. He's never been so afraid that he'd let somebody do anything to him. But I have. I've been to that point when he beat me so bad that I didn't know if I would live or die.

Then about three years after that, the year my daughter Thelma turned sixteen, she decided that she wanted to get married. She'd been dating this boy who was twenty. She came to us one night after she had been out with that boy and she said to me, "If you

308

don't let me get married, I'll *have* to get married. It's getting to the place where Ed is pushing me to have sex."

"You wait, because I waited," I told her. "That is an important thing to hang onto. It is the only thing you have to give a man that you like."

"You have to let me get married," she said. "I can't stand it any longer." We took them down to a town in Virginia where you can go and get married that same day, the same way we were married. Ed got a job working in a gas station. They got them a trailer and they lived in it. Thelma got pregnant. And soon Little Eddie come along.

When their son was nine months old, Thelma called me one day crying, "Mom, I got to come home."

"Why?"

"Ed wants a divorce." By the time the baby was a year old they were divorced. He married another girl a few weeks after that. Thelma lived on welfare. Ed had visitation rights but he didn't come around.

Then Thelma met Milt, her husband now. Ed raised a stink about that because they moved in together and they weren't married. Thelma got pregnant with Albert.

Albert came along and I thought, "I've got two grandsons and things couldn't get any better." But Albert had problems right from the beginning. There were all kinds of indications that there was something wrong, but we didn't know what it was. Thelma being young, it seemed like she didn't know what to do. She took him to the doctor and they run tests and they run tests and they run tests. That poor little child was six months old and they kept running tests and he was getting skinnier and skinnier. Finally the doctor just threw up her hands. "I don't know what else to do," she told us. "There's nothing left."

She sent us to the children's hospital in the city. They had him twenty-four hours and they knew what was wrong with him. He's got Wiskott Aldrich disease. It's an immune deficiency that's caused by genetic imbalance of some kind. They have not pinpointed it, male recipient, female carrier. If he makes it through the basic childhood diseases, he will still probably die before he is twenty of lymphatic cancer because the lymph glands get tired of fighting off these infections.

By that time Thelma realized that she was pregnant again. They told her that if she had another child and it was a boy there was ninety-nine chances out of a hundred that it would be the same way. So we prayed all the way through that pregnancy that it would be a girl. We practically begged God to let us have a girl.

But then David was born. While Thelma was still in the hospital, Albert was having some problems. With this disease the blood count drops like crazy. One day it'll be okay—not really normal because it's never normal, but okay for them. Then in a twenty-four-hour period it can drop down to life-threatening.

He developed these little freckles. That's what they looked like and that's what I thought they were. But he kept getting more and more. I noticed that he was so irritable. He didn't rest and when he did sleep he was fidgety. I got worried, so him and I went to town to the hospital. I was frantic.

I never spent such a night in my life as I spent that night. I thought my grandson was going to die. I got him to the hospital and his blood count was two thousand. Forty thousand is normal. He had a lot of fluid around his lungs. They wanted to work with him and he wouldn't let them. Finally the doctor told me, "You'll just have to leave." I got up to leave and that child screamed and carried on so bad when they tried to put the oxygen mask on him, he went into cardiac arrest. You talk about somebody being scared, I was scared.

They finally got his heart going again. I told him,

"Grandma's not going to leave you." I got down to his feet because they were working around his head and body and it was the only place I could go. I sat there for three hours and played This Little Piggy with his feet just to let him know I was still there. They got him stabilized. They brought me a chair into the isolation ward and I talked and sang to him all night long.

They let Thelma out of the maternity ward and told her to bring the new baby, so they could run tests to see if he was as sick as Albert. David was only two or three days old. I was with her when the results came in. I hope I never have to tell anybody again what I had to tell her. She kept saying, "Mom, why? Why?" I kept saying, "I don't know, I don't know." We spent two or three hours crying.

We didn't know from one day to the next whether Albert was going to live or not. Christmas came and we didn't really celebrate. We went to the hospital and spent the day with him. He was so bad he couldn't have cared less who was there. He was so sore he couldn't stand to be touched.

New Year's Eve, I wasn't going to work. I was going to go up to the hospital so Thelma could come home and rest for a day without having to worry about Albert being alone. When Billy left that morning, I told him that was what I was going to do.

I got in the shower about six o'clock that morning. I stood there and I got to crying and I couldn't stop. I got to the place where I thought to myself, "Why should I put myself through that? I don't have to go up there. She's there, she'll be all right." Then I thought, "I'll just go to work."

Billy came home from work that evening and he'd had a few beers. He was drunker than I had seen him for a while. He asked, "How was Albert?" I commenced to tell him why I didn't go. He got mad at me and he said, "Why did you lie to me?"

"Billy, I didn't lie to you. I just changed my mind.

I couldn't go.'' By that time I was getting frantic, because I thought, ''Uh-oh, here we go again.''

''You whore, why did you lie to me?''

Billy kept at me and kept at me. Finally I got mad. I stuck my finger down his face and I said, ''If you don't shut up right now, you're going to leave this house, one way or the other.''

He jumped up out of the chair, ''Who do you think you're talking to?''

''I'm talking to a stupid drunk is who I'm talking to.'' That made him mad. My God, did he get mad.

I thought afterward, maybe he was upset about Albert, too, and this was the only way he could trigger off some steam. That's the only way he knows to deal with anything. He don't know how to talk about it. He never did learn how. Nobody ever did tell him.

''If you're not leaving,'' I said, ''I am.''

''You're not taking my truck.'' He laid the keys to the truck on the banana bar.

''I don't have to take the truck,'' I said, ''I can walk.'' I was standing there by the freezer and I started to go back to the bedroom to change clothes. As I went past him, I stumbled. I reached out and put my hand on the bar to steady myself. He must have thought I was going to go grab the keys, because that's when he hit me. He took the flat of his hand, hauled off and swatted me between the shoulders. I turned around and said, ''That's it. Your ass is mud. You're going to jail.''

I calmly went over to the telephone and picked it up. He took it out of my hand and threw it out in the yard. I said, ''Don't make no difference to me. I'm leaving. But you'll be in jail before the night's over.'' I went down to the neighbors and I called the law.

I filed charges. I meant it this time. I was not going to let him get by with it. I knew that was the only way I was going to have any peace. I knew that this vicious cycle was getting ready to take off again.

In the end it cost better than two thousand dollars with counseling and everything. I let my charges go on pending because he agreed to go to counseling. But he fooled me. We only went to two sessions. I'm sure we should have went to more.

To this day, I am afraid of him. When he gets mad, he does not know what he is doing and you'd better be afraid of him. But as long as he stays away from drinking, I think I can handle it. See, he's on a year's probation, so he daren't get picked up with even an empty beer can in the car. They had took him in for drunk driving and domestic violence.

Things aren't much better. He's not drinking anymore, but he's still mad. I think the main problem is the sex business. He's not impotent completely, but partially. Then he takes it out on me and says I'm getting it someplace else. He'll ask me if I got any today at work. Who has time while I'm cooking at that restaurant? He'll ask me, "Do you love me?"

"Yes, but sometimes I don't like you." He can't understand that.

Church was something I loved doing. I loved to be with God's people. But it got to the point where every time I would go to church, when I'd come home I'd get this same thing over again—"Who'd you go to the basement with? Who'd you sit with? You only go up there to see some man." I decided why put myself through this every Sunday morning. Go to church to feel good and then come home and get this badgering.

I can't sleep at night. As soon as I lay down, I get this feeling of dread. I feel like I'm not going to wake up in the morning. Billy doesn't understand that. He wants me in bed with him every night at the same time. He won't go to bed without me. I don't know if he's afraid to go to bed without me, or what. When we do go to bed he wants to make love, but he can't. I know that's frustrating. I keep trying to tell him it's all right. But he does not believe me no matter how many times I tell him it's all right. I get so tired of saying, "It's all right."

I keep having these pains in my chest. One I had at work was so bad that they called the emergency squad and took me to the hospital. I think it scared Billy. But when he found out it wasn't my heart, he's been laughing about it. The doctor says it's stress. I'm always waiting for the other shoe to drop. I think it's going to drop sometime this summer.

Three nights ago he called me a whore.

When he left for work this morning he said to me, "What do I have to live for? We don't have anything."

"Billy," I said, "we've got more now than we've ever had in our lives." But he don't see it that way. There are things that are changing in his life and he's not willing to accept the change. I am. I'm ready for the change.

I don't know. There's this feeling of dread that something is going to happen. I think he's going to kill himself. I think he'll kill me, too.

Peg

I grew up in the hills. My mom was a schoolteacher. My dad was a coal miner. She met him at the school where she taught—he was a student, ten years younger than her.

Dad is a civilized redneck. Until his anger comes out you have no idea what a redneck he is. People admired and feared him in the community. He ended up being a leader in the town, partly because of his connection with my mother and partly because he was a real strong, clear-thinking kind of person. He didn't like dealing with bullshit. Everything was black or white.

My mom wanted me to be a schoolteacher and come back and teach in my hometown. Of course, I rejected all of that. I was the rebel in my family. From the time that I started reading books, I craved getting out of there. I would read about places and I'd think, "Gosh, I want to see that." That's what kept me from staying.

When I was thirteen, my mom said to me, "Oh, you've got to watch out for those passions. You've just got to watch out for those passions." Of course, then I wanted to know, "What passions? Tell me about these passions." There's not a book in the house except these epic romances that have women and men and sex all glorified, nothing real about it. There's nothing that has what I'm looking for. "What is this passion that she's talking about? By golly, I'm going to find out about this." Mom was very puritanical, very strict. That was all she would say.

When I was sixteen, a cousin of mine told my dad about this guy bothering me at a dance. He had kissed me and I fought to get away from him, because I didn't like the guy.

Dad asked me to go for a drive on a Sunday afternoon. Takes me with him and we walk into the restaurant where all the kids hang out. He leads me up to this guy I didn't like. He says, "You see this girl?"

"Yeah," the guy says.

"If you ever touch her again, I'll blow your brains out."

All I could say was, "Oh, Dad." If he were to tell you about that day now, he'd tell it with such pride. That's typical down there. You protect your woman.

When I was seventeen I got pregnant. I was four months pregnant when I graduated from high school. I got married. We lived there for two years and finally I got my husband to move to another state. I'm positive that subconsciously I married a person that I could get to take me out of there whether he wanted to or not. Someone I could control enough to get me out of there.

When I moved here at nineteen, everything was a treat. Freeways, I was so excited to see freeways. Wow, this is the real world. I loved finding new parts of town and going down new streets. I explored a lot of things that probably I shouldn't have been exploring. I ended up in a seedy section of town one day, and here I am going into adult bookstores. My friends said, "You did what?"

"I've never been in one. I wanted to see what it was like."

But I went through those first years until I was twenty-four like I was in a cocoon. I had this naiveté that bad things can't happen to me because I'm safe inside my cocoon. I never thought about bad things, the real world. It was just me inside this little capsule. World affairs did not affect me at all. People would talk about things and I would wonder why it upset them, since it wasn't happening here and now. There was myself, my husband, the usual getting used to each other, the fighting and loving and learning to live together, and sharing the child.

I was very content with my baby. In fact, I was very natural at parenting. I surprised myself. I instinctively seemed to know what to do without being taught. I decided when I was twenty-two and my son was four —and this was such a stupid reason—that I should probably have another child so he doesn't grow up alone. It wasn't from any real desire to have a second child. Babies didn't drive me crazy. It was when a kid got old enough to communicate that I began to really feel good about that relationship.

I was a perfect mother until my daughter came along. She changed everything. She cried and he didn't. She cried for reasons that he never cried for. She was very precise and wanted things a certain way, even when she was tiny. As I went through the experience of raising her I kept thinking to myself, "I'm supposed to be learning something here. I know I am." We clashed intensely. She prepared me for experiences that I've had later in life whereas my son didn't. With him it was comfortable, it was easy. He never challenged me. I never really had to use my head. With her I always had to try and figure out how she was thinking and where that would lead. I had to try to stay one step ahead of her.

For a long time I accepted my role and what it is to be a mother. My husband and I lived in little suburbia. We had a brand-new house in a subdivision with the perfect little environment: Kids for our kids to play with, families who were the same ages that we were—middle-class suburbia. Many of the women in that community got close together. The subdivision started its own little civic club. We started doing things to beautify the community, the whole American suburban path.

When I was twenty-five I can remember feeling dissatisfied. I couldn't pin it down. I just knew I wasn't happy. I would cry and have no idea of why I was crying. Everything was perfect. I had everything I was supposed to have, exactly like Donna Reed, smiles and all, the whole works.

I would sit and cry to my husband, tell him that something was wrong and I didn't know what and I couldn't explain it. It was just wrong.

He'd blow me off. "I don't know what you're talking about. Don't bother me; I've got to work tonight, okay?"

What he did was right for who he was. He had no way of knowing what was going on with me. That was the way he would have dealt with me back home in the mountains. That's the way his mom and dad would have dealt with it. I was just a crazy woman. I needed to talk and he didn't know how to deal with that. So he didn't. He said, "Shut up, woman."

I began to join things. I was fanatical about it. I was the super volunteer for ten years. If there was an organization that needed leadership, I was there. "Okay, yes, I'll be on that board, I'll lead that committee." So I filled my time, looking for something to make me feel better. And it did. I got social approval and all these little ego boosters. I was just fantastic. I look back now and think, "Jesus Christ, you did work miracles. But why? So you organized the block parents for 1978?" At least, I wasn't home drinking vodka or leaning over the back fence doing "Ain't it awful?"

Toward the end of that ten years, I got into a women's group that was run by a psychologist at one of the grade schools. Oh, God the times were a-changing. We read, *I'm Okay, You're Okay*. It was so standard for women my age. "Oh, wow, you want your husband to take the garbage out so you'll feel loved? Huh. So that's why I'm hurt when he doesn't take the garbage out?"

Trying to communicate that stuff to my husband was a different story. We would have get-togethers with the husbands and wives in this group. All the husbands would sit on one side of the room and look at all their wives like, "Oh, look what you've done to us. You're disrupting our happy little homes." My husband hated it, but he went . . . for a while.

We had moved in the meantime from the small house that we had first bought into a larger home. We were following the path, right up the ladder. That was really satisfying for a while.

My kids were being normal kids. My son, Bob, perfected the technique of conning Mom into thinking he was the perfect kid. Much as I had done with my mother. Now he tells me what he was really doing. My daughter, Isabel, was being the rebellious one. She didn't have to totally rebel because I was always letting loose of the reins as we went along. I was positive that if I tried to push my will on her, she'd be hitchhiking to California. This kid you can't push too far.

The thing she did consistently with me was be honest with me. When she was fifteen she was standing in front of a mirror rubbing her face and she said, "My face always breaks out when I smoke too much pot."

"Don't tell me these things," I said. "Protect me. I'm just the mom."

When the kids moved into the high school age group I got tired of doing all this volunteer stuff and not getting paid for it. There was a new agency in town, Crisis Hotline. Back in the '70s, everybody was needing drug counseling. I volunteered for that with the idea of getting a job sooner or later.

My cocoon got dented and there was an opening. I thought, "Wow, Peg, look what's out there." I was just blown away that there were drugs. That kids were doing them and dying. My kids were at the age where they were going to be exposed to all that, so it was time to wake up and see what's going on.

I felt like I should have chin straps on, so my jaw would not drop open. I was in shock. "People do that?" I wasn't dealing with suburbia anymore. There were a lot of transients, runaways, suicides. I'm real intrigued. I was very good at it.

We ran this hotline all night long. A fellow came in about two in the morning. He's tripping on something and he has a knife. The young man working with me was shocked out of his mind that I said to this guy, "Fine, you can come in and I'll talk to you, but you have to give me the knife first. We just don't do that here." The guy gives me the knife. I take it and put it in a drawer. We sat down and talked. It's exactly what my dad would have done.

A woman who was chronically coming in and threatening suicide was from my old neighborhood. She comes in on a Sunday afternoon and she's got a bottle of Darvon. She's throwing them up in the air and saying that she's going to take them. She says, "When the director is here, he takes the pills and puts them in a drawer."

"Jane," I said, "they are your pills." This was gut instinct, no one told me to do this. "I really believe that you have the right to take your life if you want to. I can't take that right from you."

She stood there and looked at me a long time and finally she said, "Oh, shit, Peggy, that's not what you're supposed to say."

"Okay, Jane, come on, let's talk."

That period in my life was an incredible education. I came in contact with so many different people. It challenged me. It was also addictive. The do-gooder who will save the world. I ended up going to work for that agency. That was my search for meaning and purpose.

Then my husband, George, began to get dissatisfied. By then I had learned about listening skills. I can listen, so let's talk about it. He would get frustrated because he couldn't put it into words. He was like I had been, exactly, except that as we talked, he began to see that we had moved to different levels. That's when he began to feel threatened and I began to feel bored. But being a good wife, I was *not* going to disturb that marriage.

George began to complain a lot about how he worked all his life and he didn't have anything to show for it. I couldn't understand it because I was happy now. I had a bigger house with a nice yard. I had a garden, and social contacts. My kids were doing fine.

I got frustrated and upset with him, because it seemed to me that he had everything. What I realized much later was that he was saying he didn't have that connection with me and his children that he wanted. The kids came to me to talk. He and the kids grew apart, partly because he was tired and didn't want to deal with them after working all day, and partly because he didn't understand them and they didn't understand him.

Those high-school years and the challenges helped put the finish on my marriage. Isabel, bless her heart, was forever confronting her father and disagreeing with him. He saw disagreement as meaning that she didn't care for him. She didn't respect him and therefore didn't love him. The older she got, he would get almost crazy because of these differences he would have with her.

My son was the kind of kid that everything he tried he did well at. It didn't matter what. George would try woodworking and it would come out a little rough. Bob would try it and it would be finished and artistic. I think George felt threatened by that.

He began to exhibit a lot of what I thought was odd behavior at that time. He became very much of a recluse. He didn't want to go anywhere or do anything, which of course frustrated me even more.

He was real possessive of me always. I had always dealt with it, but now he started doing things. Like at the job he would write my name on a 2 x 4 and then nail it into a building that they were constructing. In a moment when he was trying to make up with me after a fight, he told me that he had fantasies of locking me away so no one else could get close to me and I couldn't have contact with anyone else. Instead of hearing that as a fear of losing me like I could have heard, I thought, "Oh, wow, he's flipping out. I'm in danger."

He lost his temper a lot and that ties into my father and seeing him lose his temper. I was petrified of anger. He became very, very suspicious. He became more and more intimidated by the people I worked with. They talked a language he didn't understand. I'm sure he felt inadequate.

I had already decided that I didn't love him five

years before that. But I was going to stick it out for the kids. I always did this justification thing in my head. "Well, it's no big deal. I'm fairly happy. Who else would be out there for me? I can endure it. I have my home and my job."

But as the kids got older I began to think about just him and me, alone. It didn't frighten me, but it didn't appeal to me either. When both the kids were gone for two weeks that summer, I knew this was the time for me to see if it was going to work.

The two weeks that the kids were gone was perfect. It was *perfect*. There were no temper flare-ups. He was happy.

The night the kids got back home, there was this huge fight. He got mad at my son for some totally insignificant thing. I stood in the kitchen thinking, "Something is wrong with this picture. This is not good. I don't like this. No."

Next, he went through three suicide attempts. The first time it happened, my daughter was there by herself. I happened to call from being out shopping and she said, "I'm supposed to go to Youth Fellowship and my dad's talking about killing himself. What'd you think I ought to do?"

"Isabel, I don't know. Go to Youth Fellowship."

"Are you sure it'll be okay?"

"You've got to go. You can't stay. If he's going to kill himself you don't need to be there. So go."

I panicked; I did all the stereotypical things. "Oh, God, a suicide. My husband kills himself and the whole world is going to know that he's not happy and it's my fault." So I do the whole rescuing bit. That lasted through all three attempts, two or three weeks apart.

Finally, I couldn't deal with this. He would talk about getting professional help, but then he'd back out at the last minute. One day when it was just he and I eating supper—I was still the perfect little wife, supper at five o'clock and the whole works—I said, "I've been thinking about the fact that you want to kill yourself. I keep wondering to myself what would I tell a client if they came in with a problem like this with their husband. I have to say to you what I'd tell them. I need to hear myself say that to you: If you want to die, that's something you have to take care of yourself. I can't keep doing this. You've got a right to do it."

The attempted suicides stopped like magic. There was never even any mention of them again. It was like they never existed.

Then we went through a couple of weeks where he would come home from work and be angry about something that had happened at work and blow up at me. I'd been in the counseling profession long enough to know that those were just the symptoms of everything else, but I was busy denying to myself that this was the end. And we did have those two weeks, that magic time.

He came home one night and was real, real upset about something that happened on a job. I was sitting on the basement stairs talking to him. He jumps up, grabs me, throws me to the floor. Isabel was home and just then she opened the door. This is the first time that there had been anything that even resembled physical abuse. I thought, "This is it. He won't be able to cope with her seeing what's going on. I need to do something because it's only going to get worse." That's when I made up my mind that I was going to leave him.

I went to the attorney's and talked to my kids. It was so planned. I knew at Christmas that I was going to divorce him. The kids knew everything, but we were going to have this one last Christmas. That was kind of dirty but I did it.

He sensed that something was going on, so he

started counseling with the minister of our church and he started promising and saying things will get better.

I was not sleeping at all. I was a wreck, constantly wired. I lost thirty pounds. He was doing a lot of escapist behavior. He would come home from work and go to bed. Christmas Day, he gets up, opens gifts, goes back to bed. We both knew, but we weren't saying.

The night I had decided to tell him, I'm cleaning up the dishes and thinking, "I can still back out. I can still back out." I was in knots. "No, I can't back out. I've got to go through with it. It's destroying us both." I'd been married twenty-one years at that point.

I went into the family room. Isabel and Bob are there. They know what's going to happen. God, yes. I tell him that I'm going to get a divorce. He looks at me and says, "You can't. I own you." Isabel flips out. That was all I said. Isabel and he argued, he got mad and left the room.

The kids went to a movie. I had set it up to tell him right before he was going to a counseling session. In fact to make sure he went to the counseling session, as soon as my kids left, I went to the phone and called the minister and said, "I just told George I'm getting a divorce; he's on his way to see you." It's your problem.

George went crazy. I was real scared, because I didn't know what he was going to do. But he went ahead to the session. I told him, "When you get back, I won't be here. Isabel and I are going back home to tell Mom and Dad. We'll talk about house and all that stuff later."

My daughter and I went off the next morning, driving through a blizzard. I really dreaded telling my mom because, every time I called her and she wasn't expecting it, she'd say, "You're not having problems, are you?"

"No, Mom, everything is fine," I'd say. That last year she'd say, "You know if you got a divorce, it would kill me."

I go to my brother's house which is about another hour's drive from home. I call my dad and say, "I'm coming in." My dad, bless him, he calls the road crews to come out and clear the roads for me so I can come home. This is so classic, so down-home. "My kid is coming home."

I see my mom and she starts to cry. Of course, Mom dealt with it fine. My husband finally became the bad guy because he'd done all these bad things to me, even though she had really liked him all along. I explained to her that I was as much to blame as he was.

My dad said, "My little girl. I'm going to shoot the bastard."

We had a very stormy seven months until the divorce was final. He was very angry. He'd call friends of mine and threaten them. It was the only way he could get even and make himself feel okay about not letting me get the better of him. It ended up causing both kids to lose a lot of respect for him.

Isabel had a scene with him after the divorce in a restaurant. He used the same guilt techniques on her that he'd used on me. He said to her, "Something is wrong with you."

"No, there's nothing wrong."

"Yes, there is. Something is wrong with you."

"Just leave it alone. I don't want to talk."

He keeps on it. Then he shoves his food away, folds his arms, and starts to pout.

My son tells this story and is just embarrassed because Isabel ends up being the redneck like her grandfather. She shoves her food out of the way, she leans across the table, and she says, "You want to know what's wrong with me? You fucked up my life." And then she starts. Bob is leading her out of the restaurant and she's screaming, "If you think you're going to do this to me for $137 a month child support, you're crazy."

They have not seen him since then. He moved back to Kentucky and has been married three times since then.

In fact Mom did die soon after the divorce. She was seventy-seven. She had a stroke and she lived another week after that. That last week, I was helping to bathe her and she was telling me stories. She just can't understand how she can still have "passions."

"Mom, that's fantastic," I said. "It just shows that you and Dad can still have feelings for each other." I asked her if she had told Dad that and she said, "Oh, no."

She went into a coma and she was like that for about forty hours. I went to her bedside and I tried to think of what I could say that would make it easier for her. I stood there and talked to her. I told her that one of the things I had realized was Daddy loved her very much. She always was very afraid that he was cheating on her. I'm positive, knowing my dad, that he did. He justified it in his mind and that made it okay. But it was real important for me to tell her that I saw the love he had for her, even though she had not always been able to recognize it was there. Even though they hadn't been able to speak it, the love was there.

I don't know if she heard me. I like to think she did.

The only time my dad changed his behavior toward me was when my mother was in the hospital. Then for a short time we were peers. He could see me as an adult. But, boy, the minute she was buried it was right back to little girl.

My ex-husband called and asked if he could come to the funeral. I said, "I don't have any problem with you coming." My dad jerked the phone out of my hand, which was standard for my dad, and says, "You stay away or I'll blow your head off."

After the divorce, I got into a relationship with a

326

friend of mine who is the same age as my son—but
she is a woman. When I was working at the counseling
agency, this woman, Sandy, came on as a volunteer
when she was seventeen. I was one of the trainers and
she was one of my trainees. The thing that I always
liked about her was that she didn't put me into that
adult bracket. She invited me to do things that kids
her age were doing. We did road rallies together. God,
I loved it. This was exciting. She didn't lock me into
that parent or older person role. We had fun together.

As my marriage reached a crisis and I became willing to talk about it, she was the person I talked to. She
had some experiences in growing up that she had not
talked about with other people. We gravitated to each
other. I look back on it now and I can't even define it.

My husband was my first sexual experience and the
only male experience. On our wedding night, I remember thinking, "Humm, it's supposed to be more than
this." It was supposed to be wildfire and all that kind
of stuff. I've always been great at fantasizing, so it
was hard for anyone to live up to what I expected. My
husband and I were both very inexperienced.

In my growing years, when I was becoming this
"modern day woman," I would read articles in magazines and then hand them to my husband, saying,
"Okay, now, read this."

Sex with my husband was always awkward and not
always satisfying. He and I jockeyed for power positions. We didn't talk. I also was so concerned about
pregnancy—fanatic about pregnancy. Once I had the
two children, I was not going to have another child.
"Eighteen years from now I will be free."

Sandy was twenty and I was thirty-seven and our
relationship was everything I expected it to be. Making love to a woman was something I found very exciting. I was free, I didn't have to worry about
pregnancy. We didn't get into the power struggles that
I was in with George, so everything fit. It was perfect

for that time. We've been in that relationship for seven years.

Sandy and I went into business together because I needed a house. She comes from a family of entrepreneurs. I casually said to Sandy's father, "I think I'm going to buy a piece of land and put an A-frame up on it." He knew a distributor of prefabricated houses and suggested that we check it out. We went to the home office of this company and we literally faked our way through it. Neither one of us knew how to read blueprints. They said they wanted a distributor in our area. They asked about our experience and we bluffed.

We came back with two sets of blueprints and taught ourselves how to build the houses on paper. We went to lumber stores and we hung out at job sites. We talked to people and taught ourselves. The distributors came and visited us two months later and liked what they saw. They were selling franchises and they literally gave us this distributorship. So we started building.

My son quit school to become a builder with us. He's built more of these homes in this part of the country than anyone else. I have two businesses now, the one that sells the homes and the one that builds them. We just started a third one that will manufacture the homes to be built.

For a year and a half during this, my son, my daughter, and my lover lived together in this house. The kids were never used to me locking doors, and now I slept in a bedroom in the same bed with a woman with the door locked. They would come to the bedroom, knock on the door, and wait to come in to talk.

Neither Isabel nor my son had acknowledged the relationship I had with Sandy. I was always at family events with Sandy. We took vacations together, we had the same checking accounts, we bought cars together. We didn't talk about it. I was incredibly homophobic. Tell my own kids? No, never.

Isabel says even now that she never suspected. I think that was a conscious I-don't-want-to-know. She had one girlfriend who was gay, and she and another friend had done a film on drag queens for a video class. She kept going on about these drag queens. She'd come home and tell me about experiences going to gay bars. I thought, "Oh, God, where is this headed? I'm going to have to deal with this eventually."

She was working at her job one night and she called me. "Can you come pick me up and will you leave Sandy at home?"

"This is it," I thought. I told Sandy what was going on and she said, "So what are you going to do?"

"I'm going to lie. I'm not going to deal with this. I guarantee you, I'm not going to tell the truth."

I go and pick up Isabel. I already suspected that she and this other woman were becoming attracted to one another. I'd watched the dynamics between them. We come all the way back home doing the little small talk. We pull into the driveway and she said, "I need to tell you something."

"Thank God, it's dark," I thought.

"I think I'm gay," she said. "And I think you and Sandy are, too."

I really can't lie. I've never done it well. It's a skill I wish I had. If a situation demands finesse, I'm not the one to do it. So I looked at my daughter and I said, "You're right."

"I kind of thought so," she said. So we talked about it, then went to her room and talked some more. She wanted to know how it started, all those kinds of questions. I talked to her about her relationship.

Then she did the Isabel thing; she started speaking gigs at the university with two gay males and another gay woman. They had this little setup. If anyone asked, "What happened when you told your mother," Isabel would tell her story.

She went through a real radical period where she

was calling all straight men and women "breeders." That made me take a look at the whole radical side, because I don't think that's right. I have a son who is going to have children. I don't see him as a breeder. The relationship he has with his girlfriend is very valid and I want to have grandchildren someday. God gave us the equipment to breed.

I went through a period when I was convinced that men were no good, that I had every reason to be afraid of men, that I had every reason to be angry at men. And yet I deliberately went into a business that was a male-oriented business, home construction. I was that angry, afraid person for three or four years, until I realized that I did have more control. The fear was fear of myself and of the power that control gave me, the power I had given to my husband, the power I gave to my father.

Through this business I was exposed to men that I could generally like, either in a brotherly fashion or in an attracted fashion. I could not be where I am today if I had not been with men and learned what men have to give. And I feel like I've had some impact on them. I know that in the building business, I've taught several men what it's like to be a woman, to have women's values, and to make those as important as their values are.

Meanwhile I was hearing all this stuff from the radical lesbian community. "We need to be separatist, we need to be on our own, we need to make these distinctions and not let men have power over us." I was getting confused by that. What was going on inside of me wasn't what I was hearing. It didn't fit for me. What I've been doing is coming to grips with how I feel about men, how they could be in my life, and about the validity of how men and women need each other. I'm in a couple of groups right now where I am the only one who is saying, "I can't buy into being separatist. If that's how you're going to run the group

I can't be part of it, because men and women have too much to offer each other.''

I've pulled out of the everyday workings of my business during the last year. I decided it is time for me to reassess my life. I became a mother before I was even grown. I had to learn about my own feelings as I went along, sort of on-the-job training. When I left my husband, instead of breaking out of my cocoon, I just took Sandy and my children inside with me. Now I'm opening my arms and saying, "Okay, you guys, go away, because I need to feel what's inside there and I don't know what's ahead." I don't know if I'm going to feel the same way with my arms wide open as I did when they were enfolding other people. I don't know if I will be as independent or if I will be as strong. I don't know any of that.

I feel very lucky to have had two lifetimes already. Now I feel like a little baby bird standing on the brink of another life full of possibilities. It's exciting, but also real scary.

Sharon

First child. First grandchild. I felt special, very loved, taken care of, surrounded by people, in the center of things. I felt beautiful. People told me I was beautiful.

I was closest to my father, not my mother. My father was my mother. He was the one who took me on rides to talk about things, the one who took me fishing, who taught me things he wanted me to know. He was an attorney and he took me to his work, to the jail, to the court. He always had time. When he came home the day began for me in certain ways.

My mother was harder to reach, colder. I couldn't reach her in the same way I could reach my father.

By the time I was eleven, I discovered boys, and they discovered me. You know how they pick a girl in the classroom that all the boys love and they write you love notes and it's always the same girl? I was the girl that all the boys followed home from school. I was always in love with somebody, too. But the whole class loved me. So I became really interested in that. It became a big source of what I did with my time, thinking about boys, ducking the boys. Some of the boys tried to kiss me after school and I would have to hide.

I remember walking home from sixth grade and having half the class follow me home. I was not sexual, not sexual at all. This was 1949. It gave me this tremendous sense of, "Why me?" I also liked it.

I was pretty and my figure developed young. My father started calling me "boy crazy." Boy crazy, yeah.

By the time I was fourteen, Daddy was through, because then there were fifteen- and sixteen-year-old boys following me home. Daddy didn't like that at all. I "lost" my dad at fourteen and my mother I didn't know how to deal with. So I turned to boys, to men. I liked them back. From fourteen to sixteen, I was in love all the time.

My mother and father became very strict. Boys were asking me out on dates, but my parents wouldn't let me go out in cars. I cried every single day one summer, because I wanted to go out with a boy who had a car and they wouldn't let me. I'd fool them and let the boys come pick me up, figuring once they saw the boys they'd let me go. But they wouldn't. I cried every day.

Instead of doing something constructive during those years, I was figuring out how I could go from one man to another. My energy was focused on how I was going to go from one to another and keep everybody happy, including my parents who weren't very happy with it all and were very unhappy with me.

While I was sixteen, I was in love with a twenty-three-year-old, just back from Korea. That upset Dad.

I was popular in school, had friends, but I was finished with high school emotionally. I was not a high-school girl any longer. I wanted to go with my boyfriend who was twenty-three years old, and I did. I found ways to do it. It was still not sexual at all. Lots of necking, *heavy* necking.

One Thursday, I was going to a club meeting at school. My boyfriend would pick me up there and that was why I was going. The prettiest girl in the class was driving. She had just gotten her license. Someone had given me a copy of a test I had the next day, and I was trying to memorize it. We had a head-on collision. The thing that really saved me was that I was cheating on this test and had my head down. I went through the windshield, but I was relaxed enough not to look up and catch it right in the face. I hit my forehead.

I remember lying there all full of blood, a priest coming over and talking to me and giving me the last rites. My girlfriend was saying that she was blind. I was really angry at this. They were giving her all the attention, because she was really pretty and I was covered with blood. A boyfriend's father was there looking at me and holding my hand, not knowing who I was, feeling terrible.

I went to the hospital and they called my parents. I was in the emergency room and they couldn't sew me up because I wasn't of age. Both my parents come screaming down the hall, "Is she dead? Is she dead? Is she dead?"

I went through this whole thing with the car accident feeling lucky. Lucky that I wasn't hurt more, that I was just cut on my head and scarred on my face, my

333

nose was broken and my rib was broken, but I was walking and my face wasn't cut up too bad.

Now, I'm eighteen and graduating high school. My twenty-four-year-old boyfriend came to my senior prom and to my graduation. Everybody stared at me. I was definitely out of place. At that age, a man looks like a man and the guys in high school didn't look the same at all. My father called him an ape and a monkey. My boyfriend asked me to get married to him.

My best girlfriend got married at nineteen. I cried at her wedding, I was so jealous, so envious. Oh, my God, I thought that she had just found heaven. The first time I went to visit her, she was washing his socks and cooking spaghetti and I thought that was the most glamorous, courageous thing in the whole world.

I still had a curfew and if I didn't make it home I was punished. Although I couldn't do what she was doing, I wanted it. But then I started to think that my boyfriend was too dumb. He wasn't smart enough. I was right. He wasn't smart. But he loved me.

My father said to me, "You have to have a profession. You've got to find a way—*in case* you ever need it—to make money."

I went to college. Nothing about college appealed to me, except doing it, getting the degree and getting out. I didn't want the life of a college girl, none of it. I decided to become a teacher. I wasn't learning anything. Classes were boring. I hated the food. I hated being with the people. But I always had boyfriends.

I look back and think, "Why didn't I rebel, why didn't I get angry?" I don't know. I thought if I was out kissing and necking, I *was* rebelling. They didn't want me to do it. That's what I could do. They were always on me for that. "Boy crazy."

A guy who was a friend of mine from high school, a big man on campus, a real Mr. College, fraternity guy who was going into the Navy, said to me, "You were always the one I loved. All those other women, nothing. You and I had such an incredible friendship. I'm asking you to be my girl. Will you wear my fraternity pin?''

I was shocked. We were friends, but this was the *most* popular guy. He told me that he loved me and then I loved him.

He goes off to the Navy and I was the Ensign's girlfriend. Love letters, phone calls, all this stuff. I'm still in college. I'm supposed to be waiting for him.

Another guy comes along—handsome, gorgeous— and I start dating him. We didn't ever talk, never talked, but a lot of kissing, always kissing.

The Ensign came back from the Navy to marry me; the other guy also came to marry me and my father was mean to both of them. "How are you going to support her? What do you think you're going to do? How are you going to make a living for her?'' Terrible.

Somewhere in this, the Ensign was back in Japan and this tall, handsome guy and I got engaged. One day he comes to my house and he brings me an engagement ring. I didn't really want it, but I didn't know what to say. I was so sexually taken by him, although we weren't having sex. He was so handsome and his family lived in a big house in an exclusive neighborhood. Before I knew it, there was a wedding planned.

His family was in the men's clothing business. I was to go down and work in the men's store near the navy yards. The mother ran the store. I had to be there for sales and on Father's Day. I hated it. "This is going to be my life? In a men's store? No, not me. I don't like it. I can kiss him, I can love him, I can feel sexual, but I can't be in a men's store by the navy yards.'' I broke off the engagement.

This is 1960. I knew a lot of other men during this time. Boys, men, all wanted to marry me. I was the good girl from a nice home.

The last summer before I was to graduate, my parents let me have an apartment with another girl. I had a date every single, solitary night that summer. I had freedom.

My parents now had much more money than ever. My father was building a big house in that same exclusive neighborhood and they were planning my bedroom. I was *twenty-one*. I kept saying, "Don't plan my bedroom. I graduate from college in six months. I don't want to come live with you." But they were doing it anyway.

In August, my father told me about a man from Las Vegas who he was working with. This man had a son who was in his business. My father wanted me to go out with the son. "What a wonderful boy this is! He is so wonderful because he waits to take his mother out to dinner every night and he isn't with the chorus girls. He is really close to his father," and all this stuff. So I make a date with this boy on the recommendation of my father and his friend.

I felt real big since I had my own apartment. In walked the handsomest man I've ever seen in my whole life. The most dashing, the most interesting, the most sophisticated, twenty-eight-year-old man I ever laid eyes on. He looked like a matador. My first words to him were, "You're a matador."

Tall, dark, and handsome, he had a black Thunderbird convertible and he was a former Air Force jet pilot. We went out on that first date to an affair that both of our families were at. I couldn't even talk to him, I was so scared, so nervous, so impressed.

Then he didn't call me for a week or ten days. Finally, he called me and we did something a second time. There are two dates and there's nothing, nothing. Never kissed him, nothing.

The third date we were going to spend a Sunday at the beach. This was now the middle of September. I went out with my old fiancé the night before this and he said, "I want you to tell me tomorrow, Sunday, whether or not you're ever going to marry me. You broke our engagement a year and a half ago. I've been hanging around here. It's going to be yes or no—tomorrow.''

Sunday morning, the matador picked me up at my parents' house. I was back there by now. He came in and my parents were nice to him. My dad knew him from business. He had suggested that I go out with him.

We went to the beach. I thought he was so glamorous. He had this house that was glamorous, his business was glamorous. He was older, had been in the service. As we're driving to the beach in the Thunderbird convertible with the top down, he said to me, "Buddy, what do you look so nervous about?"

"I've got to make up my mind today," I said. I wasn't playing jokes. I was really serious. "I know this guy that I've been engaged to and I've got to tell him today if we're going to get married. This is it." I was not being manipulative. I was really thinking about it.

"You're not going to marry him," he said, "you're going to marry me."

"I am?"

"Yeah, but first of all, I have to know some things: How much is your college tuition to finish college and do you have your teeth fixed?"

We spent the day at the beach. Went back to his parents' penthouse apartment and he said to his mother and father, "I want you to meet the girl I'm going to marry. I'm going to marry Sharon." That was it.

I was on a cloud, in a dream. Here this Prince Charming had come along, this dashing who-knewwhat. He came over to my parents that night and told them we were getting married. I still hadn't really been alone with him, I still hadn't kissed him. I said to myself, "Even if it doesn't last, I'm going for this ride."

We got married in December. Big wedding. Five hundred people. Both families. I was scared of him. I was intimidated. I didn't feel I was gorgeously attractive enough. I didn't think I was interesting. I was a schoolgirl. I had to drink wine to be able to talk to him at night.

He wasn't a good boy. He was a bad, bad boy. He had a tragic life as a child, which he never told me about until I married him. His mother died real young. He ran away from home. He rode the rails. He tried to join the Marines. He was a brilliant student, but was always a rebellious kid. He'd run away from home for six months at a time and they'd find him carhopping in Arizona.

He was *my* bad boy, too, and I was the good girl. Chorus girls, show girls. Racy people. He was racy to me. I was fascinated by him.

We went on our honeymoon to his parents' house in Palm Springs. I was still a virgin. After all these engagements and all these men, I was a virgin when I got married. I was almost twenty-two years old and I had started with boys at thirteen years old. I was nervous having to get undressed in front of him. I had to go into the other room.

I didn't know if he loved me or not. Maybe it was just the right thing for him to do. I didn't care. I remember saying to myself, "I don't care if it doesn't last for six months, I want it. I want to be his wife. I want to know him. I want to get on the roller coaster."

He went away to his sophisticated job and I started my student teaching, which was really hard for me with lesson plans and all that shit *and* trying to be a wife. I'd never cooked a meal, I'd never done anything. I thought I had to cook, entertain, have dinner parties, polish the silver. It took me a week to have a dinner party.

I was tired. I can never remember being as tired in my whole life. My husband never came home from work until late—nine-thirty or ten o'clock at night—so we ate then every night. We had candles and wine, because he wanted them every night. I had to keep up this romantic illusion, I thought. So I'd do my school-work, and then have wine and candles and people over every night.

I cried every night sexually. He was handsome, daring, sexual. He didn't want to make love to me. I used to count the times he wanted to make love to me when we first got married. I wanted to make love to him every single night. I had held all this in for twenty-two years. I got married a virgin. He was getting a gift, right? "I did something special for you. I held it in." But when I made love to him it seemed like he was doing it out of duty. It wasn't something that he felt.

He was always coming home tired, working hard, exhausted, traveling a lot. I was frustrated and upset and angry. I had nobody to talk to about it. Nobody talked about their sex lives. I had no girlfriends. I couldn't go to my parents. I would cry myself to sleep every night or go into the other room and cry. He had a very bad temper, and if he heard me crying, he would get angry. I had nobody.

I wanted to get pregnant, because my husband was going to be thirty, I was going to be twenty-three, and I didn't know what I was going to do with my life. I didn't want to go to work as a schoolteacher. I didn't want to not do anything. I didn't know what else I could do except be a mother. So I got pregnant.

I loved being pregnant. I had this incredible feeling that no one else had ever done it. I was the only one. I had a secret no one else could have. I was carrying this person I loved so much inside of me. It was mine. I was connected to this love in me in a deep way.

In July, I gave birth to my daughter, which was probably the happiest moment of my life, seeing her born. When I saw her I thought, "That's my child. I'm her mother." I felt so complete.

Coming home with the baby was really hard. My husband wasn't available. I was disappointed he wasn't sharing it with me. Family was over all the time, because it was the first grandchild. My mother told me it was the best time in my life. The best time in my life? I'd watch my husband get dressed, put on his cologne, and go to work and I was jealous. I was cleaning up the baby stuff.

I loved my baby, but I didn't like the role. I never said it, because everybody was telling me, "This is the best time in your life." I didn't know that to be unhappy or to feel tired was accepted. I had no one to say that to.

We built our own home, this great home. I got a housekeeper. I didn't know what to do, thought I was going to get pregnant again. I was twenty-four years old, and I thought I was a good wife. I knew I wasn't getting the kind of attention I deserved and my child wasn't getting it. But we were the perfect couple. I really idolized this guy. I was still fascinated by him and he was very magical to me.

I go out one night with a girlfriend of mine to a movie—which I never did when my husband was working. I was driving home with her and I saw my husband with another woman.

I was in shock. Coming home, I felt like someone put ice water in my veins. *Ice water in my veins.* I was hysterical, crying, couldn't control myself.

I must have seen him at ten or eleven o'clock at night. He got in about two-thirty or three. He was one of the boys and drank a lot. He'd been drinking. I asked him where he was. He told me this or that.

"I pulled up next to you in a car," I said.

He didn't say anything. Then he hit me. A lot. He was caught. He felt trapped. I don't think he knew what to do.

The next day I was black and blue. I go in to my father. My father knew my husband hit me. He said, "Men are this way. Men will always do this. All men do this. If this is the reason you want to leave a marriage, you go ahead, but all men do it."

I went to a doctor. He was a very unsophisticated doctor, and I think he was shooting through his hat, but he said to me, "You know, if you leave him, you'll be okay. He won't." Those words were such a revelation to me. I'll be okay. I'm this girl who's just trying to take care of a kid, who just went to college and doesn't have a career or even a job. He's this glamorous man, the most sophisticated man in the world. I'll be okay, and he won't? Those words changed me. I saw it differently after the doctor said those words. I had a fit, went to his office, and threw down the ring.

The next weekend, he came to me and said, "Please, get in the car with me and go to Palm Springs." I was thinking about getting a divorce, but I knew I wouldn't. We went to Palm Springs. We never talked about it at all. We were just in Palm Springs together. We didn't talk about anything, so we didn't talk about that.

We got back to the marriage. Still entertaining and polishing silver and all this crap. Still didn't like it. I was really not a good mother to my child at this time. I was acting out on her. I was angry at her. She was a tough child and I was hitting her. Horrible. I was really horrible.

We took fun vacations to Mexico. We were around a lot of people. We were traveling. His business was going well. There was a lot of excitement there for a young woman.

I decided then that my marriage was safe enough that I could have a second child. When they told me I had a daughter, I said, "You're kidding me. Two girls. How could I be so lucky to have daughters?"

My second daughter came into the world very precious, very laid back, totally different than my first child. I treated her differently than my first daughter. I wasn't as angry with her. I wasn't pulling at her. I wasn't arguing with her. She was easy for me.

My husband still was not there for us, but I was more adjusted to that. He used to take my older daughter to his office on Saturday. I don't think he was ever alone with her. When she graduated from kindergarten, he took her to a fancy watering hole, a place where people drink rum drinks on Saturday afternoon.

By this time he had a motorcycle. The daredevil guy, the jet pilot, was coming out that way. He was running motorcycles all the time. He was still the hero of all the guys, because he was dirt biking. He loved speed. I'm not speedy. I'm real conservative. I don't take risks. I'm afraid of danger. But I certainly let him do all that, which I loved.

I found him with a woman again. I was going through his pockets and I found a name and address of a woman. I was suspicious. I was always jealous, very jealous. I called her up and it turned out that she worked near his office. I went to see her. She told me not to think anything about it, that he really wasn't there. Then I told him my friend saw him coming out of that place. I said, "I also found this piece of paper."

"Oh, I just went there for a meeting," or some crap. Both of the women I caught him with were older women. A lot older than me.

Finally came the time around 1971, my husband got promoted to a really big job with a big company that was on the New York Stock Exchange. It was talked-about, dramatic stuff. He was in with the big boys. I don't know who they were. They were Big. My husband was made president.

Our tenth anniversary was that December. He wrote me this beautiful letter. I have it. He says how

I taught him about family and about home, that he'd learned so much from me. He'd never had a home since his mother died when he was a child. He was grateful to me. How much he cared about our life, our children. How I was like a rock for him.

Then several months after that, my husband quit his job with this big public company with the big guaranteed income. I thought it was the best thing that ever happened in our life. He wasn't going to be on this treadmill, a workaholic, running, going, tired, no time for me, all planes and meetings. His priorities are going to be straight. My children were six and nine years old by this time. We didn't know what we were going to do. I didn't care. This was going to be the beginning of our life.

He retired from the job—which made the newspapers—and he went into the hospital. He was losing weight and thought he had cancer. He didn't.

He really never functioned after that. Virtually went to bed. Nights became days, days became nights. He talked about seeing a psychiatrist, and he went once or twice. He didn't like it. He was not the kind to talk about feelings. Believe me, that was not his thing.

I went to see the doctor once, because I didn't know anything about psychiatry or therapy. The psychiatrist said to me, "Kill himself."

"What?" I said. "Kill himself? This guy's got everything. We've got money, we've got two kids, we've got our health."

I asked my husband and he said, "The guy's nuts, Sharon. What would I want to kill myself for?" I know now he was in a serious depression. He wasn't functioning.

For my daughter's birthday in August, he went on a river rafting trip with her on the Snake River. They told me when they got back that it was really awful. He'd wander off at night. He was afraid he was going to hurt people. They had to really watch him.

Back home one night after that, it was midnight, and he said to me, "You've got to call your father. I'm really afraid to be in the house right now."

I called my father and my father sat outside our bedroom door all night long, just in a chair. Another friend came and they rotated during the night.

The next morning when the light came, he told me, "I was afraid I was going to kill you and kill the children." He was afraid to be alone with us and he wanted protection.

I had a birthday party for my daughter. He would come out of the bedroom and make comments like, "This is the last birthday I'll see her." I didn't know what he meant.

Later that month, it was his stepmother's birthday, and there was a big party for her. He was supposed to be there to greet the guests and do the polite things. But he had really not been functioning since June.

I took my children to an art lesson in the morning that day, and when we came back, the house was locked and we couldn't get in. I went hysterical. I called my father and my uncle and we broke down the door. We went to the bedroom. The bedroom door was locked. We screamed for him, and he came out.

"Oh, I must have fallen asleep," he said. "I didn't know I put the chain on the front door."

My father sat down and told him, "You can't do this to Sharon and the children. This is exhausting. It frightens them when the door is locked. You can't do it."

My parents took my children home with them for a while. I lay down and took a nap with my husband. He just stared at me and told me how beautiful I was when I was sleeping. He wouldn't stop looking at me.

My parents brought my children back and we got up. We had to go to this birthday party that night. He came into the kitchen while I was cooking my kids' dinner. I told him, "If you don't want to go to that party, you don't have to go. If it's too much pressure for you, don't go. You matter. The birthday party doesn't matter."

"No, no, no," he said, "I want to go." He went into the bedroom. I was feeding my children peas. I went to the door and couldn't open it. I tried to get hold of my dad, but he was on the way to the party already. I tried the door again, but I couldn't get in. There was no sound in there. I still didn't know what was wrong. I called another friend of ours. Finally, they tracked down my father and he came over with this other friend of ours. This all took place within ten minutes of when I saw him in the kitchen. The two of them couldn't open the door. They broke through a window.

He was dead. He shot himself.

I had to make a decision that second whether I wanted to live or I wanted to die. I really wanted to die. I remembered how in India the women jump into the fire of the funeral pyre. I said quickly to myself, "I can't do that. I've got kids. I've got to live and I've got to be okay."

I had a choice whether to go in and see him or not. I decided not to do it. If I had gone in the room, I would have fallen apart trying to bring him back to life. I knew I couldn't do it.

Everybody was waiting at his mother's house for the birthday party when they got the call that he was dead. Everybody just ran over in black tie and formals. He had money, this house, friends, family, wife, these children, in-laws. He was the guy all the guys looked up to. It was just shocking. He was the idol of everybody.

At the funeral, I got an image of myself like Jackie Kennedy and the two kids standing on the hill. I dressed us in long gingham gowns. I clearly thought that I had to be together for my kids. I couldn't fall apart. I went to Hawaii with my children after the funeral. When we came back and I was walking my children to school, all the people were staring at us because their father had committed suicide. I had to hold my head up high.

Looking back now, from eighteen years later, I didn't feel guilty then and I don't feel guilty now. He had ten really good years, the best he could have had. He was obviously a person always in turmoil, always running. But whatever he had with me was really good and I feel okay about it. I don't feel like I could have done anything different or should I have. Whatever I knew, I knew. And that's it.

This guy who was my student in the ninth grade when I was student teaching, ten years younger than me, came to the door two days after my husband died and he said, "I remember when I was a boy in your class, I was in love with you. I remember what your smile did for me, and someday that smile will do for another man what it did to me then."

He was in college going to medical school. He'd come and hang around, play with my children. We called him The Kid.

I took another vacation to Hawaii with my children. The Kid was there and knew we were coming in. He met us with leis. We picnicked and swam. I was having fun. Another guy could be nice to my kids. Another guy can play. Then we became sexual.

When I came back home, it was really tough, but The Kid and I ended up living together for six years. My family was against it. Everybody was against it. I didn't care. It was wonderful for my children, wonderful for me.

He was finishing his last year in medical school, doing his internship and residency. Because my kids were in school and he was in school working hard, I went back to graduate school. I'm a therapist now, a marriage, family, child counselor. It took three thousand clinical hours plus a master's degree plus board exams. We were all working, we were all studying.

I was thirty-five and he was twenty-five when we started together. He was a product of the '60s, a different generation. I liked the cultural difference and I felt more in tune with that generation. During Vietnam he had been smoking dope and protesting. I liked that consciousness and I felt much more comfortable with it.

We took vacations together with the kids, because we were all out of school at the same time. He got a summer job in Europe, so we all went to Europe together and lived there. We had a great time. There was no authoritarian father in the house making all these kinds of rules.

He was also from a very upper-middle-class family which fit in with me, too. I didn't have to be embarrassed that I had a lot of money, that I had a nice house. The Kid knew all about that. He was from that, too. I didn't have to cover up.

Then I started getting worried, because he never put a lot of rules on me. I'd date other people while I was living with him. I was sleeping with other men. I thought, "I have to find a husband. The Kid's not really going to be my husband." We got a marriage license once, we both took blood tests, but we chickened out. The age difference was really becoming a problem. He wanted to have children. I didn't. That became the issue, although I'm sure it really wasn't.

I started seeing another man—a doctor. He was an ob-gyn with my uncle. I became very sexually involved with him. An affair. The Kid was out to lunch then anyway. During his residency, he was on call, working days and nights.

That summer I thought I was pregnant, but I didn't know whose it was, this doctor's or The Kid's. I came home after two months on vacation with my parents and children, feeling shitty, nauseous, having no one to tell. I'm thirty-eight years old and I'm afraid to tell anyone.

I came home and told The Kid. My being gone had been good for him. He'd been with young people. I told him and he ran.

Then I did the worst thing I ever did in my life. I told the ob-gyn. He said to me, "I'm not going to marry you, but you have the baby. I don't want you having an abortion."

I then had to grow up real fast. I did not want the baby. I realized I had told the two men who might be the father and neither one of them was there for me for different reasons.

I got my kids off to camp, and a girlfriend took me to have an abortion. I had it by myself and I came home by myself.

The ob-gyn then started feeling terrible about it. Awful, wanted to be there for me. His life changed. He wanted to marry me. He started performing abortions to earn money so everything would be all right. He'd come over here crying every time he did one. I was through with him by this time.

The Kid and I ended up back living together. It was a forgotten issue that I was ever pregnant. He forgot it. I buried it. But I really knew it was over. He was letting me go too much. I wanted him to give me rules and he wasn't. He was letting me do things and be with people and I didn't like it. I wanted him to say, "You're my woman." And he never did. I think he was really scared. We split up. It was tough on me, just awful, although I knew it was the right thing.

Now I was forty-two and getting scared. I was dating a lot, but I didn't like anybody. I was tired of meeting men, tired of being out there. I was scared of my age. My oldest daughter was going off to college, my younger daughter was going to be sixteen. I was with an out-of-work writer. It was a very sexual relationship, but he was a real negative kind of guy who was forty-five and had never done anything but write one book. He was a loser and I was going with losers. I was hitting bottom.

Along came this guy—in August—six foot four, Princeton, Yale, neurosurgeon, another jet pilot in a way. He had a real bad track record. He had four children from former marriages. He knew how old I was and I was very conscious of that. The first time I met him, he said, "Will you marry me?" One date. I said yes and we got married on New Year's Eve, five years ago.

I got married out of my head, not my heart. I got married because he had all the things I wanted in a husband: brains, good education, talent, and he was used to being around people with money. I was tired. It had been ten years since my husband had died. And I was scared.

I was taking my final exams that December. I got married New Year's Eve. The day my daughter left for college was the day I started studying for my board certification. That was the way I took care of myself.

I'd been to graduate school and done all my hours, but I still didn't realize I was going to be actually doing this thing. I turned around and there it was before me. The real thing. I passed my boards. What am I going to do, put a shingle out?

In the meantime, I went to a party with my husband that I didn't really want to go to. I complained and bitched that I wasn't going to be the doctor's wife. But I met a man there who changed my life. He is a man who opened a community for people suffering from life-threatening diseases. He met me and thought I was a dilettante, just a woman who really couldn't come to work with his clients.

I made an appointment with him and told him, "I'm not like that. I want to work there."

"You can't get paid, even though you're a licensed therapist," he said. "You have to be an intern." I was upset about that. I had my papers. But I took the internship and I got a job at the same time at a community health agency starting a foster care program. It was my first paying job in my life. I got paid twelve dollars an hour. I was forty-five years old.

Because of my work with cancer patients, my whole life changed. I always wanted to understand death. To be honest with you, my first husband had an influence on that. I wanted to understand people who went through the most horrifying kind of personal situations and survived. What was this human need to live? Why was living so important? What was the beauty? I've become dedicated to this job, this work. I find it the best place for me in the world.

They didn't put me on staff for a while. I was there a year and they were hiring other therapists outside. I came to the director one day and I said, "I've been here for a year. Why haven't you just hired me?"

"I'm not your daddy," he said. "You tell me you're ready for it." That was an awakening for me.

"I'm ready for it," I said. It was a big thing to be ready. I wasn't sure. When they put me on staff it was the most incredible moment in my life. Found out I'm good at it. I'm a group therapist there with four ongoing groups. I also have a nice private practice. I work really hard now. I didn't think I would ever be getting a paycheck. I get two weeks' vacation a year. I have patients I feel committed to.

I'll be forty-nine this week. I have a very hard marriage now. My husband has severe emotional problems. He's erratic. You never know what's going to set him off.

He hates the fact that I'm independent and he loves it, too. I was financially independent since my first husband died. I have very wealthy parents—rich parents, rich, rich. I've got my work and there's no way anybody can take my independence away. I do not need a man in those kinds of ways.

Financially, it's really hard for him, because he doesn't earn enough money to take care of himself as a neurosurgeon, which shouldn't be. I pay for everything. He hates me for it, yet he's attracted to it. He decided to get his own office and went into debt to open it. Our marriage bargain was that he could do that and I would be supportive. I thought being supportive meant paying for the house, paying the bills, doing all that. He thought being supportive was paying for his new office and taking out loans. He's real angry at me that I didn't do that.

It's been tough. I've been separated from my husband twice. We're separated now, but sort of going back. I always go back. I should leave, but I don't have the courage to leave. The reality of being forty-nine and being a woman alone in the world, wondering if that's how I'll live my life, is frightening to me, I must admit it. I see women my age out there now and I don't feel age-appropriate meeting them. I don't feel age-appropriate looking for men.

I don't seem to want to cross him either. I'm connected to him sexually. We've kept that going even though we've been apart. We both returned to our religion together. It has become an important part of our life. The spirituality is very much there. We're committed politically. He's committed to his work as a doctor, which I'm very proud of. I'm committed to my work with cancer patients. So we really blend in a lot of ways. These are hard things for me to give up, intellectually.

We were apart last year for three months. I was a basket case. I hated being alone. I started dating and I hated that. I spent all the holidays—Christmas, New Year's—alone. I spent my anniversary alone.

I've been living by myself this time for almost four months. Day to day, I feel better than I ever felt in my life. I don't feel lonely this time. I have wonderful friends. I have not wanted another man for the first time in my life. I haven't looked for a man at all these four months. It's really weird all alone in this big house. But I have in mind living on my own this time.

Part of me thinks I may go back with him. I don't like even saying it, but I may. I'm real scared, I'm getting nervous, because my husband's on real good behavior right now. He's courting me again.

I'm not good with men. I thought I was great. I'm the worst. I've done everything okay except make relationships with men. I have solid relationships with my female friends, with my children, and with my children's friends. But the area I thought I was best in, I fucked up in. Boy crazy. I don't get it. I don't know. I don't know. I don't understand it.

Grace

My mother was very young when I was born—she was about fourteen. During those times, people would just not even hear of a teenage girl having a baby. Since my mother's family was one of those real proper southern families that did everything that they thought was right, my mother held that pregnancy for nine months without letting anyone know what was going on. I was born in the house and they rushed me over to the hospital to have my umbilical cord tied and cut. Then they whisked me off to live with an aunt, so that it would never be known that my mom had a baby.

Coming up as a young girl, there were a lot of questions that were unanswered for me. I came up kind of wondering who was who here. My aunt was my real family and I had already learned to call her Big Mama.

My mother was very talented and she became a dancer and singer. She used to travel around with a lot of famous crowds like Lena Horne and Louis Armstrong in these big revues. I used to hear a lot of things about her, but at that time, no one didn't tell me that she was my mother.

I was six years old when my father ran a lawsuit and I had to go live with him. He showed me all these pictures and everything. "This is really your mother, not your sister."

My father was West Indian, so then I became very Jamaican. I picked up an accent and everything. Their culture was entirely different than my grandmother's and my aunt's, because those women were Southerners. Southerners base everything on being proper and right. Jamaicans have a class system where you have to be a number one important person to be able to be looked up to. My father used to gnarl that into my head, the importance of being someone important.

I didn't get to really see my moms until I was about eight. She came to visit and she brought me an outfit. It was a pretty blue skirt with a pretty ruffled blouse, a polka-dot vest, patent leather shoes, and white tights. I thought I was the prettiest girl on the block.

Whenever she did come, it was a holiday, either Thanksgiving or Christmas. She would bring gifts and I remember each gift that she brought. The first time it was the outfit. The next time that she brought me anything from afar, it was a doll, a porcelain doll. It had pretty hair and clothing and shoes. I cherished those things. She used to write and she would call. She would send autographs of famous people in her letters.

When I was a little girl, I thought it was something personal that my mother didn't want me. That I wasn't good enough, like I had to have hair like the doll baby she brought me. I wished I could be like other girls. A lot of times in school when both parents should be there, I'd wish then that my moms could have come for just a little while. I hated her for that. She was putting me out of her life and never doing things for me.

As I grew older, I was able to try and understand a little better as to why my mother wasn't there and why she hadn't raised me. I realized she didn't have any other choice. She was just a baby and didn't realize what it meant to be a moms and to keep a baby, herself. She had no say-so in the matter. So I didn't hate her.

I had a father. Who says you have to be raised by your mother? Lots of times the father leaves. The mother can leave, too. Fathers have done it, still come back, and are still daddy.

My father and I were very close. He was trying to overdo his part as a father. I was close to him more because he was so strict, than close just because I wanted to be there. He didn't want me to have a baby like my moms had one so early. He wasn't thinking about all the great things that he was teaching me and what I had seen and learned. I wasn't going to go out and do this with myself. I wasn't perfect, but I decided that I would never have a baby when I wasn't ready, out of fear of knowing what it feels like to be that kind of child.

When I met my husband I was eighteen years old. He was just somebody that I had met at a party once. We started talking. He was such a nice person during that time. My father was truly against that marriage, because my husband didn't fit his class system. I resented him telling me that. So I married him. I was going to show my father that people just don't think about things like that anymore. Because he didn't have the proper education that you're looking for or because he didn't fit your critique of what a man should be, doesn't mean that I can't care for him. That was one reason why I got married to him.

And, of course, I had to get married. My daughter

was going to be born. The baby should be able to have a real father.

I don't know what happened exactly. After we became husband and wife and we had a baby, it was like my whole world fell in. He became a monster. He was changing little by little, a little here and a little there. He became more obsessive. He was beginning to drink and he was beginning to say things. We would have a lot of arguments. But he would never hit me.

But by the time my second daughter was born, he was beginning to strike me. Even though he had a better job now, he'd strike me. Anything that happened on the job, I would become the person that made that happen, because I was so stupid yesterday. Or we had dinner late and everyone got in the bed too late and my kids was crying too much and I was stupid for having another baby—it was too much on one person; now I won't be able to work. He would just get mad and blame me for it. If I didn't have a receipt for a certain thing, he would hit me. Little things like that.

I was trying to be the perfect neighbor and the perfect mother to my children, not letting my neighbors know what was really going on next door. I was a community worker. I sat on the community board. Everyone knew me. I didn't want people actually knowing what was going on in my life. I wouldn't even cry for fear that would draw attention to what was going on in my house. That would only make him angrier, the fact that I wouldn't give in, that I wouldn't cry.

This went on for fourteen or fifteen years. Finally it reached a point where he was threatening me with harm, like with knives, or real gruesome things. He'd throw a knife that would land in the floor so near that it could have hit me. One time he made me lay the baby down on the floor and he took the knife and threw it. It went right near her head. He dared me to move her. I couldn't help it, I screamed bloody murder.

The cops came. But by then he'd thrown the knife into the garbage pail and then took it to the incinerator. I couldn't prove that it's been there or nothing. They took him out and around the block. During that time in the late '70s, police didn't really take a lot of men downtown. The baby wasn't crying, she wasn't nervous. So it really didn't happen. They talked to him and he came back.

So that night was the first time I left home. I waited for him to go to sleep, I got the kids dressed, and I left. I stayed away about three weeks.

He finally found me at my sister-in-law's house. He tracked me down and came bearing glad tidings. He had gifts for us. He looked great. He hadn't drank any. He was being the perfect husband. He cried and carried on something awful. He agreed to go to AA, he agreed to be counseled by a marriage counselor. We went and we did it. Everything went real well for a whole year, almost.

Nine months to be exact. He started this act up again and would come home drinking. He was expecting to be promoted to a different level in his job and he didn't get it. That just threw him right back to where he was, thinking small of himself and thinking that his failure was going to change the way I felt about him.

In the meantime, he never did strike one of the children, or beat them with his hands. They were so afraid of him because of what he was doing to me, they wouldn't do anything to anger him anyway. If he said, "Go to bed!" everyone just got into their pajamas and went to bed. That was it.

It was just me. He would get them into their bed and I knew what was coming up. He was going to argue, and he was going to do something real mean. Like I would go into the bathroom, and he would lock the door from the outside, so I couldn't come out. He would let this go on for two hours, three hours. If I found a way out, that would have really, really irritated him then.

You start out just getting slapped, then it turns into real stuff, where you begin to get scars here and there and everywhere. I was so afraid. He used to choke me a lot. He kicked me back here on my spine and that was causing me a lot of problems. Headaches. He used to always hit me in the head. This was to knock out whatever sense that I did have—like getting rid of it, not being able to let me think.

Then one night, a couple days before Thanksgiving, after a real terrible beating, I just could not deal with it anymore. He beat me up and he told me, "When I come back from the store, I might just kill you." So when he left out to go to the store, I got all the kids ready, put them in their coats and everything. My youngest child was two months old by then. When I left out of there that night, I didn't know from hide nor hair where I was going, but I knew I was going to get out of there.

I went to the train station, called the cops, and told them where I was. They came and got me. They gave us cab fare to get to Victim Services. I went to Victim Services and they told me there was nowhere that they could put me that night that would have been safe. Did I have a friend? I had *one* friend I met at a meeting I had gone to once and who I began to talk to about what was happening to me. She's the one used to tell me all the time, "Get out before you die." She knew what I was suffering. She experienced the same thing, because her husband was a city policeman and she didn't dare ruin his life. Finally, she had got out and she gave me shelter the first couple of nights.

I stayed with her until Thanksgiving Day. Then she left. She'd gone to her mother and sister for the holidays. There was no food in her house, no baby formula, nothing whatsoever. There was a neighbor next door that she told to check on us. The neighbor found that there was no food there, nothing. The neighbor said, "You're sitting there and there's no milk, no food?" So she gave the baby some milk, and she gave us a turkey leg, a can of peas, and a box of Rice-a-Roni. This was for me, five children. But we had to make that work, because that was all there was.

The person who was counseling me from Victim Services wouldn't be in until the next morning. All we had was the clothes that we wore and about eighty cents left from the cab fare that the cops had given us. Victim Services didn't give me money, which they were supposed to have done. Just part of getting lost in the system. It was my first real meeting with that. I didn't know it was going to be like this. Thanksgiving dinner was one turkey leg, a can of peas, a box of Rice-a-roni, and two cans of Carnation milk.

The day after Thanksgiving, the counselor called, told me that the cab would pick me up across the street. It was outside by eight o'clock. We got in and the driver took us to our destination thirty-five miles across town to a shelter.

Victim Services rented six apartments in this facility to shelter women. The only people who knew we were battered women were the people in management. No one else knew. They said, "You can't talk to anybody." You're all alone, you can't talk to anybody on the floor and I didn't even have a can opener.

Going into these shelters, it sounds great. It sounds like, "This is it. This is your haven." Of course, you won't be beaten. No one will be beating you, but it's absolutely hell.

The way they make you feel is, you're stupid. You should have never left your home, because here's what you got. You cannot socialize. You cannot have any outside contact with anyone whatsoever, besides the other women here in this program. These women and you have one thing in common: You've all been beaten, you're all running. So the only thing that you can talk about is your problems. You can't talk about anything else. You go to counseling twice a week, sit in a session with other women, and talk about how this man beat you, while a counselor sitting in the corner says, "Well, why did you do that? Why did you let this happen?"

You're feeling so vulnerable at that time, and no one has yet to say, "Welcome." No one has yet to say, "We're going to try to help you." No one has yet to sit you down and say, "It's going to be rough going, all uphill right now, but you're going to get there."

You come in scared and you leave feeling like shit. I thought, "This is really weird. This is supposed to be where I find myself and do something better."

You only get ninety days, and at the end of that, you have to find housing. You're out. That's it. You're out in the street or you go back to your battery. They told me I could not apply for city housing because they did not cater to battered women. We were in a class by ourselves.

The only thing that you get very fast is aid from the Department of Social Services. You can get that Day One. They'll give you some food stamps and some money, but it may be forever before you get that next check. They gave me $58. That looked pretty good because I hadn't had any money in a month almost by this time. They said that within five days I would have $274 in the mail for food stamps, but it took that another month to get there. So I had $58 to juggle with. The shelter only gave me some canned food that they had gotten as a donation from a church, dried soup mixes and stuff. The oatmeal and dry goods had worms in it, so none of that was usable. This was enough to last five children and me about three days. There wasn't any type of meat whatsoever.

The day after I arrived they gave me carfare to go

to register with welfare and carfare to go get my photo ID taken. But they expected me to take my five children with me. It was just crazy.

To them, it was, "How dare you be upset? We're giving you a place to live." I had to take it in stride, because I didn't know enough about what was happening to me or where I was going. But I was getting mad. My anger was giving me the strength that I needed to keep going.

Then I watched the other women falling apart, being told, "We're going to call the Department of Children Services and your kids are going to be placed in foster care." Some of the women were actually agreeing to that.

I just could not see this as being a reality. How dare you give me the indication that you're going to really help me and you haven't done anything but make me feel even worse about what I've done? You're making me feel guilty about what I've done to my children. You're not giving me anything to hold onto. No tomorrow to look forward to. The only thing you've told me is what I can't do.

After about three weeks, I knew exactly where I was going and I let them have it. I called a meeting with them. They were surprised. I told them to come talk to me or talk to someone in the press, because I had seen and heard enough. I just didn't think it was fair. We went over a whole list of things I had found when I came there, things that had been done and how I felt that these things were totally wrong. These people who were beaten at home were being abused by the system. They were driving women back out to be killed, but at least at home, your things were there and you had food.

We had several of these meetings and I had meetings with the other women every day. Everything changed while I was there. But it didn't stay that way.

It went right back as soon as I wasn't there to carry on so bad.

That's Phase One of being manipulated by the system. Phase Two: I had nowhere to live after my ninety days was up.

I did a whole lot of thinking. My kids were really unhappy. They'd suffered a great trauma, the loss of all the familiar things that were theirs, their own real home. There'd been a lot of running and shoving and doing things the system's way. They couldn't take anymore, so I was going to go back home and try to make a go of it.

I kept calling the phone at home, but I wasn't getting any answer, so I went back over there. I found out that my husband had lost the apartment. He hadn't paid the rent for a whole ninety days. He split and finally they just took everything away that he had left in the apartment. Most of it he had already sold, because I had never stayed away from home that long before, and no one knew where I was. So there was no home to go back to. That was a knockdown.

I was blaming myself, "You shouldn't have gone." But I took a good look in the mirror and there was a great change since I had been gone. I was *me*. My kids were not dead. I felt whatever went down, I could get a hold of it, once we got out of this place into our own again.

Nobody wants to hear that you're a single mother with five children on welfare. That's totally out. You don't live in apartments then. The shelter had no housing advice, no specialist connected with city housing. They did not refer you to anything. They wanted you to find someone to keep your kids and go looking for a place on your own. Are you jiving?

I finally ended up down at the Department of Social Services. Because I had been a battered woman, they thought they would "look out for" me, so they sent me to the Martinique Hotel in midtown Manhattan.

You hear a lot about that place, if you read the news-papers.

I had laid away a color TV while I was living in that shelter. I owed seventy dollars on it, so I went and I got it out. That was the one thing good that I had to offer my kids, so that's why I splurged and I did that. That was our prized possession along with whatever clothing we had. I had about three hundred dollars worth of food stamps and some canned foods, and I brought that to the hotel.

Oh, God. When we arrived there, that was the be-ginning of the end to me. Oh, my God. There was people standing there looking like they were going to jump at us any minute. But this is because of my own inner fears, things that I had heard. "People are going to rob you. People are getting killed there." But I had to go there. Where else was I going to go?

This man ran over to the cab and opened the door. Right away I thought he was attacking us, because of my own fears and because of the fact that I've never really witnessed this type of atmosphere. We had lived in a very middle-class neighborhood. I grabbed the door and snatched it back closed.

"I just want to help you, miss," he said, "to carry your bags. You got all those babies and I want to help you carry those bags up. I won't charge you anything."

Then I felt so small. I said, "Oh, I'm sorry. I'm very nervous. Please excuse me."

"It's all right," he said. "All people think we're going to kill them just because we're standing outside. But welcome to the Martinique Hotel." At least he said *welcome*.

We went in, and he took our bags on over to the desk. I was getting ready to give him money and he said, "You don't have to give any money to me. You'll find out. You don't have a dime to spend. If I can be of any help to you later, let me know."

The lady gave me two keys and said, "This is it. You have to go up there by yourself." So we had to get in the elevator with everyone staring at us. My kids were like up *under* me, scared to death.

We went upstairs into this room. When you stepped on the floor, the floor stuck to your feet. The rug was just gook. They had tried to shampoo it, but it was so filthy the only thing you got was sticky stuff as a result of the soap and water and the dirt. Oh, God, it was so horrible. But it was home. The only thing that kept me going with a sane attitude—some hope—was, "This is home. I don't have to answer to anyone."

It was dinnertime. I'm looking for the stove. There is no stove. So I called downstairs with the phone. Somebody answered and says, "Yeah?"

"Is there any cooking? Anyplace to cook?"

"Miss, this is a *ho*-tel." Bam! That was it.

"My God, how do I ask questions?" I thought. So I went across the hall and knocked. Somebody was calling, *"Qué?"* I thought they was calling me Kate. I didn't know *qué* meant "what" in Spanish. So I'm saying, "No, it's Grace, your new neighbor."

Finally, a girl came to the door and said, "No English." As I was coming back to my room, there was this black family and I called to them, "Miss, what do you do when you have to eat?"

"Oh, you have to go to the store and buy yourself a hot plate and cook it in your room. But don't let the management know that you're doing that. Is this your first night?"

"Yes," I told her.

"If you want, you can heat things up on my hot plate."

But I didn't want to impose. I wanted to be alone. I was feeling so damn bad.

I went back to my room and got my money. I took all the kids, I went across the street, and it cost me sixty dollars to buy food for everyone. I bought juice, milk, and cereal for the next morning. I put the milk outside on the ledge so it would stay cool—it was early spring and there was still a nip in the air. I bought bread, peanut butter, and jelly. I bought hot Chinese food. I could have gone to the grocery store and bought the same things for less than twenty dollars. The prices are high because of the hotel and the fact that there was nothing else available.

I took it back upstairs and the kids didn't eat any of it, because it was horrible. They ate the peanut butter and jelly. They drank milk and juice and they ate cookies. I bought them some pretzels and they watched color TV. That was some solace to them.

The next day out of my anger, I just couldn't stand seeing that room being that way. I started ripping up the rug left and right, pulling the carpet up off the floor. It took me about five days to get all of that rug up. The next weekend, after I got another check, I went out and got stuff to do the floor. I pulled the nails up. I rearranged the furniture. I bought sheets for the bed, our own sheets and pads and everything.

I went downstairs one day and asked the man there to tell me where I could get a refrigerator. I had to have milk for my baby. I had read through my pamphlet and it said that I was entitled to a refrigerator, having a baby living in any hotel facility. He said, "We don't give refrigerators anymore. That was years ago." But I had passed through the halls at night and could see the backs of refrigerators in certain rooms through the windows.

"Well, right now I have an infant and I do need one."

"Uh, Miss, if you can find a refrigerator, you can have it."

So I started climbing floors and I looked and looked. By the time I got to the fifth floor, there was an empty room with a man in there painting. There was a refrigerator in the middle of the floor and I took it. That was my attack to get a refrigerator. Later on, I went through a whole lot of channels and I got them for the whole hotel. Someone donated refrigerators for every apartment.

Pretty soon, our room was a haven for other people, because it *was* an apartment. We made a closet into a kitchen. I hung pots and pans, bought a two-burner hot plate and a microwave oven. I did the works. We had ourselves a place to prepare food. After that, lots of people started doing the same thing. It became like an epidemic, everyone was doing it.

I became the spokesperson for the tenants. I did things that other people only dreamed of doing, simply because I was angry and I had the guts to do it. Who were they in management to treat us so bad? I was bringing in all this money to them for rent, so I was a rent-paying tenant who deserved better than what I was getting. It was taxpayers' money. But some of that was mine I had earned for years. I'd paid taxes. That money was there for me to use when I needed it.

Of course, the money being paid for me to live there was just unbelievable. Every time I went to pick it up, I just would get angrier. They have you wait there from eight-thirty in the morning to four o'clock in the afternoon, before you are given that check and allowed to leave, take it back, and give it to the management of the hotel. The whole thing was insane. All day long, you're sitting there thinking, "What I could do with this month's money. I could get a nice apartment and the furniture to go in it." But it wasn't your money, it was theirs.

I attended a lot of meetings. I sat on a lot of panels. I went to City Hall to have things changed. I played a great part in voicing things for the homeless.

What I walked into, I just couldn't see it happening to another person. It was a piece out of my life that I will never forget. How could the system, who was paying out all this money to these hotels, allow this to happen to real human beings? That was a real knock in the butt.

Of course, one of the reasons I was able to do some good was that nobody knew at any of the agencies I was dealing with that I was homeless. Everybody on the outside is saying, "Look at them!" It was like, this is a planet called "Hotel for the Homeless" and these are its inhabitants. These people were no longer looked upon as people. They were hotel kids, hotel men, hotel families. Everyone exploited you because of that. Kids were treated on a different level in the schools. "You aren't equipped to learn, because you're from the Hotel for the Homeless."

They never stopped to think that these people came from a real house at one time. I myself came out of one where there was a salary of approximately forty thousand dollars a year. We lived decent lives. I knew what a kitchen was. I knew what it was like to have a washing machine and an ironing board. It's not like these are all brand-new to me.

How does it feel to be homeless? You breathe. You eat. You live. You sleep. You go to work. You go to school. If you cut me, I'll bleed. I'm a real human being. The only difference between you and me is that you are stabilized at this minute where you want to be, and I'm currently living in a place that I don't want to be. But I'm just like you. I think. I live on my own motivations, my dreams.

My case was not a unique one. I was a battered woman who was forced to be homeless. I wasn't there because you have termed me as being lazy or shiftless or a Welfare burden. You don't know me. The only thing you know is my address.

If you saw me shopping in the department store across the street—which I did a lot for bargains—I was just one of you. But if you saw where I returned to, all of a sudden I became someone else, of a different background and culture, from a different planet.

WOMEN

These are the things that hurt the most. It would make people such as myself reluctant to search for help for themselves. It makes you think twice before you would go to an agency and say, "I don't have enough food, because the food stamps ran out, or the welfare did not provide us with a check for this period." You are afraid of being found out.

A lot of things happening with the younger people living in these hotels is that they react to what they think is expected of them. You are rejected from Day One, so they say, "You think that I'm the Big Bad Wolf, so I'm going to be one. You don't want me here, so I'm going to make life miserable for you. You're scared of me, so I might as well enjoy that. I'm me. I'm somebody. I'm for real. You're afraid of me. So what? At least you see me as a person—the person you're afraid of. So what?"

I was awful worried about my children. There was lots of nights when I would go to bed very dismayed, very angry with myself, angry with the system. But my anger had to be my stomping grounds, my energy. This is the thing that made me go out and fight, not just for me, but for others around me who were less articulate and could not say what needed to be said. For two years I didn't think of anybody above myself. I helped people to get where they were going. I felt, "When I'm ready, I'll just get up and go."

But my main problem was fear of rejection from my old neighborhood. I couldn't tell people where I was or what had really happened. I was embarrassed. I had my pride. I would help other people to get housing and to get out, but I was afraid to go back to my old neighborhood and say, "Look, I need an apartment. I need help." I didn't want anyone to know. I just wanted them to look up one day and say, "Where have you been?"

I wouldn't say anything. Maybe just, "On vaca-

367

tion.'' Out of this need to do for others, I was also hiding my own needs.

I felt, too, that if I walked out on these people, they'd had it. There wouldn't be anyone there to answer their questions, no one to give them a helping hand. I used to go to the grocery store and buy lots of food, just so I could come home and bag up beans or rice to give out to other people to keep them from going to bed hungry. They may not have been using their money right, because of drugs or whatever, but they still had kids that needed to be fed. It got so bad and people became so dependent on me that they started calling me the Martinique Mother. That was wild. I don't want to be that.

Finally, I had to let the story be told. I told myself, ''You have to live, too.'' I had to let someone know where I was.

Ironically enough, one woman on the board of directors of the organization that I helped start used to live about three blocks from my old home, where I left from. She saw me. She kept looking at me and I kept looking at her. I knew who she was, but I thought, ''She can't recognize me, because I'm not going to let her.'' So I would always turn my back or leave so she couldn't see me.

One day she had to see me, because I was coordinator of a hot meals program and she needed to talk to me about the menu. Finally I go to meet her in the hotel.

''Oh, my God. What are you doing here?'' she said. ''Do you live here?''

''Yeah.''

''You can't live here. You can't do that. How could you?''

''Easy. I go home upstairs every night and I turn the key in the door. That's my home.'' I took her upstairs to my room. She was amazed that what she had read in the newspapers was where we actually lived. This was our world right now. This was what we had to deal with. Behind this door was my haven.

Anyway, she contacted the right people and I bought into a low-income ownership building with money I had saved from the jobs I was working. We moved out of the hotel on the week before Mother's Day. That was my Mother's Day present to my children. The happiest day of my life. I could breathe. I was home again.